THE **COMPLETE IDIOT'S GUIDE** ® TO

Value Investing

by Lita Epstein

ALPHA

A member of Penguin Group (USA) Inc.

ALPHA BOOKS

Published by the Penguin Group

Penguin Group (USA) Inc., 375 Hudson Street, New York, New York 10014, USA

Penguin Group (Canada), 90 Eglinton Avenue East, Suite 700, Toronto, Ontario M4P 2Y3, Canada (a division of Pearson Penguin Canada Inc.)

Penguin Books Ltd., 80 Strand, London WC2R 0RL, England

Penguin Ireland, 25 St. Stephen's Green, Dublin 2, Ireland (a division of Penguin Books Ltd.)

Penguin Group (Australia), 250 Camberwell Road, Camberwell, Victoria 3124, Australia (a division of Pearson Australia Group Pty. Ltd.)

Penguin Books India Pvt. Ltd., 11 Community Centre, Panchsheel Park, New Delhi—110 017, India

Penguin Group (NZ), 67 Apollo Drive, Rosedale, North Shore, Auckland 1311, New Zealand (a division of Pearson New Zealand Ltd.)

Penguin Books (South Africa) (Pty.) Ltd., 24 Sturdee Avenue, Rosebank, Johannesburg 2196, South Africa

Penguin Books Ltd., Registered Offices: 80 Strand, London WC2R 0RL, England

Most Alpha books are available at special quantity discounts for bulk purchases for sales promotions, premiums, fund-raising, or educational use. Special books, or book excerpts, can also be created to fit specific needs.

For details, write: Special Markets, Alpha Books, 375 Hudson Street, New York, NY 10014.

Publisher: *Marie Butler-Knight*
Editorial Director: *Mike Sanders*
Senior Managing Editor: *Billy Fields*
Senior Acquisitions Editor: *Paul Dinas*
Development Editor: *Nancy D. Lewis*
Production Editor: *Kayla Dugger*
Copy Editor: *Krista Hansing Editorial Services, Inc.*

Cartoonist: *Steve Barr*
Cover Designer: *Bill Thomas*
Book Designer: *Trina Wurst*
Indexer: *Brad Herriman*
Layout: *Brian Massey*
Proofreader: *John Etchison*

Contents at a Glance

Contents

Introduction

When the stock market is volatile, with rapid swings up and down, most people run for the hills and get out. Smart investors watch for the lows and find good stocks that have been beaten down unjustifiably. These value investors learn how to find the intrinsic value of a company and determine when to buy a stock at or below its intrinsic value.

In this book, we show you the various styles value investors use to find the intrinsic value of a stock and how they build their portfolios—value style. Some focus on buying cheap stocks, some like to take the contrarian view, and still others believe in concentrating their portfolio.

Let's take a look at what you'll find in the book:

In **Part 1, "Exploring Value Basics,"** you'll learn the basics of value investing and how to develop your investing muscle so you can stick to your guns as a value investor.

In **Part 2, "Digging Deep—Reading Financial Reports,"** you'll discover how to read between the lines of financial reports and dig for the information you need to make an informed decision about a company.

In **Part 3, "Analyzing the Fundamentals of a Company and the Market,"** you'll explore market behavior and learn how to analyze the numbers on financial statements.

In **Part 4, "Discovering How to Use Investment Vehicles for Value Investing,"** you'll be introduced to the various vehicles you can use to invest—bonds, stocks, mutual funds, convertibles, and warrants. You'll also review the risks of investing using these vehicles.

In **Part 5, "Value Investing Strategies,"** you'll delve into the various strategies value investors use to build successful portfolios.

We've also developed some little helpers you'll find throughout the book:

Value Visions

You'll find quotes from key value investors that will help you improve your value investing skills.

Losing Value

You'll find warnings for things you should avoid as a value investor.

Finding Value

You'll find tips for how to improve your value investing skills.

def•i•ni•tion

You'll find meanings to words you might not understand.

Acknowledgments

First, I want to thank Paul Dinas, my acquisitions editor, for his continuing support and his ability to find just the right topics for me. I also want to thank Nancy Lewis for her excellent work developing the book, Krista Hansing for her careful attention to detail as she copyedited the book, and Kayla Dugger for her efforts to keep the book on its production schedule. Also, I can't forget my agent, Jessica Faust, for her continuing support for my books. Finally, last but not least, my husband, HG Wolpin, who must put up with me—especially as panic sets in at deadline time.

Special Thanks to the Technical Reviewer

The Complete Idiot's Guide to Value Investing was reviewed by an expert who double-checked the accuracy of what you'll learn here, to help us ensure that this book gives you everything you need to know about value investing. Special thanks are extended to Kenneth Kaplan.

Trademarks

All terms mentioned in this book that are known to be or are suspected of being trademarks or service marks have been appropriately capitalized. Alpha Books and Penguin Group (USA) Inc. cannot attest to the accuracy of this information. Use of a term in this book should not be regarded as affecting the validity of any trademark or service mark.

Part 1

Exploring Value Basics

In this part, you'll start your exploration of value investing by discovering what it entails and how to get your mind-set ready for this unique style of investing. We'll also take you back in history to learn more about how the stock market got to where it is today.

What Is Value Investing?

In This Chapter

- Explore the meaning
- Discover reasons for doing it
- Invest or speculate?
- Value-investing gurus

If you're looking to make a quick buck, this is not the book for you. Value investing involves looking for a company on sale and having the patience to wait until others realize that company is a bargain. Sometimes that can take years. Value investing can also include defensive investing—an investor seeks safety when the market is too volatile by picking the right mix of bonds, commodities, and safer stocks to ride out the storm.

In this chapter, we delve into the definition of value investing and why you should do it. We also introduce you to the masters of value investing, but we take a closer look at each master's strategies in Part 5.

Defining Value Investing

Value investors buy stocks only when their market price is significantly below the calculated *intrinsic value*—essentially, they are part of a fire sale.

def•i•ni•tion

The **intrinsic value** of a company is based on the internally generated cash returns. When analyzing numbers for a stock, the common way to find intrinsic value is to calculate a discounted stream of net cash flows to find out what those cash flows are worth in today's dollars. We show you how to do this analysis in Part 3.

While growth investors chase some dream of future earnings potential, value investors want you to show them the money (actual cash flow generated from doing business) before they'll pluck down their hard-earned dollars to buy the stock.

Benjamin Graham, the granddaddy of value investing, believed the "obvious prospects for physical growth in a business do not translate into obvious profits for investors." That was his core belief.

Graham thought that buying stock based on some future, undetermined earnings potential was a sure route to ultimate financial disaster for the investor. He did not believe that anyone, even experts, had "dependable ways of selecting and concentrating on the most promising companies in the most promising industries."

Graham also thought that growth companies ultimately would not give investors a good return on their money because so much of the money earned will be reinvested to grow the company instead of being paid out to investors. While it's true that when you make the perfect choice growth investing can earn you riches in the stock market, if that company doesn't have an ongoing income stream, the profits made won't last.

Losing Value

We all saw a prime example of how growth investing can fail big time when Internet stocks crashed in 2002. Many of those darlings of growth investors shot up from IPO prices of $10 to $20 to prices of $100 and more during the late 1990s. But what were they worth in 2002? Most lost 95 percent of their value, if they survived at all. You would have to gain 1,900 percent on that money to get back the 95 percent you lost.

Even if you are a growth investor, remember never to chase the hottest stocks. By the time stocks become hot, often they are already selling for more than they are worth and it's only a matter of time before they fall back to Earth—translating into a much lower stock price and a loss for you.

Why Do It?

Value investing never gives you the type of quick returns you can get on a growth stock if you happen to get lucky and pick one just before it rockets to the top. As a value investor, you need a lot of patience to wait for the rest of the market to spot that bargain you found.

From the time you buy a stock you think is priced at a good value until the time the rest of the market agrees with you, three years or more could pass. But if you picked right, over the long term, you'll have a solid portfolio with a good cash flow that you can hold for a long time.

Finding Value

In his 1999 letter to shareholders, Warren Buffett wrote, "The most common cause of low prices is pessimism—sometimes pervasive, sometimes specific to a company or industry. We want to do business in such an environment, not because we like pessimism, but because we like the prices it produces. It's optimism that is the enemy of the rational buyer."

As you're trying to figure out whether to hold a stock, think about Warren Buffett, the sage of Omaha, a leading value investor who buys stocks (or entire companies) only when he determines he wants to hold them forever. Over the years as chairman of Berkshire Hathaway, Buffett has shifted his company's focus from buying shares of stocks to buying entire companies. Berkshire Hathaway owned more than 65 companies, according to its 2007 annual report.

Now, you may not want to hold stocks forever. You may want to take some profits during a bull market and then wait for the next bear market to buy back into the market. It's all up to you and your investment style and goals.

Consider some key things you'll need to remember when starting out as a value investor:

♦ A stock is not just a ticker symbol or an electronic blip on a screen. When you buy a stock, you are buying the interest in a business. The price of that stock may or may not be the same as the value of that business. Stock price is set by the mood of the market, not by the value of a business's assets.

- Think of the market as a large pendulum that swings from irrational exuberance (the Internet bubble) to unjustifiable pessimism (the 2002 stock market crash). If you want to become a successful value investor, learn how to sell when everyone else is buying—during the period of irrational exuberance—and buy when everyone else is heading for the doors—unjustifiable pessimism.

- The higher the price you pay for a stock, the lower your return will be when you sell the stock. For example, you'll make more on a stock for which you paid $10 and sell at $20 ($10 profit) versus a stock for which you paid $15 and sell at $20 ($5 profit). Live by the old adage—buy low, sell high. By the time the market discovers a stock as the best choice to buy, its price is already too high and it has nowhere to go but down. A value investor seeks to find that "best buy" before the market notices it.

- When evaluating the worth of a company, first look at its assets on the books (the balance sheet—see Chapter 5), then check out its current earnings power (the income statement—see Chapter 6), and possibly consider growth, but don't put too much credence on unproved earnings.

- Always buy when your analysis shows there is a margin of safety, which means don't pay more for a stock than your analysis shows it's worth, no matter how excited you may be about owing the company. We show you how to calculate margin of safety in Part 3. By holding strictly to this rule, you'll minimize your chances of picking the wrong stock. We can't guarantee you'll never make a mistake. Even the greatest stock pickers make mistakes.

- Stock trading is always a zero-sum game. Every time a stock changes hands, there is a buyer and a seller. One of them will win and one will lose. To succeed as an investor, you need to be on the winning side most of the time. Note we didn't say "all the time." You will make mistakes. Learn from them and move on.

Learn to invest with patience and with confidence in your ability to analyze stocks and pick the stocks selling at the best value. If you do, you'll discover how to find great bargains during a bear market and when to sell during a bull market.

Getting Started as a Value Investor

So how does one get started as a value investor? Obviously, the key is to find stocks that are undervalued, but how do you go about doing that? It's really a four-step process.

Step 1: Pick Your Industry

First, pick an industry in which you believe the market has unjustifiably beaten down the stocks too much. To show you how this works, we focus on the housing indus-

try in this book, since the housing market crash has certainly beaten down the stocks of all home builders. So they're all on sale. We ask this question: are any companies worth considering because the market has beaten them down too low?

You may be wondering why we chose home builders rather than financial companies. We chose not to look at financial institutions because the full extent of the damage is still to be determined, so the stock prices of these companies may still fall a considerable distance.

> **Value Visions**
>
> In his annual letter to investors released February 29, 2008, Warren Buffett said, "As house prices fall, a huge amount of financial folly is being exposed. You only learn who has been swimming naked when the tide goes out—and what we are witnessing at some of our largest financial institutions is an ugly sight."

Step 2: Pick the Top Companies

Next, when doing an analysis, pick the top three to five companies in that industry. For the purposes of this book, we focus on two home builders. Let's call them Builder A and Builder B.

We disguised the annual reports we are using throughout this book so you won't be able to recognize the builders. Normally, you would look at more than two companies, but to have enough space to do a full analysis, we just analyze two in this book.

Step 3: Determine the Best Choice

After checking out a company for its intrinsic value, determine whether either of them makes a good value choice as a purchase for a value portfolio. If they both do, then which one makes the better choice?

Step 4: Determine the Best Price

Then determine what price is a good price at which to buy the stock, while still giving you a good margin of safety in case the stock does go down. This margin of safety is the difference between what you'll pay for the stock and what your analysis shows the stock is worth, given today's condition.

You need to learn a number of things to be able to get started as a value investor:

> **Value Visions**
>
> Warren Buffett's quote on analysts tells it like it is: "We've long felt that the only value of stock forecasters is to make fortune-tellers look good. Even now, Charlie [vice chairman of Berkshire Hathaway and longtime partner of Warren Buffett] and I continue to believe that short-term market forecasts are poison and should be kept locked up in a safe place, away from children and also from grown-ups who behave in the market like children."

♦ Read between the lines of the financial statements and annual reports. Most companies prepare annual reports with dramatic pictures and a lot of marketing fluff. That is not what you'll be looking at to find out whether a company is worth considering. Just like with any legal contract, you need to scour the small print. You can't depend on analysts. You must learn how to do this yourself. We show you how to do that in Part 2.

♦ Analyze the numbers you find in the financial statements. Value investors employ some of the same analytical tools as growth investors, but they use some tools unique to finding out a company's true value. We show you how to do that in Part 3.

♦ Explore various value investing strategies. You'll need to pick the strategy that you're most comfortable using. This can include asset and capital allocation, defensive investing, contrarian investing, concentrating your portfolio, and buying cheap. We introduce you to all these types of strategies and the investor gurus who use them in Part 5.

In Part 4, we review the different types of investments from which you can choose, including a closer look at bonds, stocks, and mutual funds. We also take a look at the risks you face when you invest. Before you start looking at strategies you can use, it's important for you to understand the various types of investments available to build a portfolio and how they work.

Meet Today's Top Value Investors

Value investing is an art, and there's no reason for you to reinvent the wheel. Get to know the leading value investors and build on their successful strategies to find your own success as a value investor.

Warren Buffett

While Benjamin Graham earned the title of the granddaddy of value investing, Warren Buffett is by far his star pupil. Known as the sage of Omaha in investing circles, Buffett took the principles he learned as Graham's student and built an empire that is the envy of all who don't own stock in his company—Berkshire Hathaway. You had to pay $140,000 for one share of stock at the end of February 2007. People who stuck with him from the beginning of his company are all millionaires today.

In his recent letter to shareholders, Buffett said his company has two major areas of value. The first is its investments in stocks, bonds, and cash equivalents, as well as his insurance businesses. The second is the earnings from his 66 other noninsurance businesses. Berkshire Hathaway's most well-known insurance company is GEICO.

Buffett looks for companies that meet these criteria:

- A business we understand
- Favorable long-term economics
- Able and trustworthy management
- Sensible price tag

Sounds pretty simple, doesn't it? We take a closer look at Buffett and his investing style in Chapter 18.

Mario Gabelli

Mario Gabelli is the chairman and chief executive officer of GAMCO Investors, a company that provides investment advice regarding alternative investments and offers mutual funds. His individual clients are primarily institutional and high-net-worth investors. Gabelli founded the firm in 1977 as an institutional broker-dealer and built it into the diversified financial services corporation it is today.

Like Buffett, Gabelli is a disciple of Graham and a pioneer in applying Graham's principles to the analysis of companies in a wide

Finding Value _____

Gabelli definitely believes we are in a buying season for value investors. He told investors in a February 2008 letter to shareholders, "Many companies are selling at reasonable valuations. 'Mr. Market' prices in emotions and fear during disruptive market periods, and we aim to take advantage of this by buying companies that are trading at unwarranted discounts."

range of industries. He developed his own Private Market Value with a Catalyst™ methodology, which is now an analytical standard in the value investing community. We take a closer look at Gabelli's methodology in Chapter 22.

Glenn Greenberg

Glenn Greenberg founded Chieftain Capital Management with his partner, John Shapiro, in 1984. His disciplined investment strategy compounded the accounts of his clients at 22.5 percent (before management fees) during the period from 1984 through 2004, versus 12.9 percent for the S&P 500. Greenberg invests in the same portfolio as his clients.

Greenberg maintains a highly concentrated portfolio that he describes as a "defense against ignorance." He believes that the more companies you own, the less you will know about each, and the less you know about a business, the more likely you are to make mistakes due to fear and greed.

His style of investing is highly concentrated. Greenberg usually owns fewer than 10 stocks. He invests in companies with little competition and places a great deal of emphasis on return on invested capital. We take a closer look at his investment strategy in Chapter 23.

Michael Price

Michael Price used value investing to build his portfolio and earn him his spot as the 271st richest person in the world, according to *Forbes*. A renowned money manager, Price learned finance as a $200-a-week research assistant. He's known for buying undervalued companies and raising hell. He'll battle it out with management in the companies whose stock he buys if he disagrees with their decisions.

Price manages the private firm MFP Investors. With $1.6 billion under management, much of it is his own money, he believes in a value-based approach to investing. Price buys stock in out-of-favor small-cap companies that he determines are good values. We take a look at his investment strategy in Chapter 24.

Walter Schloss

Walter Schloss, also a student of Benjamin Graham, started his limited partnership in the middle of 1955 and beat the market for 45 years, from 1956 to 2000, providing investors who stuck with him a compounded 15.3 percent annual gain, compared to 11.5 percent for the *Standard & Poor's Industrial Index*. Every $1 an investor decided to put under Schloss's management in 1956 was worth $662 in 2000. Anyone would be happy with that return.

Schloss follows a deep value investing philosophy, focusing on stocks that are statistically cheap measured against key value-analytical tools. We delve more deeply into his investing style in Chapter 24.

def•i•ni•tion

The **Standard & Poor's Industrial Index** is an index of 500 stocks chosen based on market size, liquidity, and industry groupings, among other factors. It's designed as a leading indicator of the U.S. stock market and reflects the risk/return of large stock companies in the market.

Value investing can sometimes be counterintuitive, because you're buying stocks that everyone else is exiting. But that's what makes it a fire sale and what gives you a good chance to make a profit by buying low, being patient, and waiting for others to recognize the good buy—and then when they do, you sell high to start the cycle all over again.

The Least You Need to Know

◆ Never forget that when you are buying a stock, you are actually buying a share of ownership in a business, not just a blip on a screen.

◆ Start your search for good stocks to buy by choosing an industry that the market has beaten down, and then select three to five good stocks to analyze for possible purchase.

◆ Don't buy stocks when everyone else is buying them. Instead, look for those great bargains everyone is missing.

2

Avoid Your Biggest Enemy— Yourself

In This Chapter

- ◆ Getting into the right frame of mind
- ◆ Controlling your emotions
- ◆ Running against the crowd
- ◆ When to buy and sell
- ◆ Getting yourself organized

If you want to be a value investor, you have to get used to the idea that you'll always be buying against the crowd, and you'll usually have to wait three to five years to see the fruits of your labor. You won't get those large quick returns you hear about from traders or folks riding the growth wave. In this chapter, we talk about how to get yourself into the right frame of mind for being a value investor.

Develop the Value Mind-Set

Value investors must think long term and not think that making a quick profit is their first priority. You must realize that you won't be investing in the same types of stocks as your friends, and you won't be able to compare quarter-to-quarter returns.

Finding Value _____

In the preface to Benjamin Graham's *The Intelligent Investor* (Harper Business Essentials, 2003), Warren Buffett writes, "To invest successfully over a lifetime does not require a stratospheric IQ, unusual business insights, or inside information. What's needed is a sound intellectual framework for making decisions and the ability to keep emotions from corroding that framework."

You'll also need to enjoy digging into the annual reports of the companies that interest you and be prepared to analyze everything you see. Successful value investors are those who enjoy researching and learning everything about a company before diving in and investing.

The key tools you'll need as a value investor are …

◆ Patience to wait for the market to realize you found a gold mine in a beaten-down stock.

◆ Discipline to spend the time researching your choices and not get caught up in the mob mentality as people push stocks higher and higher above their true value.

◆ Desire to learn all you can about choosing the right industries to explore, picking the right stocks within those industries that are unjustifiably beaten down, and then having the courage to wait until the market realizes what a great investment it is missing.

◆ Ability to check your emotions at the door. Don't get emotionally involved in your stocks. Your value portfolio is a way to make money. Don't fall in love with it or the stocks in it.

◆ Expectation of adequate profits but not extraordinary performance. Historically, the average annual return for stocks in any 20-year period is about 10 to 12 percent per year. That doesn't mean you'll earn that amount each year: some years will be higher, some lower, but that's the average return you should expect with a long-term stock portfolio.

◆ Ability to calculate what a stock is worth, based on a careful analysis of the business. Don't gamble on how much the stock may go up because someone else is foolish enough to pay that. Eventually, the fools disappear and you could be left holding the bag.

♦ Ability to think for yourself. Unless you've found a friend who is also dedicated to the idea of becoming a value investor, don't count on those around you for support. You must learn to think for yourself.

Investment vs. Speculation

Essentially, you need to change your mind-set from one of speculator to one of investor. Too many people look only at the movements of a stock price, not at the fundamentals of the business whose stock they are buying. This type of speculation is practiced daily by day traders and has been picked up by many who thought they were investing.

Speculators are the ones who drive stock prices to unsustainable heights. During the inflating of the Internet bubble, speculators drove the stock prices of Internet businesses so high in the late 1990s and led to the crash of those same stocks in 2002.

As a value investor, you would have looked at those Internet stocks and seen that those companies had absolutely no income, and you would have realized that investing in these stocks was like buying fool's gold. In the late 1990s, even stars like Amazon, which is one of the very few Internet companies still alive today, were losing millions every year. In fact, Amazon's earnings per share are still pretty meager—only $1.12 per share, as of December 2007.

Most of the Internet companies had no well-thought-out plans regarding how they would actually create an ongoing cash flow. Instead, they were totally dependent on the venture capital funds that were feeding their business. Their plans were pipe dreams, and their dreams got smashed. Speculators jumped on the bandwagon when these dogs made it to their *initial public offerings (IPO)*. Many speculators even borrowed money to get in on the action, using options and margin accounts.

def•i•ni•tion

An **initial public offering (IPO)** is the first time a stock is sold on the public markets. Companies sell stock to raise cash for the company operations and growth.

These IPOs helped the venture capitalists get their money back. They helped the investment bankers earn millions of dollars in fees. But small investors who got suckered into these deals lost most of their money when the market crashed.

As the speculative fever grew, prices were driven higher and higher—a classic recipe for an asset bubble. Eventually, the bubble will burst.

Value investors, like Warren Buffett, knew better and stayed out of the frenzy. They didn't ride the wave up, and many thought they were fools in the late 1990s for staying out of the game. But when the real speculative fools turned their 401(k)s into 201(k)s, as they lost half their portfolios when the market crashed in 2002, the true value investors learned the value of sitting on the sidelines of that type of asset bubble.

At the time the bubble was inflating, Buffett told his investors that he would not buy any stock of a business he doesn't understand. That's a key lesson you need to learn as well. Everyone makes their best investment decisions when they invest in an industry they know well. The more you understand the fundamentals of the industries in which you invest, the better stock choices you'll be able to make in that industry.

In 2002, Buffett's impression of Internet speculation finally proved right. Berkshire Hathaway never touched an Internet stock, and the company's performance beat the S&P 500 by 32.1 percent. Buffett did warn his investors not to expect this every year and that he usually expects to beat the S&P by only a few points, at most. He also warned that, in a bull market, Berkshire Hathaway would likely not do as well as the S&P. Buffett prefers a safer and steadier path using core value investing techniques.

> ### Value Visions
>
> In his 2000 annual letter to investors, Warren Buffett said, "The line separating investment and speculation, which is never bright and clear, becomes blurred still further when most market participants have recently enjoyed triumphs. Nothing sedates rationality like large doses of effortless money. After a heady experience of that kind, normally sensible people drift into behavior akin to that of Cinderella at the ball. They know that overstaying the festivities—that is, continuing to speculate in companies that have gigantic valuations relative to the cash they are likely to generate in the future—will eventually bring on pumpkins and mice. But they nevertheless hate to miss a single minute of what is one helluva party. Therefore, the giddy participants all plan to leave just seconds before midnight. There's a problem, though: They are dancing in a room in which the clocks have no hands."

Investors who've stuck by Buffett have been very happy with his results. He took over Berkshire Hathaway in 1965. If you had invested $10,000 in the stock of that company at that time, it would be worth $50 million today.

Harness Your Emotions

Getting a grip on your emotions can be the hardest thing you'll do as you move toward value investing. Everyone loves to win and hates to see the market constantly beat down their choices. You need to turn that mind-set around and think instead that you're shopping in the bargain basement; in the long term, your wise, carefully researched choices will pay off.

But don't fall in love with your choices, either. Sometimes you will have to admit that you made a mistake and you must sell a stock before you've made a profit or after you've already taken a loss.

You'll find it easy to fall in love with a stock, especially after spending hours analyzing the industry and the company, as well as looking at the fundamentals of the sector and determining the price at which you want to buy the stock. The stock becomes almost like a child that you nurtured. You may feel like a failure if you made the wrong choice.

Well, get over it. You will make mistakes, and the faster you own up to those mistakes, the better your long-term results will be. If you think you've made a mistake, don't respond emotionally. Don't get depressed, and, above all else, don't panic. Remember, patience is your biggest virtue as a value investor.

If you think the company is taking too long to turn around, take the time to research the company's fundamentals again. Take a close look at the numbers and determine whether anything has changed since you did your first analysis of the company. Run an analysis again (we show how to do this in Part 3).

In fact, it's a good idea to run this type of analysis at least yearly on all stocks you hold in your portfolio. You need to know when it's a good time to buy as well as sell.

Have the assets that they hold changed drastically in value? Do they have a lot less cash and a lot more debt? Are their net profits and cash flows still looking as good as they did when you chose the stock? If the answer is yes, calm down—it just means you need to have a bit more patience for the market to find the bargain. If the answer is no, cut your losses, accept your mistake, and sell the stock.

You will feel some pangs of failure, but don't let that get you down. You may find it a bitter pill to swallow that you made a mistake, but sometimes it's better to just find a better stock in which to invest.

If you've made a mistake, take a careful look to figure out what went wrong. Take some extra time to analyze how you made the mistake so you don't make that mistake again. You may find that the first time you looked at the stock, full information had not been reported to the public. Or leadership of the company might have changed and decided to move the company in a direction that you don't think will be a good one for the company. If you see a management change and you don't support the direction the company is now taking, definitely sell that stock.

Don't Run with the Crowd

As a value investor, you never want to choose the stocks everyone else is buying. If everyone is already buying the stock, no matter how good the stock looks, it will eventually hit a top and tumble down.

> **Value Visions**
>
> Warren Buffett told his investors in his 2004 annual letter, "Investors should remember that excitement and expenses are their enemies. And if they insist on trying to time their participation in equities, they should try to be fearful when others are greedy, and greedy when others are fearful."

If you like the company after you've done the analysis, be patient. Wait until that stock tumbles and buy it at its low instead of its high.

Don't get caught up in trying to find the absolute bottom. Many try, few succeed. Instead, do your analysis, find what you think is the right price with the right margin of safety, and buy the stock when it reaches your target. We talk more about how to find that right price with the right margin of safety in Part 3.

Bull Sell, Bear Buy

While we can't guarantee you'll always find the perfect price, the one thing we can guarantee is that you'll always be selling stocks during a *bull market* to lock in your profits. Likewise, you'll always be buying stocks in a *bear market* when the stocks are on a fire sale.

Yes, this goes strongly against the crowd, but if you can get yourself into the right mind-set to do that, you can have a long, successful run as a value investor, provided that you put in the time to do the research necessary to find the companies with the best value prospects.

def•i•ni•tion

A **bull market** is a market in which most stocks are going up in price. A **bear market** is a market in which most stocks are going down in price.

Luck vs. Discipline

Value investing certainly requires a bit of luck, but it's mostly based on perseverance and discipline. Since you will be taking some risk as you pick beaten-down companies, you do need the luck that most of these risks will pay off. You also need the discipline to stick with your choice, knowing it will eventually pay off even if things don't look good immediately. And, yes, some of those risks won't pay off.

Luck plays a part in every investor's life, but few credit their success to being lucky. So don't count on luck to get you where you want to go.

Discipline is the key to the door of success for value investors. You have to know how to set your investing goals and stick to them. You must have the ability to develop your own road map to success without having to worry about taking directions from others. You also need to become an accumulator of wealth and have the discipline to not spend as much as you make, so you have money to invest when you find a good bargain.

 Finding Value

Remember, disciplined people are not easily side-tracked. They set their sights on a series of lofty goals, figure out strategies for meeting those goals, and have the discipline to not lose sight of those goals, even if they stumble and fall along the way. They get up, fix the problems, and continue to stay focused on their ultimate goals.

Staying Organized

You also need to be well organized to manage the research you'll be doing on all the companies you follow. You must be good at developing research plans and stay organized enough to keep those plans on target. Learning how to manage your time and organize your day so you are able to get everything done on your to-do list is a basic skill that you must develop.

Each time you review your goals, whether it's daily, weekly, or monthly, make a to-do list of the items you need to get done to complete your immediate goals for the day, week, or month. You don't need a fancy system. While many people use a personal digital assistant or software on their computer, a simple pad of paper can work just as well.

Check off the to-do list as you get the items done. If you seem to be avoiding something that needs to be done, encourage yourself to push through whatever is preventing you from completing the task. Don't let yourself procrastinate because it's something you find distasteful to do.

The key to being organized is developing a system for automating where everything goes in the room. Start by figuring out exactly what you plan to do in your office and how you plan to do it. Group the things you do into five or six categories, such as general paperwork, creative work, financial work, reading material, and family tasks.

Your list of tasks should be clearly delineated so there isn't overlap among your categories. That way, when you pick a place for each of these categories of materials to go, you'll be able to automatically place something into the right place without thinking about it as you work through your day.

Next, determine what types of equipment or furniture you need for each of the tasks you plan to do. As you set up your space with zones for each of your tasks, try to have as little overlap as possible so you don't have to even think about it when you need to put an item someplace to stay organized.

People who lack organization tend to just put things down anywhere and then have a hard time finding them later. They end up wasting a lot of their life just looking for things.

To help you get started in organizing your life, look at the five or six categories of activities you want to do in your office and design the perfect workspace to accomplish all those tasks. For now, don't worry about costs—just think about use of space.

Sketch out what that perfect workplace would look like, with a work zone and storage place to satisfy each of those categories. Next, try to lay out your office as close to the perfect space as you can. If you find you do need some additional items for the space, buy what you need within your budget.

You may end up buying cheap storage bins and file cabinets at a discount store initially until you can afford the ideal furniture, but getting organized is more important than an attractive office space with expensive furniture that you can't afford. You also can save a lot of money on office furniture if you want to assemble it yourself.

As you start to work in your newly designed space, you may find that you're still losing stuff. Figure out what kind of stuff that is. Probably you're putting things in the wrong category or you don't have your categories clearly enough defined in your mind.

You may need to reorder your initial plans to work the most efficiently. Revise your plans to match your actual work habits until you find you are efficiently using your space and your time. In the long run, this will save you a lot of time, money, and effort, and is especially important for tax planning and payment.

Throughout this book, we show you how to read between the lines of the annual reports and financial statements, as well as how to analyze those reports to determine whether a stock you're interested in purchasing makes a good choice for a value investor.

The Least You Need to Know

- Work on learning how to be more patient. Patience will become your biggest virtue as a value investor.

- Concentrate on learning to become an investor. Don't get caught up in a speculative swing in the market.

- Get your emotions under control. They won't help you, and they could encourage you to make the wrong investment moves.

Travel Back in Time—Market History

In This Chapter

- ◆ Cycling through time
- ◆ Bubbling up
- ◆ Avoid repeating market mistakes

You may not enjoy a history lesson, but it's important for you to understand how the market has behaved in the past so you have an idea of what you can expect to find in future markets. No, you won't find that two markets are exactly the same, but you will see that similar patterns repeat themselves.

In this chapter, we review how the stock market grew up to what it is today. Then we look at the basics of market cycles. Finally, we explore those huge market missteps—asset bubbles—and look at how you can avoid being caught up in a future major misstep.

From Butttonwood Tree to Major Financial Market

The U.S. stock market didn't start with a formalized plan. It actually had very meager beginnings.

On May 17, 1792, 24 brokers signed an agreement forming the first organized stock market in New York under a buttonwood tree at what is now 58 Wall Street. They agreed to sell shares, or parts of companies, among themselves and charge people a commission or fee to buy and sell shares for others.

This agreement was not formalized until March 8, 1817, when a formal constitution was adopted and the first stock exchange was formed under the name New York Stock & Exchange Board. From the late 1700s until about 1860, brokers made markets outdoors. The first stock ticker was introduced in 1867.

Formal membership in a stock exchange first became salable in 1868, and it wasn't until 1869 that the New York Stock Exchange (NYSE) started to require the registration of securities by its listed companies to prevent overissuance.

The New York Stock Exchange was not the only way to buy stocks at that time. Stocks that were not good enough for the NYSE were traded outside on the curbs. This so-called "curb trading" became what is today known as the American Stock Exchange, which finally moved indoors in 1921.

After the crash of 1929, the government stepped in and began regulating the stock market under the Securities Act of 1933, to provide full disclosure to investors and prohibit fraud in connection with the sale of securities.

Finding Value

The stock market took many years to rebuild itself and recover from the crash of 1929. Not until 1954 did the stock market finally rise above its 1929 peak—but during that time, there were some great buys for value investors.

Then numerous additional pieces of legislation were enacted to fix the 1933 act. The Securities Exchange Act of 1934 provided for the regulation of securities trading and established the Securities and Exchange Commission (SEC). In the 1940s and 1950s, trading in commodities and monetary instruments became part of the stock exchanges, along with automated trading functions.

Believe it or not, the NYSE wasn't incorporated until 1971. The first member organization listed was Merrill Lynch, in July of that year.

Today's market is dominated by institutional trading, which includes mutual funds and pension funds. In 1960, institutions and other professional investors controlled about half of the shares traded on the NYSE. By the 2000s, this number jumped to almost 90 percent of trades controlled by institutional investors.

Most people today do invest through mutual funds or their employer retirement plan, but more individual investors are choosing to do it themselves. How much of an impact this will have on these numbers is still a big unknown.

Creating the OTC Market

Until the 1960s, the over-the-counter (OTC) stock market was a disorganized group of stocks that did not trade on either the NYSE or the American Stock Exchange. The market was ripe for fraud, and the U.S. Congress decided the SEC should take a closer look at it.

So in 1961, the U.S. Congress asked the SEC to conduct a study of the securities markets. The completed study was finally released in 1963. The SEC concluded that the OTC securities market was fragmented and obscure. The report called for automation of the OTC market and gave the responsibility to the National Association of Securities Dealers (NASD) to implement the project.

In 1968, the NASD began construction of this system, called the National Association of Securities Dealers Automated Quotation (NASDAQ). The first trading day for the world's first electronic stock market, the NASDAQ, was February 8, 1971, which included more than 2,500 securities. Today it's the fastest-growing stock market.

In the 1990s, we saw individual investors reassert themselves. Online investing and the extensive information that you can find on the Internet certainly helped to fuel this shift. This helped in the movement toward the SEC pushing for analysts' calls, where key corporate personnel discuss significant new company information with a select few analysts, to be available to large and small investors at the same time. We talk more about how you can take advantage of these analysts' calls in Chapter 12.

Continuing the shift, we have been seeing a more even playing field for individual investors. Consumer empowerment has never been stronger. Today consumers have greater choice in how to invest, what type of investing instruments to use, and how to access the market.

You can invest directly in stocks yourself using an online trading system, or you can work with a broker at a brokerage house. You can buy mutual funds directly from a mutual fund company, or you can buy them from a mutual fund supermarket, which is usually run by a brokerage house that lets you put together a mutual fund portfolio from several different mutual fund companies. We talk more about your investment options in Part 4.

Market Cycles

Even with all these new purchase options and investment tools, the market still goes through the same types of business cycles. As a value investor, it's important to know how to recognize these cycles and at what point in the cycle the current market sits. Every business cycle has four key parts—peak, recession, trough, and expansion/recovery.

The ups and downs of a business cycle.

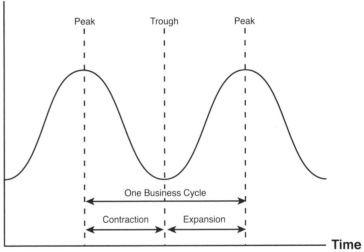

Peak

During a peak, the economy is growing at a fast pace, with the *gross domestic product* (*GDP*) near its maximum output and employment levels. Income and prices are increasing, and the risk of inflation is great and may already have set in. Businesses and investors are in good shape financially and are delighted with how things are going.

def•i•ni•tion

The **gross domestic product (GDP)** represents the monetary value of goods produced during a specific period of time, such as a quarter or a year, and shows how fast the economy is growing. The U.S. government releases its GDP numbers quarterly.

This is the type of market in which value investors look to take profits made on earlier investments and stash cash for the next big sale. When the market is at or near its peak, don't buy anything; it's just a matter of time until its next fall.

Recession/Contraction

A recession/contraction is the opposite of what you'll see during a peak period. As the economy falls from its peak, employment levels begin to decline. Production and output eventually decline. People have less money to spend or fear they may lose their jobs. Wages and prices level off but likely won't fall unless the recession is a long, deep one.

Stocks are usually on sale during a recession, and that's when it's time for value investors to go bargain shopping. Just because a stock is cheap is no reason to buy it. You must be very careful when picking stocks that are a good buy and selling below their true market value.

Often during a peak market, stocks are sold beyond their true value, so just because a stock is on sale does not mean it's worth the price. You can know if the stock is truly worth its price only by scouring the annual report (we show you how in Part 2) and analyzing the numbers (we show you how in Part 3). We also discuss pricing strategies in Chapter 24.

Trough

When a recession/contraction finally hits bottom, it's called a trough. If this period at the bottom stretches out too long, it can become a depression, which is a severe, prolonged recession. The most recent depression in the United States was between 1929 and 1932. During a depression, the economy sits at the bottom of a trough, wages and employment stagnate, and everyone impatiently waits for the next expansion.

This can be the best time to do your research and look for those bargains. Research companies carefully determine the best price at which to buy, and buy the stocks when they reach that price. Of course, everyone hopes for the lowest price, but it's almost impossible to time that properly. You can wait until you see the stock start to move up, but you always risk the possibility that a good news announcement will send that stock price above what you are willing to pay. We talk more about value investing strategies in Part 5.

Expansion/Recovery

When the economy starts to grow again, employment picks up, along with factory outputs. The economy moves out of a trough and up toward its next peak. During this period, the economy heats up.

Finding Value

As the market nears its peak, it's time to sell and take profits. If you like the company, you can always buy the stock again during the next contraction or trough.

If you are a value investor, as the economy climbs toward its next peak, it's time to pull back on buying new stock. Hopefully during the contraction and while the market was at the trough, you found some great bargains and are watching your profits grow. Don't get too greedy. While you might want to wait until the stock hits it peak, the fall could be fast, so it's best not to try to time the peak when you're looking to take profits.

How can you tell when a market is nearing its peak? That's when everyone else is buying into stock and the stock prices for the companies you hold no longer look reasonable based on the financial statements. We talk more about stock pricing strategies in Chapter 24.

How to Recognize Parts of a Cycle

Learning how to recognize the parts of a cycle is difficult even for economists. In fact, officially, you won't even know when the economy hits a peak or a trough until months after the economy has passed that key part of the cycle.

The National Bureau of Economic Research (NBER) can make the official declaration of a recession or recovery only when all the numbers are in. Those numbers won't be available until about six months or more after the new part of the cycle begins.

For example, the NBER declared on November 26, 2001, that the current peak of the business cycle was reached on March 2001, about a year after everyone now believes the Internet stock bubble burst in March 2000. The NBER made another announcement on January 2004 that the peak may actually have been as early as November 2000. Now that we are far enough away from the event, economists believe the Internet stock bubble burst in March 2000.

An experienced value investor should never have gotten caught up in the Internet stock bubble. Anyone who did his or her homework would know that since the Internet companies had no cash earnings, they would not make good value investment choices. As you learn about value investing analysis tools, you'll see that it was a no-brainer to avoid the purchase of these stocks.

Finding Value

You can see a chart of the peaks and troughs for business cycles throughout history at the National Bureau of Economic Research's website, www.nber.org/cycles/cyclesmain.html.

But unfortunately, it's also just as hard for the NBER to figure out the end of a trough so you know when to start buying stocks again. The end of the trough after the Internet stock bubble burst was November 2001, but the NBER didn't declare this date until July 17, 2003. If you waited for the NBER announcement, you would have missed the best buying opportunities.

Why does it take the NBER so long? The information the NBER needs to make an official announcement is not available until months after the cycle ends. Then the NBER must take the time to collect and analyze the data.

The declaration of a recession/contraction or an expansion/recovery is based on at least six months of data. One quarter of good or bad news is not declared as a recession of good or bad news. For example, for a recession to be declared, there would need to be solid economic data that the economy contracted for the last two quarters in a row. By the time the NBER gets the data it needs for that six-month period, the economy is already likely moving toward its next step in the cycle.

Your best bet to try to determine where the economy is in a recession is to watch some key economic indicators. When the economy is at the earliest part of a recession, consumer expectations fall sharply and productivity levels drop.

You can follow two key indexes to get a quick look at the country's economic health and what consumers and businesses are spending.

- **Consumer Confidence Index (CCI)**—The Conference Board, a nonprofit business group, releases this index monthly. The CCI surveys the results of the spending of more than 5,000 households and gauges the financial health, spending power, and confidence of the average consumer. You can read the monthly press announcement from the Conference Board at www.conference-board.org/economics/consumerConfidence.cfm.

- **Durable Goods Report**—This report by the Census Bureau provides data on new orders received from more than 4,000 manufacturers of durable goods. Durable goods are higher-priced capital goods orders with a useful life of three years or more, such as cars, semiconductor equipment, and turbines. More than 85 industries are represented in the sample, which covers the entire United States. This report gives you an indication of business demand. You can view this report monthly at www.census.gov/indicator/www/m3/adv.

We take a closer look at market behavior and how it impacts stock prices in Chapter 10.

Big Booms, Big Busts

When the market hits a peak and keeps going, that's when an asset bubble is formed. You never, ever want to buy stock when you believe a bubble is forming. The most recent asset bubble was the U.S. housing market, when prices kept going up and up in the early 2000s until the bubble finally burst in 2006.

> **Value Visions**
>
> Burton Malkiel, who wrote the classic book on the stock market *A Random Walk Down Wall Street* (W. W. Norton & Company, 1996), describes asset bubbles as "greed run amok" and says they have been an "essential feature of every spectacular boom in history."

History continues to prove that skyrocketing markets depend on the support of crowd psychology. This "greed run amok" will succumb to the financial law of gravitation. While unsustainable prices may persist for years, eventually they will crash.

Frequently, when someone discusses investing bubbles, they talk of the tulip-bulb craze of the 1600s in Holland. Tulips were brought to Holland in 1593 from Turkey. They became very popular in Dutch gardens, until it turned into tulip mania. In January 1637, there was a 20-fold increase in tulip-bulb prices, which was followed by an even greater decrease in February of that year. This started a snowball effect that soon turned to panic, bankrupted many dealers, and finally resulted in a prolonged depression in Holland.

If you're interested in learning more about classic asset bubbles, you can search on the Internet for these key words: the South Sea Bubble of the 1800s in England, the Florida Real Estate Craze of the 1920s, and of course the bubble that ended with the 1929 stock market crash.

How Nonstock Bubbles Can Impact the Stock Market

In the early 2000s, we all saw the market crash with the bursting of the Internet bubble. A stock bubble is not the only kind of bubble that can cause the stock market to take a nosedive, as we all witnessed in horror in 2008. The Dow Industrial Average plunged in one year from a high of 13,930.01 in October 2007 to below 9,955.50 at the close of market on October 8, 2008—just two business days after the passage by Congress of the $700 billion bailout package to try to shore up the markets.

You would have to go back to September 2003 to find a month where the stock market closed below that point. In other words, the Dow lost 3,974.50, or 28.5 percent. Anything below 20 percent is the sign of a bear market. If you held on to your stocks, you would have lost all gains for a five-year period between 2003 and 2008. As a value investor, you should have pulled out when the bulls were running in 2003 and let the stocks fall off the cliff, then looked for bargains when the stocks hit bottom.

How did we get into this mess? The usual way the markets behave before and after a bubble. Easy money helped people buy homes that they really couldn't afford. Investors took advantage of this easy money as well to buy homes with little or no money down and quickly flipped them for a profit. These lending practices helped to inflate the bubble.

Unfortunately, the party that inflates an asset bubble can never last. As the bubble started to deflate, the people who got loans that couldn't really pay for them began defaulting on those loans, which led to record numbers of foreclosures. As foreclosures mounted, the value of homes across the country started to drop. This led to a lot more people than just the subprime borrowers stuck with homes that were worth less than their mortgages, and a dramatic increase in the number of foreclosures.

On top of that mess, the banks developed securities that they sold to help raise additional cash to loan money during the inflating of the bubble. It's these securities that the banks were not able to sell in 2008 because no one could put a market value on them. That doesn't mean they are worthless, but they can't be sold because no one knows what they are worth and they won't be able to figure that out until the entire mortgage mess is unraveled, which could take years. This created a credit market freeze, which meant not only it was difficult to get a mortgage, but it was also difficult for all types of businesses to get loans.

It's this credit freeze spreading through the market as a whole that caused the wider stock market meltdown. Since all types of companies can't get credit, they are having trouble paying their bills or taking steps toward growing their companies. Many retailers can't get credit to buy the products they need to sell for the upcoming holiday markets. Others are questioning whether they even need to buy the products because with the unemployment rate rising every month for the past eight months, many don't think there will be much of a holiday season.

The $700 billion bailout plan passed in October 2008 will enable the U.S. government to buy up the subprime mortgages and other mortgages in trouble to free up cash with the hopes that banks can start lending money again. Only time will tell whether this bailout plan will work. I'm writing this just after the passage of this bill, so the jury is out on how effective it will be.

Value investors should use this time at the bottom of the market to find the best bargains. Stocks are on sale, but the big problem is figuring out how much lower they can go. In these types of markets, watching and waiting can be your best bet until you see a clear sign that a recovery is on the way. You may miss the absolute bottom, but if you do a good job of research you can still find a lot of good bargains as the market regroups and starts back up.

Use History So You Don't Repeat Its Failures

The key lesson to learn about asset bubbles is how to recognize them. When did you realize the Internet stock bubble of the late 1990s was inflating? Did you get caught up in the frenzy to buy Internet stocks before they crashed in 2001?

If so, you need to learn from that mistake and begin to follow the core principle of value investing—buy stocks when they are a true bargain and learn to recognize business cycles. Buy when the economy is near the end of a contraction and stocks are on sale. Be sure to buy before the market starts moving too far up the curve to its next peak.

Take the time to research stock history further if you're not sure you can recognize the four parts of the business cycle. If you can't, you'll get caught up and repeat the failures other investors have learned throughout history.

The Least You Need to Know

- ◆ A value investor looks for bargains among stocks that are beaten down unjustifiably.

- ◆ The best time to buy value stocks is when the market is heading down into a trough or just starting its climb to the next peak.

- ◆ The best time for value investors to sell stocks is when the market is at or near its peak for a particular market cycle.

Part

Digging Deep—Reading Financial Reports

In this part, you'll learn how to use a key value investing tool—the financial reports provided by the companies. You'll explore the anatomy of a financial report, then focus on the key parts you should scour—the auditor's report, the financial statements, the notes to the financial statements, and management's discussion and analysis.

Chapter 4

Explore the Anatomy of Financial Reports

In This Chapter

◆ Meeting the parts

◆ Discovering the keys

◆ Recognizing the games

As an investor, your primary source of information about a company is its annual report. Value investors must scour those reports, and I'm not talking about the pretty pictures and glossy, well-designed text.

Don't be fooled by the easy-to-read sections that give you a glowing report about all the company's successes over the last year. That's not where you'll find the information you need to look at closely as a value investor. In this chapter, we explore the key parts of an annual report, highlight the four key parts you should digest in depth, and then alert you to some of the numbers games many companies play.

The Four Key Parts of an Annual Report

Every annual report has four key parts you must read. We suggest you read them in this order:

Part 1—The auditor's letter or auditor's report. The auditor's letter or auditor's report (either terminology can be used) is a one- or two-page section of the report signed by the auditors. You usually will find this letter either immediately before or immediately after the financial statements.

def•i•ni•tion

An **audit** is the examination and verification of a company's financial and accounting records. Audits for major corporations are performed by certified public accountants (CPAs). Auditors don't look at every piece of paper related to financial transactions, but instead review a sampling of the materials involved, as well as count the cash on hand.

The auditors highlight any problems they found during their *audit* in the financial reports in this letter. If they state they have "going-concern problems," watch out. This company may be headed for bankruptcy and you may not want to spend too much time researching it unless you want to specialize in buying stock in bankrupt companies. Some people do, but we don't recommend it unless you are a true specialist in this field. We talk more about what you can expect to see in the next part.

Part 2—Financial statements. The financial statements include the balance sheet (Chapter 5), the income statement (Chapter 6), and the statement of cash flows (Chapter 7). That's where you'll find a summary of the financial results for the company, but you'll need to dig deeper to find out what's behind these numbers.

Part 3—Notes to the financial statements. The notes to the financial statements is the section where you'll get all the detail about what's behind the financial numbers you see in the financial statements. We take a closer look at what you can expect to find in the financial statements in Chapter 8.

Part 4—Management's discussion and analysis. The company's managers discuss both their successes and failures during the year in this section. In addition, you'll find a discussion of any long-range future plans in the works. We talk more about what you can expect to find in this section of the annual report in Chapter 9.

After scouring these financial reports, you'll be able to analyze the numbers. We show you the formulas to use to measure profitability, liquidity, and cash, and how much you should pay for the stock in Chapter 11.

Breaking Down Parts of the Financial Reports

In most financial reports, the first thing you'll see is the letter to the shareholders from the chairman and CEO or president of the company. Those letters are written by the marketing and public relations staff, so don't think you'll get any juicy bits of information there. What you will find are carefully worded phrases that shout out the good news and try to hide the bad.

Even in these letters, you can find clues to some key types of trouble by watching for the red-flag words:

- **Challenging**—When you see this word used in the letter to shareholders, expect to find that the company was facing some significant difficulties with a particular product, service, or market. Look for further details in the not-so-glossy section of the report.

- **Restructuring**—This word lets you know that something wasn't working. You need to look for details in the not-so-glossy section of the report to find out what didn't work, what was done to fix it, and how much it's going to cost.

- **Corrective actions**—These words are used to gloss over mistakes in the opening letter. You'll find the details and the plan for fixing them in the sections usually printed in small type.

- **Difficulties**—This word is another sign of trouble, but you won't find the details in the opening letter—again, you'll need to scour the small print.

What you will find worth reading in the opening letter is information about key new initiatives, a general statement about the company's financial condition, performance summaries of key divisions or *subsidiaries*, and the initiatives or subsidiaries that are the future stars.

def•i•ni•tion

A **subsidiary** is any company for which a majority of the voting stock is owned by another company, known as the holding company.

So don't be fooled by these letters to shareholders that focus on the positive news and try to gloss over any bad news.

After the letter to the shareholders, you'll find pretty pictures and more glowing reports of the successes for the year. As with the opening letter, the marketing and public relations team wrote these pages. You will get a good idea of the successes for the year and find out more detail about any new initiatives, but don't count on this letter to give you the full picture of the financial state of the company.

These pages are then followed with one or two pages about who's in charge of the company and who's serving on the board of directors. Take some time to review the backgrounds of the people in charge. These are the ones you'll be paying if you decide to invest in that company, so it's good to know who they are and how they rose to a leadership position in the company.

Auditor's Letter or Report

As mentioned, the auditor's letter is an important part of the annual report that you should read before you spend any time looking at the core financial data. That's because if you see a statement indicating that the auditors found a "going-concern problem," you may not want to spend too much more time researching that company.

Losing Value

As a value investor, you'll look for companies that have experienced some bad years but that you think will turn around. Turnaround may not be in the cards for a company with a "going-concern problem," however. A "going-concern problem" means that auditors question whether that company has the financial means to continue operating. Often this statement appears just before the company announces the intention to file bankruptcy.

You'll find the auditor's report either just before or just after the financial statements. The auditor's letter has three key paragraphs—introductory paragraph, scope paragraph, and opinion paragraph.

Introductory Paragraph

In this paragraph, you'll find details about the time period the audit covers and who's responsible for preparing the financial statements. In most cases, the auditors state that management is responsible for the financial statements and that the role of the auditors is only to express an opinion about the statements based on their audit. Yes, the auditors are protecting themselves just in case problems are found in the financial statements and made public later.

Scope Paragraph

In the second paragraph, the auditors describe how they conducted the audit, including a statement that they used generally accepted audit standards. These standards require auditors to plan and prepare the audit to be reasonably sure that the financial statements are free of material misstatements. A material misstatement involves an error that could significantly impact a company's financial position.

Opinion Paragraph

In the third and, in most cases, final paragraph (sometimes this could be more than one paragraph if the auditors raised a number of questions), the auditors state their opinions about the financial statements. If no problems were found, this paragraph will be short and sweet and include a statement such as "The financial statements were prepared in conformity with *generally accepted accounting principles*" (*GAAP*).

When the auditors find no problems, all paragraphs are relatively short and sweet. This type of auditor's report is called a standard auditor's report. You'll find no qualifiers or red flags.

If you do find questions or red flags that limit the auditors' opinion, it's called a qualified or nonstandard report. Since, as a value investor, you are seeking to find beaten-down companies that you believe show good signs of recovery, you should expect to find some qualified auditor's reports when you do your research.

def•i•ni•tion

Generally accepted accounting principles (GAAP) are thousands of very detailed opinions developed over the years to establish how various transactions should be reported in the financial statements. The Federal Accounting Standards Advisory Board produces and manages GAAP rulings. You can learn more about GAAP at www.fasab.gov/accepted.html.

Finding Value

When you do see a nonstandard auditor's report, be sure to find a discussion of the problem cited by the auditors in the management's discussion and analysis (Chapter 9). Discover how the management team is handling the problem and how the problem could impact the long-term recovery of the company. Don't hesitate to call the investors relations department to ask questions before you decide to invest your hard-earned dollars in the company.

Value investors must dig deeper into the report to find out why the auditors had problems and try to determine whether you think the company can overcome its problems. As you read the other chapters in this part of the book, we'll give you a good idea of the red flags you might expect to find and how to interpret what you do find.

Some problems you may expect to find in a nonstandard auditor's report include these:

Work performed by another auditor. In most cases, this is not the sign of a major problem. Companies do change auditors, and the new auditor must depend on historical information from the previous auditor.

Look for an explanation in the annual report that states why the company changed auditors. Sometimes a company can get beaten down just because it changed auditors and Wall Street gets nervous.

Accounting policy change. Whenever a company decides to change an accounting policy or its accounting methods, the auditors must note the change in a nonstandard auditor's report. This may or may not be a sign of a problem.

If the auditors disagree with the change, though, watch out. Look for more information about the change in the notes to the financial statement (read Chapter 8 to find out more about the types of changes), and look to find out more about the reason for the change by reading the management's perspective in the management discussion of analysis.

Going-concern problem. This is the biggie. When you see this in any auditor's report, you are seeing the largest of the red flags. This means the auditors question whether the company has the ability to continue operating.

Specific disclosures. Sometimes the auditors question just one or two specific financial matters but still give the company a nonqualified opinion (see the following for an explanation of qualified opinions). In these instances, the auditors highlight a financial matter they believe investors should know about, but don't think these are signs of a significant problem. An example of this type of disclosure may be that the company is doing business with another company that has officers on the boards of both companies.

Qualified opinion. Whenever the auditors issue a nonstandard report, they also issue a qualified opinion in the final paragraph of the auditor's report. You don't always have to be alarmed by a qualified opinion, but you definitely should see it as a sign that you must research more carefully whatever the auditors question.

Now that you know what to look for, you understand the reason we recommend you read the auditor's report first—that's where you will find any significant red flags you must research further as you read the other key parts of the annual report. You'll find details about any problems the auditors found in the notes to the financial statement and in the management's discussion and analysis.

If you don't find enough information in these two sections of the annual report, you can ask for more information. Call the investors relations department and ask additional questions before you make an investment decision.

Number Games to Keep Your Eye On

Not all companies are straight shooters, and some even turn to extensive game playing to report positive numbers. While most times an outsider must depend on a whistleblower to expose these games, sometimes you can see some signs of trouble just looking at the numbers.

Up until the 2007 bank scandals, we thought Enron was the leader in creative accounting scandals. But many banks used similar tricks to hide their losses in the 2007 scandals.

The kings of using off-the-books transactions in the 2007 scandals were Merrill Lynch and Citigroup. In both cases, they found creative ways to manage their risky derivative trading by selling bonds to hedge funds or setting up other types of structures to keep the riskiest bond transactions off their books.

We found out about their shenanigans when the house of cards fell as subprime mortgages ended up in foreclosure and the credit markets froze. Investors saw signs of a problem, but no one knew how big it was until both companies finally spilled the beans and got rid of their chairmen and CEOs.

Companies correct many "errors" by restating their earnings. Whenever you see a company restating its earnings over several years, dig deeply into those numbers to find out what they did and how they are correcting it. Some common "errors" do involve cooking the books, and restating earnings can be a way of covering it up:

- ◆ **Big-bath charges**—Company insiders sometimes use this tactic to give their books a "big bath," which means they wash away past financial problems. In a bad year when earnings reports will be negative, that's an ideal time for the big bath. Since the company will be reporting losses, they take a bigger hit and then hope Wall Street will focus on plans for recovery.

♦ **Creative acquisitions**—Sometimes company insiders can hide problems as part of a merger or acquisition. Problems can be written off more easily if the merger or acquisition is being carried off using a stock swap instead of cash. Getting rid of the problems as part of the merger process can remove any future earnings drag and make future statements look better.

♦ **Cookie-jar reserves**—Companies sometimes hide their problems in good years by overstating liabilities, such as record higher sales returns or bad debts than the company experiences historically. Then when there is a bad year, they can take some of the liabilities out of this cookie jar and massage the numbers so they won't look so bad in a bad year.

♦ **Materiality**—Accounting rules give companies a lot of leeway as to whether a problem materially affects the company. For example, a company that has a net profit of $10 million would be impacted materially by a $1 million loss, but a $1 billion company will not be materially affected by a $1 million loss. The larger the net profits, the easier it is for companies to hide behind the issue of materiality and not have to report their losses.

♦ **Revenue recognition**—Companies frequently play games when they recognize revenues. Most often this is done when a company recognizes a sale (records the receipt of revenue in the books) even though the customer has the option to terminate, void, or delay the sale. We talk more about how you might watch for revenue-reporting problems when we dig into the income statement in Chapter 6.

♦ **Expenses**—The reporting of expenses can be used to hide problems as well. Companies can use noncash items like depreciation or amortization (where assets are written down slowly each year to show their use). Advertising expenses, research and development costs, patents, and licenses are all areas that can be used to play with the numbers. We discuss this more fully when we talk about the income statement in Chapter 6.

♦ **Oversize assets**—Assets shown on the balance sheet leave room for games, too. Accounts receivable and inventory accounts are the most likely types of accounts that can help hide problems. We discuss this more completely when we talk about the balance sheet in Chapter 5.

♦ **Undervalued liabilities**—Whenever a company undervalues its liabilities, the bottom line looks healthier. Accounts payable and certain types of contingent liabilities are two good places to hide problems. We take a closer look at this in Chapter 5 when we discuss the balance sheet.

Unfortunately, as an outsider, you will have a hard time unearthing the problems on your own. But as a value investor, you need to understand what can be done so that if you see a discussion of restructuring charges, mergers or acquisitions, or a restatement of earnings for a company you're thinking of adding to your investment portfolio, you will understand the possible implications for the past and future earnings of the company.

As we take a closer look at what is reported in each of the key parts of the annual report—financial statements (balance sheet—see Chapter 5), income statement (see Chapter 6), and statement of cash flows (see Chapter 7), the notes to the financial statement (see Chapter 8), and the management's discussion and analysis (see Chapter 9), we also point out red flags that you should watch for when researching each company.

First, let's take a look at what a company owns and owes by digging into the balance sheet in the next chapter.

The Least You Need to Know

- ◆ Get to know the parts of an annual report and be able to differentiate between the glossy good news and the small-print financial realities.

- ◆ Always look at the auditor's report first to be sure there are no red flags you must watch for in the rest of the annual report.

- ◆ Insiders can play games with the numbers. Get to know what those games are so you can read between the lines and find the warning signs.

Chapter 5

Balance Sheet—What the Company Owns and Owes

In This Chapter

◆ Assets owned

◆ Money due to creditors

◆ Owners' share

You can get a snapshot of a company's financial picture as of a certain date in time by looking at its balance sheet. The items on a balance sheet detail what the company owns, commonly called assets, and claims that are made against the company, which include liabilities (claims made by debtors) and owners' equity (claims made by owners or investors).

In this chapter, we introduce you to the financial items that make up a balance sheet. Then we show you the possible formats companies use for their balance sheets.

Balance Sheet Formula

The balance sheet is based on a core financial accounting formula:

Assets = Liabilities + Equity

To keep a company's books in balance, this formula must always be in the minds of the financial staff. In other words, for everything the company owns, the assets, there is a claim against those assets. The claim could be one made by creditors, which are called liabilities, such as a mortgage on a building. Or the claim could be one made by owners, such as shares of stock. Owners' claims are known as equity.

Just so you understand how the formula impacts a basic transaction, let's assume a company buys a new desk for $1,200 on credit. When the company enters that transaction in its books, it will look like this:

Furniture (Asset Account)	$1,200	
Credit Card (Liability Account)		$1,200

The two sides of this transaction are in balance. As we delve into the balance sheet, you'll learn more about what makes up the assets, liabilities, and equity portions of the balance sheet.

Matching Dates

As you begin to research and compare the financial position of various companies, carefully watch the dates on the financial statements you are using. You always need to keep in mind the date on which the balance sheet picture was taken. For example, if you're comparing Company A with a balance sheet prepared as of December 31, 2003, with Company B, which has a balance sheet as of June 30, 2004, you're not comparing apples to apples. Economic conditions could differ dramatically between those two time periods.

Companies can choose a fiscal year that is different than the calendar year, and many companies do. For example, many retail businesses use a fiscal year ending date of January 31, because they don't want to try to close their books for year-end in the middle of major holiday shopping in December.

So to compare two companies with different points of time on their year-end balance sheet, you'll need to use quarterly reports to get a month-by-month picture of the companies and prepare your own set of matching balance sheets as of a particular date in time. For example, suppose Company A uses a fiscal year that is the same as the calendar year ending December 31, 2007, but Company B uses a fiscal year ending October 31, 2007. You'll need to adjust for the two-month difference to compare these two companies.

If both of these companies are retail businesses, Company A would be including its sales from December 2007 in its balance sheet, while Company B would be including December 2006. Results during holiday sales change dramatically year by year.

To be able to compare the two companies and analyze their results, you need to find the monthly detail of each company's balance sheet. You'll be able to find this in their quarterly statements. Then you can create your own set of balance sheets with the exact same months.

Suppose you choose to use December 31, 2007, as the year-end for both companies. You would then need to use the first quarter reports for 2006–2007 and 2007– 2008 fiscal years of Company B to find the results for November and December of 2006 and 2007. You would take out the results for November and December 2006 and add in the results for November and December 2007. After doing this, you would have a balance sheet for Company B that matches the dates for the calendar-year results of Company A.

Finding Value

You can find the financial statements for most companies online in the investor section of their website. If they are not posted online, you can call a company's investor relations number and ask for a copy of the annual report and any quarterly reports you need.

Check for Rounding

Most companies round their numbers to make it easier for you to read the report. For example, suppose a company has over $1.5 million in cash assets. Without rounding, the cash assets could total $1,512,036. Imagine how hard it would be to read a balance sheet with sets of numbers that long. Your eyes would glaze over and you'd probably give up.

So to make things easier, companies round up their numbers and then indicate whether the numbers are rounded to the hundreds, thousands, or maybe even the millions. Smaller companies may round to the hundreds. Most public companies round to the thousands.

So how would the number $1,512,036 look on a balance sheet rounded to the thousands? It would be $1,512. That's much easier on the eyes when you're looking at pages and pages of financial statements. But do be sure you look for an indication of how the company is rounding its numbers. This can be particularly crucial if you are trying to compare a large company to a smaller company. The larger company may round its numbers to the thousands or millions, while the smaller company is rounding to the hundreds.

Formatting Differences

You'll find three different formats for the balance sheet as you start reading financial statements—the account format, the report format, and the financial position format. To make it easier for you to see the differences, I've put together samples of each format using small numbers (remember, most of the companies you'll be researching will have balance sheet accounts in the thousands or millions).

In Appendix C, you can see two of the formats for the builders we'll be analyzing. Builder A is shown in the account format, and Builder B is shown in the report format. The third format—financial position format—shows up when you are analyzing companies based outside the United States.

Account Format

The *account format*, the one you'll see most often, is presented horizontally, with the assets in the left column and the liabilities and equity in the right column. Here's what that format looks like:

Company A (Account Format)
As of December 31, XXXX

Assets		*Liabilities*	
Current Assets	$500	Current Liabilities	$300
Long-Term Assets	$200	Long-Term Liabilities	$250
Other Assets	$ 50	Total Liabilities	$550
		Shareholders' Equity	$200
Total Assets	$750	Total Liabilities/ Equity	$750

Remember, all balance sheets must show assets equal to liabilities plus equity. You're balancing out the total owned to the total claimed (by either creditors or shareholders).

Report Format

Some companies prefer to use a one-column layout called the report format. Here's what that looks like:

Company A (Report Format)
As of December 31, XXXX

Assets

Current Assets	$500
Long-Term Assets	$200
Other Assets	$ 50
Total Assets	$750

Liabilities

Current Liabilities	$300
Long-Term Liabilities	$250
Total Liabilities	$550
Shareholders' Equity	$200
Total Liabilities/Equity	$750

Financial Position Format

The format used most often by non-U.S.-based companies is the financial position format. The key difference between this format and the other two is that it has three lines that don't appear on the account and report format:

◆ **Working capital**—This summarizes the current assets the company has available to pay bills. You find the working capital by subtracting the current assets from the current liabilities on the other two formats.

◆ **Net assets**—This shows what is left for the company's shareholders after all liabilities have been subtracted from total assets.

◆ **Noncurrent assets**—This number includes long-term assets plus other assets.

Here is what the financial format looks like:

Company A (Financial Position Format)
As of December 31, XXXX

Assets

Current Assets	$500
Less: Current Liabilities	($300)
Working Capital	$200
Plus: Noncurrent Assets	$250
Total Assets Less Current Liabilities	$450
Less: Long-Term Liabilities	$250
Net Assets	$200

The net assets line item represents the portion of the company owned by the company's shareholders. On the other two formats, it was shown as "Shareholders' Equity." If you want to add an international component to your portfolio and start considering purchases of foreign stock, you will need to get used to this format.

Key Assets to Watch

Assets track everything the company owns. The item could be something as basic as cash or as massive as a factory. Essentially anything the company owns to operate the business fits in the asset category.

Current Assets

Anything a company owns that it plans to use in the next 12 months, whether it is cash in a checking or savings account or shares of marketable securities, is considered a current asset. Current assets are the lifeblood of a company's daily operations. Without these funds, the company would not be able to pay its bills and would have to close the doors. While cash is a key part of current assets, other assets will be used to operate the business during the next 12 months, including marketable securities, inventory, and accounts receivable. Let's take a closer look at each of these assets.

◆ Cash is basically the same thing you carry around in your pocket or pocketbook, or keep in your checking and savings accounts. Keeping track of the money is a lot more complex for companies, however, because they usually keep it in many different locations. Every multimillion-dollar corporation has numerous locations, and every location needs cash. A large corporation has a maze of bank accounts, cash registers, petty cash, and other places where cash is kept daily. The amount of cash you see on the balance sheet is the amount of cash found at all company locations on the particular day for which the balance sheet was created.

◆ Accounts receivable include any money due from customers who have bought on credit. This line item summarizes all individual customer accounts in which money is owed for products or services. For example, when you go to Sears and buy clothing using a Sears credit card, you have an individual account for which the money due on that credit card will be tracked. When Sears prepares its balance sheet at the end of an accounting period, it adds up all those individual accounts for which money is still due and puts that total on the balance sheet as accounts receivable.

◆ Marketable securities are a type of liquid asset, meaning that they can easily be converted to cash. They include holdings such as stocks, bonds, or other securities that are bought and sold daily. Companies buy securities primarily as a place to hold on to assets until the company decides how to use the money for its operations or growth.

◆ Inventory includes any products that the company makes or owns but plans to sell to its customers. The inventory on the balance sheet is valued at the cost to the company, not at the price at which the company hopes to sell the product.

◆ Long-term assets include assets that the company plans to hold for more than one year. Long-term assets include land and buildings; capitalized leases; leasehold improvements; machinery and equipment; furniture and fixtures; tools, dies, and molds; intangible assets; and others. Long-term assets must be *depreciated*.

◆ Land and buildings include any buildings or land. Companies must depreciate (show that the asset is gradually being used up by deducting a portion of the value) the value of their buildings each year, but the land portion of ownership isn't depreciated.

def•i•ni•tion

Depreciation is a method used to show that an asset is gradually being used up. For example, suppose that a truck the company owns must be replaced every five years because it's essentially used up—it needs more repair than is worth doing. During the time a company uses that truck, it subtracts a portion of the asset's value using depreciation, to show that the asset is no longer as valuable as it was when it was first bought.

Many people believe that depreciating the value of a building actually results in undervaluing a company's assets. The IRS allows 39 years for depreciation of a building, and after that time the building is considered valueless. That may be true in many cases, as for factories that need to be updated to current-day production methods, but a well-maintained office building usually lasts longer. A company that has owned a building for 20 or more years may, in fact, show the value of that building depreciated below its market value.

Real estate over the past 20 years has appreciated (gone up in value) greatly in most areas of the country. While we may be seeing a downturn in real estate values in 2007 and 2008, it's rare to find a commercial building that's worth less than it was 20 years ago if the building was well maintained.

So instead of a building's value going down because of depreciation, it may actually have gone up in value as the area real estate market appreciated. You can't determine the true value of land and buildings by looking at the financial reports. You have to find research reports written by analysts or the financial press to find discussion of the true value of a company's assets held.

Financial analysts often refer to this as hidden assets. That's because they're hidden from your view when you read the financial reports. You have no way to determine while reading those reports what the true marketable value of the buildings and land might be. For example, an office building that was purchased for $390,000 and held for 20 years might have a marketable value of $1 million if it were sold today, but it has been depreciated to $190,000 over the past 20 years. The value that will be shown on the financial statement is $190,000.

Sometimes a company takes possession of or constructs a building using a lease agreement that contains an option to purchase that property at some point in the future. If this is the case, you will see a line item on the balance sheet called capitalized leases. This means that, at some point in the future, the company could likely own the property and would then add the value of the property to its total assets owned. You can usually find a full explanation of the lease agreement in the notes to the financial statements.

Companies track improvements to property that's leased and not owned in the leasehold improvements account on the balance sheet. These items are depreciated because the improvements likely lose value as they age.

Other key long-term assets include these:

- **Machinery and equipment**—This includes all machinery and equipment used in the facilities or by employees. These assets depreciate just like buildings, but for shorter periods of time, depending on the company's estimate of their useful life.

- **Furniture and fixtures**—This includes all office furniture and any fixtures used in retail stores.

- **Tools, dies, and molds**—You'll find *tools, dies, and molds* on the balance sheet of manufacturing companies, but not on balance sheets for companies that don't manufacture their own products. The tools, dies, and molds listed on a balance sheet were developed specifically by the company or for the company and can have significant value.

So far, I've been discussing tangible assets. Now on to intangible assets.

Intangible Assets

Tangible assets are assets you can feel and touch. Some assets a company holds cannot be felt and touched, including patents, copyrights, trademarks, and goodwill. These are considered *intangible assets.*

Patents, copyrights, and trademarks are actually registered with the government, and the company holds exclusive rights to these items. If another company wants to use something that is patented, copyrighted, or trademarked, it must pay a fee to use those assets.

Patents give the companies the right to dominate the market for a particular product. For example, pharmaceutical companies can be the sole source for a drug that is still under patent. Copyrights also give companies exclusive rights for sale. Books that are copyrighted can be printed only by the publisher or individual that owns the copyright, unless someone has bought the rights from the copyright owner.

Goodwill is a different type of asset, reflecting things like the value of a company's locations, customer base, or consumer loyalty. Companies essentially purchase goodwill when they buy another company for a price that's higher than the value of a company's tangible assets or market value. The premium that's paid for the company is kept in an account called "goodwill," shown on the balance sheet.

Other Assets

"Other assets" is the line item where you'll find things a company owns that don't fit into one of the other asset categories on the balance sheet. The actual items shown in this category vary by company.

Some companies put *unconsolidated subsidiaries* or *affiliates* in this category.

def•i•ni•tion

Unconsolidated subsidiaries or **affiliates** involve the ownership of less than a controlling share in another company. To list an unconsolidated subsidiary or affiliate, the company must own less than 50 percent but more than 20 percent. If the company owns less than 20 percent of another company's stock, its ownership is tracked as a marketable security.

You usually don't find more than one line item that totals all unconsolidated subsidiaries or affiliates. Sometimes more detail is mentioned in the notes to the financial reports or in the managers' commentary, but you often can't tell by reading the financial reports and looking at this category what other businesses the company owns. You have to read the financial press or analyst reports to find out the details.

Accumulated Depreciation

On a balance sheet, you may see numerous line items that start with *accumulated depreciation*. These line items appear under the type of asset whose value is being depreciated or shown as a total at the bottom of long-term assets.

def•i•ni•tion

Accumulated depreciation is the total amount depreciated against tangible assets over the life span of the assets shown on the balance sheet.

Although some companies show accumulated depreciation under each of the long-term assets, it's becoming common for companies to total accumulated depreciation at the bottom of the long-term assets section of the balance sheet. This method of reporting makes it harder for financial report readers to determine the actual age of the assets because depreciation isn't indicated by each type of asset; thus, you have no idea which assets have depreciated the most—in other words, which assets are the oldest.

Yet this information can be critical to value investors. The age of machinery and factories can be significant factors when trying to determine a company's value and what its future costs may be to maintain or expand the company.

A company with mostly aging plants needs to spend more money on repair or replacement than a company that has mostly new facilities. Look for discussion of this in the managers' commentary or the notes to the financial statement. If you don't find it there, you have to dig deeper by reading analyst reports or reports in the financial press.

Crucial Liabilities You Must Care About

Companies must spend money to operate day-to-day. Whenever a company makes a commitment to spend that money on credit, whether it is short term using a credit card or long term using a mortgage, those commitments become debts or liabilities that must be repaid in the future.

Current Liabilities

Current liabilities are any obligations that a company must pay during the next 12 months. These include short-term loans, the current portion of long-term debt (for example, the mortgage payments due over the next 12 months), accounts payable, and accrued liabilities. If the company can't pay these bills, it could go out of business or go into bankruptcy.

- ◆ **Short-term borrowings** include lines of credit the company takes to manage cash flow. When a company borrows this way, it isn't much different than when you use a credit card or personal loan to pay bills until your next paycheck. As you know, these types of loans usually carry the highest interest rate charges, so if a company can't repay them quickly, it converts the debt to something longer term with lower interest rates. This type of liability should be a relatively low number on the balance sheet, compared to other liabilities. If the number isn't low, it could be a sign of trouble indicating the company is having difficulty securing long-term debt or meeting its cash obligations.

- ◆ **Current portion of long-term debt** shows the payments due on long-term debt during the current fiscal year. Any portion of the debt that's owed beyond the current 12 months is reflected in the long-term liabilities section of the balance sheet.

- ◆ **Accounts payable** summarizes the money the company owes to others that it does business with, such as vendors, contractors, suppliers, and consultants. Companies list money they owe to others for products, services, supplies, and other short-term needs (invoices due in less than 12 months) in accounts payable.

- ◆ **Accrued liabilities** have been incurred, but the company hasn't yet paid the bill at the time a company prepares the balance sheet. For example, companies include income taxes, royalties, advertising, payroll, management incentives, or employee taxes that aren't yet paid in this line item. Sometimes a company breaks out items like income taxes payable individually without using a catch-all line item called accrued liabilities. When you look in the notes, you see more detail about the types of company financial obligations included and the total of each type of liability.

Long-Term Liabilities

Any money the company must pay out for more than 12 months in the future is considered a *long-term liability*. Long-term liabilities won't throw a company into bankruptcy, but if they become too large, the company could have trouble paying its bills in the future.

Many companies keep the long-term liabilities section short and sweet, and group almost everything under one lump sum, such as long-term debt. Long-term debt includes mortgages on buildings, loans on machinery or equipment, or bonds that need to be repaid at some point in the future. Other companies break out the type of debt, showing mortgages payable, loans payable, and bonds payable.

You can find out more detail about what the company actually groups in the other liability category in the notes to the financial statement. (Guess you're getting used to that phrase!)

Look at Equity—Owners' Stake

The final piece of the balancing equation is equity. Somebody owns all companies, and the claims these owners have against the assets owned by a company are called equity. In a small company, the equity owners are individuals or partners. In a corporation, the equity owners are shareholders.

Stock

Stock represents a portion of ownership in a company. Each share of stock has a certain value based on the price placed on the stock when it was originally sold to investors. This price isn't affected by the current market value of the stock. Any increase in a stock's value after its initial offering to the public isn't reflected here. The market gains or losses are actually taken by the stockholders, not the company, when the stock is bought and sold on the market.

Some companies issue two types of stock:

- Common stockholders own a portion of the company and can vote on issues taken to the stockholders. If the board decides to pay *dividends*, common stockholders get their portion of those dividends as long as the preferred stockholders have been paid in full.

- Preferred stockholders hold stock that's actually somewhere in between common stock and a bond. Although they don't get back the principal they paid for the stock, like a bondholder does, they have first dibs on any dividends.

  Preferred stockholders are guaranteed a certain dividend each year. If a company doesn't pay dividends for some reason, these dividends are accrued for future years and paid when the company has enough money. Accrued dividends for preferred stockholders must be paid before common stockholders get any money. The disadvantage for preferred stockholders is that they have no voting rights in the company. In some cases, depending on how the preferred stock is issued, preferred stockholders do get voting rights if dividends are paid for a while.

def•i•ni•tion

Dividends are a certain portion per share paid to common stockholders from profits. A company's board of directors declares the amount of the dividend to be paid. Dividends are usually paid on a quarterly basis.

Secured debtors are debtors who have loaned money based on specific assets, such as a mortgage on a building. The asset has been promised as a guarantee against the debt. If the company doesn't pay a secured debt, the debtor could foreclose on the asset and take the property, much like banks are doing to homeowners who can't pay their mortgage.

Why does it matter whether one holds a bond as a liability or a stock? If a company goes bankrupt, the bondholders hold first claim on any money remaining after the employees and *secured debtors* are paid. The preferred stockholders are next in line, and the common stockholders are at the bottom of the heap and are frequently left with valueless stock.

Retained Earnings

Each year, a company makes a choice to either pay out its net profit to its stockholders or retain all or some of it for reinvesting in the company. Any profit not paid to stockholders over the years is accumulated in an account called retained earnings.

Now that you have a better idea of what each of the key line items means on the balance sheet, in the next chapter, we delve deeper into the line items you'll find on the income statement.

The Least You Need to Know

- A balance sheet is a snapshot of a company's financial position as of a particular date in time.

- The assets section of the balance sheet gives you a snapshot of everything the company owns.

- The liabilities section of the balance sheet gives you a snapshot of everything the company owes to its creditors.

- The equity section of the balance sheet gives you a snapshot of what portion of the assets the shareholders own.

6

Income Statement—Are There Profits?

In This Chapter

- ◆ Key parts
- ◆ Considering format
- ◆ Recognizing revenues
- ◆ Locating expenses
- ◆ Determining profits

As a value investor, you definitely want to be sure the company is earning a profit before you decide to buy the stock. Now that might sound funny to you, but a lot of people buy growth stocks that operate in the red with hopes of earning money sometime in the future.

Everyone who bought Internet stocks as the bubble inflated in the early 2000s made that mistake. No Internet stock was earning a profit during that time, yet growth investors bid some of the Internet darlings over $100 a share even though there was no income-earning stream in sight.

As a value investor, you'll learn to stay away from those bubbles because you won't even consider investing in the stock of a company that doesn't show earnings each quarter. The income statement is the financial statement that you'll check for profits and losses. In this chapter, we explore the parts of the income statement and show you what you need to look for in this statement.

What's in an Income Statement?

An income statement shows the financial results of a company over a certain period of time. This time period could be a month, a quarter (three months), a year, or some other period of time that makes sense to the business. At the top of the income statement you'll see a statement such as "Month Ended July 2008," which means the statement shows the financial results of a company for the month of July 2008. If you see "Year Ended 2008," that income statement shows you the results for the entire year of 2008.

Each statement has four key sections:

- **Sales or revenues**—This section shows you the total amount of cash the company took in from its sales of products or services.

- **Cost of goods sold**—This section shows you how much the company spent to buy the goods it sold to customers.

- **Expenses**—This section shows you how much the company spent on everything else, such as advertising, rent, salaries, and anything else related to running the business.

- **Net income or loss**—This is the bottom line—how much profit the company made or how much money it lost. If the company took in more money in sales than it spent, the bottom line is a profit. If the company spent more than the cash it took in, the bottom line shows a loss.

The name of this financial statement is not always income statement. Some companies file it with other titles:

- Statement of operations

- Statement of earnings

- Statement of operating results

Exploring How Income Statements Look

Not all companies use the same format for income statements. Some companies use a single-step; others use a multistep format. Both formats give you the same bottom-line information.

The primary difference between these formats involves whether the information is summarized to make it easier for you to analyze. The single-step format is simpler for the accounting staff to produce, but the multistep format gives you a number of sub-totals throughout the statement that make analyzing a company's results easier.

Most public corporations use the multistep format, but many smaller companies, especially those that don't have to report to the general public, use the single-step format. You can see two sample statements for the builders we'll be analyzing in Appendix C.

Single-Step Format

The single-step format groups all data into two categories: revenue and expenses. Revenue includes income from sales, interest income, and gains from sales of equipment. It also includes income that the company raises from its regular operations or from one-time transactions, such as from the sale of a building. *Expenses* include all the costs that are involved in bringing in the revenue.

The single-step format gets its name because you perform only one step to figure out a company's net income: you subtract the expenses from the revenue. Here's what the single-step format looks like:

Company A
Year-End December 31, 2008

Revenues

Sales	$5,000
Interest Income	500
Total Revenue	**$5,500**

Expenses

Cost of Goods Sold	$2,500
Depreciation	100
Advertising	500
Salaries and Wages	500
Insurance	100
Supplies	100
Interest Expense	50
Income Taxes	100
Total Expenses	**$3,950**
Net Income	**$1,550**

Multistep Format

The multistep format divides the income statement into several sections and gives you some critical subtotals to make analyzing the data much easier and quicker. Even though the single-step and multistep income statements include the same revenues and expenses information, they group the information differently. The key difference between these two formats is that the multistep format has the following four profit lines:

- **Gross profit**—This subtotal gives you the profit generated from sales minus the cost of the goods sold.

- **Income from operations**—This subtotal shows the income the company earned after all its expenses have been subtracted.

- **Income before taxes**—This subtotal shows all income earned, which can include gains on equipment sales, interest revenue, and other revenue not generated by sales, before taxes are subtracted.

- **Net income**—This total gives you the bottom line—whether the company made a profit.

Many companies add even more profit lines. Most commonly, you will see a line called EBITDA. These initials stand for earnings before interest, taxes, depreciation, and amortization. We talk more about EBITDA and what it means for your analysis of the company later in this chapter.

Using the same items as in the single-step format, here's what a multistep format looks like:

Company A
Year-End December 31, 2008

Revenues

Sales	$5,000
Interest Income	500

Total Revenue	**$5,500**
Cost of Goods Sold	**$2,500**
Gross Profit	**$3,000**

Operating Expenses

Advertising	500
Salaries and Wages	500
Insurance	100
Supplies	100
Interest Expense	50
Depreciation	100

Total Operating Expenses	**$1,350**
Net Income Before Taxes	**$1,650**
Income Taxes	100
Net Income	**$1,550**

Now that you have a better understanding of the formats, let's take a look at what's behind all these numbers on an income statement.

Revenues and Their Direction

Sales are not always sales. Sometimes revenue is recognized before cash is received. Sometimes revenue must be reduced because of discounts or returns.

When a Sale Is a Sale

When a company recognizes something as revenue, it doesn't always mean that the company has actually received any cash. It may not even mean that the product was actually delivered to the customer. Companies use something called *accrual accounting*, which leaves room for deciding when revenue is actually recorded.

def•i•ni•tion

Accrual accounting, which is a method of accounting businesses commonly use, recognizes revenue when it's earned, not necessarily when the money is collected. It also recognizes expenses when they are incurred, even though they may not yet have been paid for.

Because accrual accounting doesn't require that a company actually have the cash in hand to count something as revenue, senior managers can play games to make the bottom line look the way they want it to look by either counting or not counting income. Sometimes they acknowledge more income than they should to improve the financial reports; other times, they reduce income to reduce the tax bite.

When a company wants to count something as revenue, it can use different factors to decide whether a particular sale should be counted. Here are some rules that must be followed:

♦ If the seller and buyer haven't agreed on the final price for the merchandise and service, the seller can't count the revenue as collected. Suppose you're the owner of a car dealership and you want your sales to look good at the end of a month. You've been working with a customer, and your customer has even picked out the car she wants, but you're still negotiating the price. You can't include that sale until you both agree to a price and sign a contract.

♦ If the buyer doesn't pay for the merchandise until the company resells it to a retail outlet (which may be the case for a company that works with a distributor) or to the customer, the company can't count the revenue until the sale to the customer is final. Suppose you sell books to bookstores but allow bookstore owners to return unsold books within a certain amount of time. So there's a good chance some of those books will be returned unsold. You must take this into account when reporting revenues on these types of deals. For example, a publisher would likely use historical data to estimate what percentage of books will be returned and adjust sales downward to reflect those likely returns.

♦ If the buyer and seller are related, revenue isn't acknowledged in the same way. (No, we're not talking about a husband and wife here—we're talking about when the buyer is the parent company or subsidiary of the seller.) Companies must handle revenue as an internal transfer of assets.

◆ If the buyer isn't obligated to pay for the merchandise because it's stolen or physically destroyed before it's delivered or sold, the company can't acknowledge the revenue until the merchandise is actually sold. For example, a bookseller works with a distributor or other middleman to get its books into retail stores. If the distributor or middleman doesn't have to pay for those books until they're delivered or sold to retailers, the manufacturer can't count the books that were shipped to the middleman or distributor as revenue until the distributor or middleman sells the books.

◆ If the seller is obligated to provide significant services to the buyer or aid in reselling the product, the seller can't count the sale of that product as revenue until the sale is actually completed with the final customer. For example, a computer manufacturer might offer installation or follow-up services for a new product as part of a sales promotion. If those services are a significant part of the final sale, the manufacturer can't count that sale as revenue until the installation or service has been completed with the customer. Items shipped for sale to local computer stores under these conditions wouldn't be considered sold, so they can't be counted as revenue.

Adjusting Sales

Not all products sell for their list price. Companies frequently use discounts, returns, or allowances to reduce the prices of products or services. As a financial report reader, you won't see the specifics about discounts offered in the income statement, but you may find some mention of significant discounting in the notes to the financial statements. These are the most common types of adjustments companies make to their sales:

◆ *Volume discounts* are offered by manufacturers to retailers to get more items into the marketplace. For example, one of the reasons you get such good prices at discount stores like Wal-Mart and Target is that the companies buy products from the manufacturer at greatly discounted prices for their thousands of stores. When a company offers volume discounts, their revenues are reduced.

def•i•ni•tion

Volume discounts are offered to retailers by a manufacturer to encourage the retailers to buy a large number of the manufacturer's product, to save a certain percentage of money off the price.

◆ **Return** arrangements between the buyer and seller allow the buyer to return goods for a number of reasons. You've probably returned goods that you didn't like, that didn't fit, or that possibly didn't even work. When you return these products, they must be subtracted from revenue.

◆ **Allowances** include gift cards and other types of accounts that a customer pays for up front without taking merchandise. Allowances are actually liabilities for a store because the customer hasn't yet selected the merchandise and the sale isn't complete. At some point in the future, merchandise will be taken off the shelves and additional cash won't be received. When allowances are given, revenues are collected up front. When the merchandise is actually taken, no revenue is recorded.

Most companies don't show you the details of their discounts, returns, and allowances, but they do track them and adjust their revenue accordingly. When you see a *net sales* or *net revenue* figure (the sales made by the company minus any adjustments) at the top of an income statement, the company has already adjusted the figure for these items. Internally, managers see the details regarding these adjustments in the sales area of the income statement, so they can track trends for discounts, returns, and allowances.

Costs and Their Impact

Like the sales line item, the *cost of goods sold* line item has many different pieces that make up its calculation on the income sheet. You don't see the details for this line item unless you're a company manager. Few companies report their cost of goods sold details to the general public.

def•i•ni•tion

Cost of goods sold summarizes what it costs to manufacture or purchase the goods that a business sells to its customers.

Items that make up the cost of goods sold vary depending on whether the company manufactures the goods in-house or purchases them from another company. If the company manufactures them in-house, the costs are tracked from the point of raw materials all the way through the manufacturing process, including the labor involved in building the product. If a company purchases the goods it plans to sell, it needs to track only the cost of purchasing those goods and shipping them to the retail stores or other locations at which they will be sold.

Even if a company is only a service company, it likely has costs for the services provided. In this case, the line item may be called "cost of services sold" rather than "cost of goods sold." You may even see a line item called "cost of goods or services sold" if a company gets revenue from both the sale of goods and the sale of services. For example, a computer consulting company may provide services to customize a software program to better match the workings of the company planning to use it. The consulting firm did not sell the product; it sold the services of customization.

Gauging Gross Profit

The gross profit line item in the revenue section of the income statement calculates net revenue or net sales minus the cost of goods sold. With this number, you see the difference between what a company pays for its inventory and the price at which the company sells this inventory. You can see at a glance how much profit a company makes selling its products before deducting the expenses of operation. If there's no profit or not enough profit here to cover the operating expenses and make some money, it's not worth being in business—and it's definitely not worth investing in the company.

You should watch the trend of a company's gross profit because it indicates the effectiveness of a company's purchasing and pricing policies. Analysts frequently use this number not only to gauge how well a company manages its product costs internally, but also to gauge how well a company manages its product costs compared to other companies in the same business.

If profit is too low, a company can do one of two things: find a way to increase sales revenue or find a way to reduce the cost of the goods it's selling.

To increase sales revenue, a company can raise or lower prices to increase the amount of money it's bringing in. Raising the prices of its product obviously will bring in more revenue if the same number of items is sold, but it could bring in less revenue if the price hike turns away customers and fewer items are sold. Lowering prices to bring in more revenue may sound strange to you, but if a company determines that its price is too high and is discouraging buyers, doing so may increase its volume of sales and, therefore, its gross margin. This scenario is especially true if the company has a lot of *fixed costs* (such as manufacturing facilities, equipment, and labor) that aren't being used to full capacity. A company could use its manufacturing facilities more effectively and efficiently if it has the capability to produce more products without a significant increase in *costs* such as raw materials or other factors, such as overtime.

A company can also consider using cost-control possibilities for manufacturing or purchasing if its gross profit is too low. The company may find a more efficient way to make the product or may negotiate a better contract for raw materials to reduce those costs. If the company purchases finished products for sale, it may be able to negotiate better contract terms to reduce its purchasing costs.

If you think the gross profit looks low when you read the income statement, look for a discussion of what management is planning to do in the management's discussion and analysis section of the financial report. We talk more about that section in Chapter 9.

Keeping Expenses Under Control

Once a company calculates its gross profit, it must take a closer look at the expenses incurred in operating the business. A business needs administrative offices, advertising, retail stores (for which one must pay rent), and other expenses to sell the products or services to its customers.

Expenses include the items a company must pay for in order to operate the business that aren't directly related to the sale and production of specific products. These differ from the cost of goods sold, which can be directly traced to the actual sale of a product. Even when a company is making a sizable gross profit, if management doesn't carefully watch the expenses, the gross profit can quickly turn into a net loss.

Expenses make up the second of the two main parts of the income statement; revenues make up the first part.

Advertising and promotion, administration, and research and development are all examples of expenses. Although many of these expenses impact the ability of a company to sell its products, they aren't direct costs of the sales process for individual items. Here are some key expenses you'll find on the income statement:

- ◆ **Advertising and promotion** can be one of the largest expenses for a company. Advertising includes TV and radio ads, print ads, and billboard ads. Promotions include product giveaways, such as hats, T-shirts, or pens with the company logo on them, or name identification on a sports stadium. For example, if a company helps promote a charitable event and has its name on T-shirts or billboards as part of the event, these expenses are included in the advertising and promotion expense line item.

- **General office needs** include administrative salaries, expenses for administrative offices, supplies, machinery, and anything else needed to run the general operations of a company. Expenses for human resources, management, accounting, and security also fall into this category.

- **Royalties** include payments to individuals or other companies for use of property owned by someone else. Companies most commonly pay royalties for the use of patents or copyrights owned by another company or individual. Companies also pay royalties when they buy the rights to extract natural resources from another person's property.

- **Research and product development** includes any costs incurred to develop new products. Most likely, you'll find detail about research and product development in the notes to the financial statements or in the management's discussion and analysis. Any company that makes new products incurs research and development costs because it must always look for ways to improve its product or introduce new products, to avoid losing out to a competitor.

- **Interest expenses** include expenses paid for interest on long- or short-term debt. You usually find some explanation for the interest expenses in the notes to the financial statements.

- **Interest income** includes interest income for any savings accounts or bonds it holds. If the company loans money to another, any interest income from this loan is shown in this line item.

- **Depreciation expenses** show the usage (or depreciation) of buildings and machinery.

- **Insurance expenses** include any expenses for insurance, including protections against theft, fire, and other losses. In addition, companies usually carry life insurance on its top executives and *errors and omissions insurance* for its top executives and board members.

def•i•ni•tion

Errors and omissions insurance protects executives and board members from being sued personally for any errors or omissions related to their work for the company or as part of their responsibility on the company's board.

- **Taxes**—yes, even corporations pay taxes on their income, although they do have lots of tax breaks to minimize the expense. In the taxes category, you find the amount the company actually paid in taxes.

Exploring Profit

When you listen to business news reports about a company on TV, you'll usually hear mention of earnings or profits. The financial news reporters usually are discussing the net profit, net income, or net loss. For readers of financial statements, that bottom-line number doesn't tell the entire story of how a company is doing. If you rely solely on the bottom-line number, it's like reading only the end of a book. You may know how the story ends, but you have no idea how the characters got to that point.

As value investors, you need to understand the many different charges or expenses unique to a business's operations. We talk more about analyzing these numbers in Part 3, but you do need to understand the different types of profit lines on the income statement so you can do the analysis.

In this chapter, we briefly review what each of these profit line items includes or doesn't include. For example, gross profit is the best number to use to analyze how well a company is managing its sales and the costs of producing those sales; however, you have no idea how well the company is managing the rest of its expenses. Using operating profits, which show you how much money was made after considering all costs and expenses for operating the company, you can analyze how efficiently the company is managing its operating activities, but you don't get enough detail to analyze product costs.

EBITDA

When you read or listen to financial news, you may hear mention of another commonly used type of profit line called EBITDA, which stands for earnings before interest, taxes, depreciation, and amortization. You can use this number to compare profitability among companies or industries because it eliminates the effects of the companies' activities to raise cash outside of their operating activities, such as by selling stock or bonds. EBITDA also eliminates any accounting decisions that could impact the bottom line, such as the companies' policies relating to depreciation methods.

You can more easily focus on the profitability of each company's operations by using EBITDA in your analysis. If a company does include this line item, it will appear at the bottom of the expenses section but before line items listing interest, taxes, depreciation, and amortization. If it's not included on the income statement, you'll need to calculate it to be able to compare apples to apples. You can easily calculate it by adding the line items for interest, taxes, depreciation, and amortization back to the net profit shown at the bottom of the income statement.

How a company chooses to raise money can greatly impact its bottom line. Selling equity has no annual costs if dividends aren't paid. Borrowing money means interest costs must be paid every year, so a company will have ongoing required expenses.

EBITDA gives financial report readers a quick view of how well a company is doing without considering its financial and accounting decisions.

Finding Value

EBITDA became very popular in the 1980s when leveraged buyouts were common. In a leveraged buyout, an individual or a company buys a controlling interest (which means more than 50 percent) in a company primarily using debt. Many times, the individual or company pays 70 percent or more of the purchase price using debt. This fad of the 1980s left many companies in a situation in which investors had to carefully watch that the company earned enough from operations to pay its huge debt load. When you're considering a company as a potential value investment, look carefully at that debt load.

Companies can get pretty creative when it comes to their income statement groupings. If you don't understand a line item, be sure to look for explanations in the notes to the financial statements. If you can't find an explanation there, call investor relations and ask questions.

Nonoperating Income or Expenses

Sometimes a company earns income from a source that isn't part of its normal revenue-generating activities. In that case, it usually lists this income on the income statement as "nonoperating income."

For example, suppose a company sold one of its buildings or divisions and made a profit. That gain on the sale of a building or division is income that wasn't made in the normal course of operations, so it should be listed in the nonoperating section of the income statement. Other types of nonoperating income include interest from notes receivable and marketable securities, dividends from investments in other companies' stock, and rent revenue if the company subleases some of its facilities.

Companies also group one-time expenses in the nonoperating section of the income statement. Suppose the company decided to close one of its factories or a division of the company. Costs involved in this one-time restructuring would be listed in this section of the income statement. Other types of expenses that you may find in this section of the income statement include casualty losses from theft, vandalism, or fire; loss from the sale or abandonment of property, plant, or equipment; and loss from employee or supplier strikes.

You usually find explanations for income or expenses from nonoperating activities in the notes to the financial statements. You should always carefully consider this non-operating income and expenses when you're thinking about buying or selling stock in a company as a value investor. You want to be able to differentiate profit made from ongoing activities versus one-time profit or loss for an unusual event.

It's important to understand how well a company is doing with its core operating activities. The core operating activities line item is where you find a company's continuing income. If those core activities aren't raising enough income, the company may be on the road to significant financial difficulties. You definitely don't want to buy the stock of a company whose core operating activities are not producing a profit.

Net Profit or Loss

The bottom line of any income statement is the net profit or loss. This number means very little if you don't understand the other line items that make up the income statement. Few investors and analysts look solely at the net profit or loss to make a major decision about whether a company is a good investment.

Calculating Earnings per Share

Another number you'll hear frequently in the financial news is the earnings per share number. While we don't recommend you make decisions about a company based on that number, you should understand what it represents. Many companies show this number at the bottom of their income statement.

Earnings per share is the amount of net income the company made per share of stock available on the market. For example, if Company A earned $1 million and there are 1 million shares on the market, the earnings per share was $1. If you own 100 shares of stock in Company A, $100 of those earnings would be yours unless the company decided to reinvest it in the company for future growth. In reality, a company rarely pays out 100 percent of its earnings. It usually pays out a very small fraction of those earnings.

You find the earnings per share calculation after net income on the income statement or in a separate statement called the statement of shareholders' equity. The calculation for earnings per share is relatively simple: you divide the number of outstanding shares (which you can find on the balance sheet) by the net earnings (which you find on the income statement).

Many companies break down this figure further according to their income statement subgroups, so you find an earnings per share from continuing operations, an earnings per share from discontinued operations, and an earnings per share from net income. If the company has even more groupings on an income statement, you're likely to find even more breakdowns for its earnings per share.

Now that you're familiar with the income statement, we have one more key financial statement to explore—the statement of cash flows. This statement focuses on the cash that flowed into the business and the cash that flowed out. We take a closer look at that statement in the next chapter.

The Least You Need to Know

- The income statement has two key sections: revenues and expenses. The revenues section shows you how much money was made by selling the products or services of the company, and the expenses section shows you how much money was spent operating the company.

- An income statement comes in two key formats. The single-step format shows the two key sections—revenue and expenses. The multistep format groups the key numbers into smaller steps, to make it easier for you to analyze how well the company is doing.

- Always look for details about profits made from operating activities versus profits made from one-time events. It's the profits made from operating activities that you can count on year after year, as long as the company continues to be well managed.

Chapter 7

Where the Cash Goes

In This Chapter

- Cash inflows and outflows
- Cash from operations
- Cash from investments
- Cash from borrowing

Every company needs cash to operate, but the balance sheet and income statement don't actually show you how much cash came into the company and how much cash went out of the company to pay obligations. If you want to actually track the cash flow, the only way you can do that is with the statement of cash flows.

In this chapter, we explore what you can expect to find on the statement of cash flows and what it means.

Show Me the Cash

On the statement of cash flows, you'll find a summary of all the cash receipts, cash payments, and changes in cash that a company holds, minus the expenses that were incurred from operating the company. In addition, the statement looks at money that flows into or out of the company through investing and financing activities.

When reading the statement of cash flows, you should be looking for answers to these three questions:

◆ Where did the company get the cash needed for operation during the period shown on the statement? As a value investor, it's important to know whether the cash came from revenue generated, funds borrowed, or stock sold. You definitely want to steer clear of a company that gets most of its cash from borrowing money. That means it's not generating enough cash to operate.

◆ How much cash did the company actually spend during the periods shown on the statement?

◆ How did the cash balance change during each of the years shown on the statement? You will usually find a summary of three years of cash flow on a statement of cash flows.

By knowing the answers to these questions, you can determine whether the company is financially healthy and has the cash it needs to continue operating or whether the company appears to have a cash flow problem. Hefty borrowing could be a sign that the company is nearing a point of fiscal disaster.

Transactions shown on the statement of cash flows are grouped into three parts:

def•i•ni•tion

Capital improvements are upgrades to assets held by the company. For example, if the company buys a new building or rents new space, any renovations done to get that new property ready for use are a capital improvement.

◆ **Operating activities** includes cash transactions that summarize revenue taken into the company through sales of its products or services and expenses paid out for operations.

◆ **Investing activities** includes the purchase or sale of the company's investments. This can include the purchase or sale of long-term assets, such as a building or a company division. Spending on *capital improvements*, such as the renovation of a building, also fits in this category, as does any buying or selling of short-term invested funds.

◆ **Financing activities** involves raising cash either through borrowing through long-term debt or by issuing new stock. It also includes using cash to pay down debt or buy back stock. Companies also include any dividends paid in this section.

Looking at Formats

Companies use one of two methods to prepare their statement of cash flows. In the end, the total is the same, but they get to it from two different directions:

- **Direct method**—This method groups major classes of cash receipts and cash payments. For example, cash collected from customers is grouped separately from cash received on interest-earning savings accounts. Dividends from stock owned by the company are also shown separately. Other key types of cash payments shown include cash paid to buy inventory, cash disbursed to pay salaries, cash paid for taxes, and cash paid to cover interest on loans.

- **Indirect method**—While the direct method is the one the regulators prefer, most companies (90 percent) use the indirect method. This method focuses on the differences between net income and net cash flow from operations and tends to allow the companies to reveal less than the direct method, leaving their competitors guessing. The indirect method is easier to prepare.

The direct and indirect methods differ only in the operating activities section of the report. The investing activities and financing activities sections are the same.

For the indirect method, here are the line items of the operating activities section:

Cash flows from operating activities
Net income (loss)

Adjustments to reconcile net income (loss) to net cash provided by (used in) operating activities:

Depreciation and amortization

Provision for deferred taxes

Decrease (increase) in accounts receivable

Decrease (increase) in inventories

Decrease (increase) in prepaid expenses

Increase (decrease) in accounts payable

Increase in other current liabilities

Exchange (gain) loss

Net cash provided by (used in) operating activities

Here's the format of the operating activities section for the direct method:

Cash flows from operating activities

Cash received from customers

Cash paid to suppliers and employees

Interest received

Interest paid, net of amounts capitalized

Income tax refund received

Income taxes paid

Other cash received (paid)

Net cash provided by (used in) operating activities

You can see that the direct method reveals the actual cash it receives from customers, the cash it pays to suppliers and employees, and the income tax refund it receives. Companies prefer not to give that information to their competitors, for good reason. That's why most companies use the indirect method.

In addition to having to reveal details about the actual cash received or paid to customers, suppliers, employees, and the government, companies that use the direct method must prepare a schedule similar to one used in the indirect method for operating activities to meet FASB requirements.

So companies save no time preparing the direct method, must reveal more detail, and must still present the indirect method. Why bother? That's why you most likely see the indirect method used in the financial reports you read.

The investing and financing activities sections for both the direct and indirect methods include these line items:

Cash flows from investing activities

Additions to property, plant, and equipment

Investments and acquisitions

Other

Net cash utilized for investing activities

The financing activities section looks similar to this:

Cash flows from financing activities

Proceeds from borrowing

Net proceeds from repayments

Purchase or sale of common stock

Stock option transactions

Dividends paid

Net cash utilized by financing activities

Cash and short-term investments at the beginning of the year

Cash and short-term investments at the end of the year

Now let's take a closer look at what goes into each of the line items of the statement of cash flows.

Operating Activities

You'll find a summary of how much cash flowed into and out of the company during the day-to-day operations of the business in the operating activities section of the statement of cash flows, which is the most important section of this financial statement. If a company isn't generating enough cash from its operations, it isn't going to be in business long. As a value investor, if cash generation is low or nonexistent, it's time to pass on this investment.

 Losing Value _____

You saw a clear example of how important having cash on hand can be when the Internet bubble burst. Many newly minted Internet companies raised millions of dollars in cash in the late 1990s, which helped them stay in business for two or three years. But once this investor capital dried up, they could no longer find the cash to operate and many went bankrupt. In fact, over 850 Internet companies closed their doors between January 2000 and January 2002.

The operating activities section adjusts the net income by adding or subtracting entries that were made to abide by the rules of accrual accounting that don't actually require the use of cash. The sections that follow describe some of the key line items that are adjusted.

Depreciation

Depreciation is an accounting tool used to show when an asset is being used up. For example, suppose a company owns a truck that cost $35,000. It expects the truck to have a useful life of three years and that then it will be sold for $5,000. Each of the three years the company owns that truck, it will show its use in the books by taking a $10,000 depreciation expense. That depreciation expense will show on the income statement, but it doesn't mean that any cash was actually spent. The expense is offset by setting up a line item called accumulated depreciation in the asset section of the balance sheet, which will be subtracted from the value of vehicles listed in that section.

Since no cash is used, an adjustment is shown on the statement of cash flows that adds cash back in. That gives you a better idea of how much actual cash was generated by operations because the company didn't have to pay out cash to pay for depreciation expenses.

Inventory

The amount spent on inventory can sometimes be another adjustment shown on the statement of cash flows that can add cash to the net income figure. If a company's inventory on hand is less in the current year than in the previous year, some of the inventory sold was actually bought with cash in the previous year.

But that's not always the case. If a company's inventory increases from the previous year, the company spent more money on inventory in the current year, and it subtracts the difference from the net income to find its current cash holdings. For example, if inventory decreases by $20,000, the company adds that amount to net income.

Accounts Receivable

Accounts receivable, through which a company tracks the accounts of customers who bought their goods or services on credit provided directly by the company, can be another item that needs adjustment on the statement of cash flows. Customers who bought their goods using credit cards from banks or other financial institutions aren't included in accounts receivable.

For example, if someone goes to Sears and buys using a Sears credit card, Sears must carry that account as part of its accounts payable. But if someone uses a MasterCard or Visa, the purchase can be counted as cash because Sears doesn't have to worry about collecting the money from the customer.

When accounts receivable increases during the year, a company sells more products or services on credit than it collects in actual cash from customers. In this case, an increase in accounts receivable means a decrease in cash available. The opposite is true if accounts receivable is a lower number during the current year than the previous year. In this case, a company collects more cash than it adds credit to customers' credit accounts. In this situation, a decrease in accounts receivable results in more cash received, which adds to the net income.

Accounts Payable

Another key account that might require a cash adjustment is accounts payable, which summarizes the bills due that haven't yet been paid. This means that cash must still be paid out in a future accounting period to cover those bills.

When accounts payable increases, a company uses less cash to pay bills in the current year than it did in the previous one, so more cash is on hand. When accounts payable increases, it has a positive effect on the cash situation. Expenses are shown on the income statement because they have been incurred, which means net income is lower. But in reality, the cash hasn't yet been paid out to cover those expenses, so an increase is added to net income to find out how much cash is actually on hand.

Conversely, if accounts payable decreases, a company pays out more cash for this liability. A decrease in accounts payable means the company has less cash on hand, and it subtracts this number from net income.

Summing Up the Cash Flow from Activities Section

To give you a taste of what all of these line items look like in the statement of cash flows in the table here, I roll together the information from the previous sections.

Company A
Statement of Cash Flows
Year Ended December 31, 2008

Cash from Operating Activities

Line Item	Cash Received or Spent
Net Income	$300,000
Depreciation	20,000
Decrease in Accounts Receivable	40,000
Increase in Inventory	(15,000)
Increase in Accounts Payable	5,000
Net Cash Provided by (Used in) Operating Activities	$350,000

You can see from this portion of the statement of cash flows for Company A that the company actually received $50,000 more in cash than is reported on the income statement. So the company actually generated more cash from operations than you thought after quickly scanning the net income shown on the income statement.

Investment Activities

The investment activities section of the statement of cash flows focuses on the purchase or sale of major new assets. For most companies, this section reduces the amount of cash available. In this section you will find the following:

◆ Purchases of new buildings, land, and major equipment

◆ Mergers or acquisitions

◆ Major improvements to existing buildings

◆ Major upgrades to existing factories and equipment

◆ Purchases of new marketable securities, such as bonds or stock

If a company sells any major assets, such as its buildings, land, major equipment, or marketable securities, the sale is shown in the investment activities section as a cash generator.

As a value investor, the primary reason to check out the investments section is to see how the company is managing its *capital expenditures* and how much cash it's using for these expenditures. If a company shows large investments in this area, be sure to look for explanations in the management's discussion and analysis (see Chapter 9) and the notes to the financial statements (see Chapter 8) to get more details on the reasons for the expenditures.

def•i•ni•tion

Capital expenditures include money spent to buy or upgrade a company's assets. This can include, for example, the purchase of a new building or another company's stock. Or it can be a major improvement to buildings already owned.

If you believe a company is making the right choices to grow the business and improve profits, investing in its stock may be worthwhile. If the company is making most of its capital expenditures to keep old factories operating as long as possible, it may be a sign that the company isn't keeping up with new technology. Either way, if you see significant adjustments in this section, you need to look for more detail about what the company is doing in the management's discussion and analysis and notes to the financial statements to help you determine whether the stock is a good investment for your individual portfolio.

Finding Value

When trying to determine which company to pick in a particular industry, compare companies in that industry to see what type of expenditures each lists in investment activities and the explanations for those expenditures in the notes to the financial statement. Compare each company to its peers to determine whether the company is using its cash wisely.

Financing Activities

Sometimes companies need an infusion of cash that is much larger than what they can raise from their day-to-day operations. A company can raise that cash with certain financing activities. Any cash raised through activities that don't include day-to-day operations can be found in the financing section of the statement of cash flows.

Issuing Stock

When a company first sells its shares of stock, it shows the money raised in the financing section of the statement of cash flows. The first time a company sells shares of stock to the general public, it's called an *initial public offering* (*IPO*). Whenever a company decides to sell additional shares to raise capital, all additional sales of stock are called *secondary public offerings*, which are similar to an IPO but involve offering new shares of stock for a company that already sells its stock on the stock market.

def•i•ni•tion

An **initial public offering (IPO)** is the first time a company sells stock to the general public. Only when the company directly sells shares of stock to the public does it generate cash. When shares of stock are sold by one investor to another, it does not impact the cash flow of the company whose stock is sold.

A **secondary public offering** is when the company sells shares of stock directly to the public at some time after the IPO.

Usually, when companies decide to do a secondary public offering, they do so to raise cash for a specific project or group of projects that they can't fund by ongoing operations. The financial department must determine whether it wants to raise funds for these new projects by borrowing money (new debt) or by issuing stock (new equity). If the company already has a great deal of debt and finds that borrowing more is difficult, it may try to sell additional shares to cover the shortfall.

Buying Back Stock

Sometimes you see a line item in the financing activities section of the statement of cash flows that shows the company bought back its stock. Most often, companies that announce a stock buyback want to accomplish one of two things:

- Increase the market price of their stock. (If companies buy back their stock, fewer shares remain on the market, which will likely raise the value of shares still on the market or available for purchase at a later date in a secondary public offering.)

- Meet internal obligations regarding employee stock options, which guarantee employees the opportunity to buy shares of stock at a price that's usually below the price outsiders must pay for the stock.

Sometimes companies buy back stock with the intention of going private, which means the company no longer wants to offer stock to the general public. In this case, company executives and the board of directors decide they no longer want to operate under the watchful eyes of investors and the government. Instead, they prefer to operate under a veil of privacy and don't have to worry about satisfying so many company outsiders.

For many companies, an announcement that they're buying back stock is an indication that they're doing well financially, and the executives believe in their company's growth prospects for the future. But buying back stock can also mean the company doesn't have any better ideas for use of the cash it's generating. Because buybacks reduce the number of outstanding shares, a company makes its per-share numbers look better, even though a fundamental change hasn't occurred in the business's operations.

Losing Value

If you see a big jump in earnings per share, it may or may not be a reason to get excited. Check for a stock buyback in the financing activities section of the statement of cash flows. If the primary reason for the jump in earnings per share is that fewer shares are on the market, the earnings per share increase is nothing more than smoke and mirrors to make the company's stock look better. A stock buyback does mean that there are fewer shareholders who have claims on the company's assets.

Paying Dividends

Whenever a company pays dividends, it shows the amount paid to shareholders in the financing activities section of this report. Companies don't have to pay dividends each year, but a company rarely stops paying dividends once it has started doing so. Shareholders get used to their dividend checks and don't like to see them cut.

If a company decides to stop paying dividends or to pay out less in dividends, the market price of the stock is sure to tumble. A company's decision not to pay dividends after paying them in the previous quarter or previous year usually indicates that it's having problems, and it raises a huge red flag on Wall Street.

This could be a buying opportunity for value investors because other investors will run as soon as there is any sign of problems. As a value investor, it's time to consider whether this stock is a good bargain buy or a company not worth considering. In Part 3, we talk about the resources and analysis you can use to make that decision.

Incurring New Debt

When a company decides it must borrow money for the long term, this new debt is shown in the financing activities section of this financial statement. This new debt can include the issuance of bonds, notes, or other forms of long-term financing, such as a mortgage on a building.

When you read the statement of cash flows and see that the company has taken on new debt, be sure to look for explanations about how the company is using this debt in the management's discussion and analysis section of the annual report (see Chapter 9), as well as in the notes to the financial statements (see Chapter 8).

Paying Off Debt

Debt payoff is usually a good sign for a company. It often indicates that a company is doing well. However, it can indicate that a company is simply rolling over existing debt into another type of debt instrument.

If you see that a company paid off one debt and took on another debt that costs about the same amount of money, this sign likely indicates that the company simply refinanced the original debt. Hopefully, that refinancing involved lowering the company's interest expenses. Look for a full explanation of the debt payoff in the notes to the financial statement.

When you look at the financing activities on a statement of cash flows for younger companies, you usually see financing activities that raise capital. Their statements include borrowing funds or issuing stock to raise cash. Older, more established companies begin paying off their debt when they start generating enough cash from operations.

Discontinued Operations

If a company decides to close down a part of its business, you usually see a special line item on the statement of cash flows that shows whether the discontinued operations have increased or decreased the amount of cash a company takes in or distributes. Sometimes discontinued operations increase cash because the company no longer has to pay the salaries and other costs related to that operation.

But frequently, discontinued operations can be a one-time hit to profits because the company has to make significant severance payments to laid-off employees and has to continue paying the costs of the manufacturing and other fixed costs related to those operations. For example, if a company leased space for the discontinued operations, the company is contractually obligated to continue paying for that space until the contract is up or the company finds someone to sublease the space.

You won't find any detail on the statement of cash flows. If you see a line item for discontinued operations, look for a full explanation in the notes to the financial statements. You may also find a discussion about why the company decided to discontinue operations in the management's discussion and analysis.

Foreign Currency Exchange

Whenever a company has global operations, it's certain to have some costs related to the cost of moving currency from one country to another. The U.S. dollar, as well as currencies from other countries, can experience changes in currency exchange rates—sometimes 100 times a day or more.

Each time the dollar exchange rate changes with a specific country, moving currency between those two countries can result in a loss or a gain. Any losses or gains related to foreign currency exchanges are shown on a special line item on the statement of cash flows called "effect of currency exchange rate changes on cash."

Getting to the Bottom Cash Line

The bottom line of the statement of cash flows is called "cash and short-term investments at end of year." This number actually shows you how much cash or cash equivalents a company has on hand for continuing operations during the next year.

Cash equivalents are any holdings that can be easily changed into cash, such as cash, cash in checking and savings accounts, certificates of deposit that are redeemable in less than 90 days, money market funds, and stocks that are sold on the major exchanges that can be easily converted to cash.

The top line of the statement of cash flows is net income. Adjustments are made to show the impact on cash from operations, investing activities, and financing. These adjustments convert that net income figure to actual cash available for continuing operations. Remember, this is the cash on hand that the company can use to continue its activities the next year.

Now that we've looked at the three key financial statements—balance sheet, income statement, and statement of cash flows—let's dig a bit deeper in the notes to the financial statements. That's where you'll find out what went into those numbers, to help you get a better understanding of how well the company is doing.

The Least You Need to Know

- The statement of cash flows helps you to find out how much cash the company actually has on hand for the next year's operations.

- The key section of this report is the cash from operating activities. That's where you find out how much cash the business actually generates from day-to-day operations.

- You can see whether the company is using its cash wisely when you review the investment activities section of the report.

- You can see whether the company is having trouble generating enough cash from its operation when you review the financing activities section of the report.

8

Taking Notes on the Financial Statements

In This Chapter

- ◆ Looking for change notes
- ◆ Determining values
- ◆ Understanding debt obligations
- ◆ Finding events and red flags

You'd never sign a contract without reading the fine print—or at least, you shouldn't. Well, the same is true when you're thinking of investing in a company by buying its stock.

When you read those glossy pages of an annual report, a company is telling you about the successes it wants to highlight. As you look at the fine print in the notes to the financial statements, you'll find all the detail you need to make an informed decision about the company.

In this chapter, we review the issues covered in the financial statements, highlight the key areas you want to scour closely as you research companies that interest you, and talk about what will be unique based on the type of companies you are considering.

Diving Into the Small Print

You may need magnifying glasses to read the fine print of notes to the financial statements. Federal regulators require this detail about the key line items in the financial statements, but most companies would prefer not to even disclose the detail. So they do it in a way that they hope most people won't even look at and in jargon you may find difficult to understand.

Yes, reading the notes to the financial statements could be difficult, but it is well worth the effort to learn the key terms you'll face and how to interpret them. Even though a company makes these notes difficult to understand, it still fulfills its obligations to the Securities and Exchange Commission.

Even if you find it daunting to read the notes, don't give up trying. You'll find lots of important information that you need to know to make a decision about whether the company is a good one to add to your portfolio. You'll get details about the company's accounting methods used, red flags about the company's finances, and any legal entanglements that might threaten the company's future.

When you look at any one of the financial statements, all you see is a list of numbers, but you'll have no idea what went into making up those numbers. To analyze how well a company did financially, you need to understand what the numbers mean and what decisions the company made to get the numbers.

The notes have no specific format, but you're likely to find at least one note regarding several key issues in every company's financial report.

Accounting Policy Changes

Most companies start their notes to the financial statements with details about their accounting policies. This note explains the accounting rules the company used to develop its numbers. The note is usually called the summary of significant accounting policies. Issues discussed in the notes include these:

- **Asset types**—The company explains the types of things it owns, as well as how the company values its assets and what methods of depreciation the company uses.

- **Revenue and expenses**—The company explains how it records the money it takes in from sales and the money it pays out to cover its expenses.

◆ **Pensions**—The company details its obligations to its current and future retirees.

◆ **Risk management**—The company discusses what it does to minimize its risk.

◆ **Stock-based compensation**—The company explains its employee incentive plans involving stock ownership.

◆ **Income taxes**—The company details its income tax obligations and the amount the company paid in taxes.

After reading the accounting policies section of the notes, if you don't understand a policy, research it further so you can make a judgment on how this policy may impact the company's financial position. You can either research the issue yourself on the Internet or call the company's investor relations office to ask questions. Also compare policies among the companies you're analyzing. You want to see whether the differences in the ways companies handle the valuation of assets or the recognition of revenues and expenses make it more difficult for you to analyze and compare the results.

For example, if companies use different methods to value their inventory, this could have a major impact on net income. Many times, you won't actually have enough detail to make an apples-to-apples comparison of two companies that use different accounting policies, but you need to be aware that the policies differ as you analyze the company's financial results. Be alert to the fact that you might be comparing apples to oranges.

We point out three accounting policies that will help you understand how differences in these policies can have a major impact on the company's net income. Those three policies are depreciation, revenue, and expenses.

Depreciation

One significant difference in accounting policies that can affect the bottom line is the amount of time a company allows for the depreciation of assets. One company may use a 15- to 25-year time frame for the depreciation of a building; another may use a 10- to 40-year span. The time frame used for depreciation directly impacts the value of the assets involved, which is recorded on the line item of the balance sheet called "cost less accumulated depreciation." A faster depreciation method reduces the value of these assets more quickly on the balance sheet.

Depreciation expenses are also deducted from general revenue. A company that writes off its buildings more quickly—say, in 25 years rather than up to 40 years—has higher depreciation expenses and lower net income than if it allows for a longer time to write off its buildings. So if you're comparing two companies that use different depreciation methods, take careful note of the depreciation expenses line on the income statement.

Revenue

You will find key differences between companies when reading the notes. For example, you might find differences in the timing of revenue recognition, which could impact the total revenues reported. Suppose one company indicates that it recognizes revenue when the product is shipped to the customer. Another company indicates that it recognizes revenue upon the customer's receipt of the product. If products are shipped at the end of the month, a company that includes shipped products will include the revenues in that month, but a company that recognizes revenue only when its products are received might not recognize the revenue until the next month.

Other revenue-recognition differences you should pay attention to include these:

♦ **Sales price**—Some companies sell products with a fixed sales price. Others indicate that prices aren't fixed and are determined between the company and the customer. Since we're using builders' financial statements, you'll probably find that most builders do set price on a customer-by-customer basis—every customer chooses different extras.

♦ **Contract completion**—A builder will indicate when he records income and expenses. For most builders, you will find this line: "Revenues and cost of revenues from these home sales are recorded at the time each home is delivered and title and possession are transferred to the buyer." If you find a builder that recognizes income on homes at a different point in time, take careful note when you start doing your comparisons.

♦ **Land development and other costs**—Builders can have significant costs before they even start selling homes in a project. Most builders spread these costs among all the future homes to be built. A common line you'll find in the notes is, "Land, land development, and other common costs, both incurred and estimated to be incurred in the future, are *amortized* to the cost of homes closed based upon the total number of homes to be constructed in each community."

def•i•ni•tion

Amortization is a method that permits a company to spread out the expenses of a project over a number of years rather than take off the full cost in the first year.

◆ **Percentage of completion method**—If you are looking at the financial statements for builders who build commercial buildings or apartment buildings, they will likely talk about this method of accounting because these larger projects span several years of financial statements and, in most cases, the builder receives payments as he completes various stages of construction.

◆ **Land sales**—When you're reviewing a builder's notes to the financial statement, you also could see information about revenue from land sales. The builder could sell land that has been apportioned into lots without building right away. Or it could sell land that was partially developing to another builder. If you see revenue from land sales, look for the detail in the notes to the financial statement.

◆ **Inventory valuation**—While this can be a relatively simple calculation for most companies, for builders this can get very convoluted, especially as the value of homes continued to drop in 2008. You should find one or more charts in the notes to the financial statements that detail how the company determined the value of its inventory. Most builders state their inventory value based on the lower of cost or fair market value. For many builders, in recent years, the fair market value was less than the costs of building the homes if they were building in one of the hard-hit areas where prices dropped as much as 40 percent to 50 percent. If the market value is less than the costs of building a house, the houses in inventory lose value. The builders report this loss by showing an "impairment" in value. When you look at the statement of cash flows for Builder A and Builder B in Appendix C, you'll see a line item for inventory impairment.

Expenses differ widely among companies. As you read this part of the accounting policies note, be sure to notice the types of expenses a company chooses to highlight. Sometimes the differences between companies can actually give you insight into how the company operates. Here are two key areas where you may see differences in how a company reports expenses:

◆ **Product development**—Some companies develop all their products in-house. Others pay fees to inventors, designers, or other types of vendors to develop and market new products. In-house product development is reported as research and development expenses. If the company primarily develops new products using outside sources, these expenses are shown based on the service offered. For example, a builder may have professional fees for an architect or an engineer.

◆ **Advertising**—Some companies indicate that all advertising is expensed at the time the advertising is printed or aired. Others may write off advertising over a longer period of time. Companies that depend on catalog sales are likely to spread out the expense of this type of advertising over several months or even a year if they can prove that sales continued to come in during that longer period in time.

As you compare two companies' financial reports, look for both the similarities and differences in their accounting policies. You may need to make some assumptions regarding the financial statements, to compare apples to apples when trying to decide which company is the better investment. For example, if the companies depreciate assets differently, you must remember that their asset valuations aren't the same, nor are their depreciation expenses (based on the same assumptions).

New Borrowing and Standing Commitments

How a company manages its debt is critical to its short- and long-term profitability. You can find out a lot about a company's financial management by reading the notes related to financial commitments.

You always find at least one note about the financial borrowings and other commitments that impact the short- and long-term financial health of the company. Most companies break down their notes into two sections: long-term borrowings and short-term borrowings. The long-term borrowings involve financial obligations of more than one year, and the short-term borrowings involve obligations due within the 12-month period being discussed in the financial report.

Long-Term Obligations

On the financial statements, you will see two types of debt—current and long-term debt. Current debt is due over the next 12 months. Long-term debt includes debt that will not be paid over the next 12 months. Both medium- and long-term notes and bonds fall into the long-term debt category. Medium-term notes or bonds are debt that a company borrows for 2 to 10 years. Long-term notes or bonds involve debt borrowed for over 10 years.

In the section of the notes on long-term financial debts, you find two key charts. One chart shows the terms of the borrowings, and the other shows the amount of cash that a company must pay toward this debt for each of the next five years and beyond.

Use these charts to compare the long-term obligations of the companies you are analyzing. You may find that one company does a good job of managing its debt and that most of its long-term debt has low interest rates and long payout periods. Another company may be having a harder time getting low interest rates.

Losing Value _____

If you see a significant difference in interest rates, dig deeper into the notes to find out why one company must pay so much more to borrow money. It could be a poor credit history, but it also could be that one company borrows a lot more than another company and the banks consider a company in deeper debt to be more of a credit risk. Obviously, the company that the banks consider more of a credit risk also is not likely to be a good investment.

Short-Term Debt

Short-term debt can have a greater impact on a company's earnings each year, as well as on the amount of cash available for operations, than long-term debt. The reason is that a company must pay short-term debt over the next 12 months, while for a long-term debt, a company must pay only interest and sometimes part of the principal in the next 12 months.

The type of short-term debt you see on a company's balance sheet varies greatly depending on the type of company. Companies whose sales are seasonal may carry a lot more short-term debt to get themselves through the slow times than companies that have a consistent cash flow from sales throughout the year.

Seasonal companies carry large lines of credit to help them buy or produce their products during the off-season times so they can have enough products to sell during high season. This is true for many retail businesses that get most of their business at the key selling seasons—Christmas and Easter. A business that primarily sells items for use in the summer, such as a swimsuit company or surfboard company, may need to carry a lot of short-term debt to produce enough inventory during their key selling months.

Another way that companies raise cash if they don't have enough on hand is to sell their *accounts receivable*. To get immediate cash, the company can sell the receivables to a bank or other financial institution and get immediate cash rather than wait for the customer to pay. They will of course take a discount on their money. For example, they may get only 92 cents for every dollar of receivables sold, which is similar to an 8 percent cost of borrowing.

def•i•ni•tion _____

Accounts receivable is the account that tracks credit extended to customers. The amount shown in this account on the balance sheet summarizes all these customer accounts. You may find more detail about this account in the notes.

Be sure to look for a statement in the financial obligations notes that indicates how a company is meeting its cash needs and whether it's having any difficulty meeting those needs. Some companies use "financial obligations" in the title for the note, while others may have one note on short-term debt obligations and another on long-term debt obligations.

Lease Obligations

Many companies lease plants, equipment, and facilities rather than purchase them. You usually find at least one note to the financial statements that spells out a company's lease obligations. Many analysts consider lease obligations not shown on the balance sheet to be just another type of debt financing that doesn't have to be shown on the balance sheet. Whether the lease is shown on the balance sheet or in the notes depends on the type of lease.

- **Capital leases**—These leases provide ownership at no cost or at a greatly reduced cost at the end of the lease. This type of lease is shown as a long-term debt obligation on the balance sheet.

- **Operating leases**—These leases offer no ownership provisions or provisions that require a considerable amount of cash to purchase the leased item. This type of lease is mentioned in the notes to the financial statements but isn't shown on the balance sheet as debt.

Companies that must constantly update certain types of equipment to avoid obsolescence use operating leases rather than capital leases. At the end of the lease period, companies return the equipment and replace it by leasing new, updated equipment. Operating leases have the lowest monthly payments.

When reading the notes, be sure to look for an explanation about the types of leases a company has and what percentage of its fixed assets are under operating leases. Some high-tech companies have higher obligations in operating lease payments than they do in long-term liabilities.

When you see operating leases that total close to 50 percent of a company's net fixed assets or that exceed the total of its long-term liabilities, be sure to use at least two thirds of the obligations, if not all of the payments, in your debt measurement calculations. The fact that these obligations are mentioned only in the notes doesn't negate their potential role in creating future cash problems for a company.

Mergers and Acquisitions

Sometimes one company decides to buy another. Other times, two companies decide to merge into one.

If a company acquired another company or merged during the year covered by the annual report, a note to the financial statements is dedicated to the financial implications of that transaction. In this note, you see this information:

- The market value of the company purchased

- The amount paid for the company

- Any exchange of stock involved in the transaction

- Information about the transaction's impact on the bottom line

When a company acquires another company, it frequently pays more for that acquisition than for the total value of its assets. The additional money spent to buy the company falls into the line item called "goodwill." Goodwill includes added value for customer base, locations, customer loyalty, and intangible factors that increase a company's value. If a company has goodwill built over the years from prior mergers or acquisitions, you see that indicated on the balance sheet as an asset.

Sometimes a company must reduce the amount of goodwill if there is a decline in the market. For example, one builder indicated an impairment of goodwill because of a decline in one of its markets. In the notes to the financial statements, you will find a reason for the goodwill impairment and which acquisition was impacted. You should also find out whether there is any goodwill left for that particular merger.

While information about goodwill impairment will not have a major impact on a company's bottom line, it does give you a glimpse of the market difficulties the company is facing. Pay close attention to an indication of goodwill impairment and how the company sees that impairment impacting future growth. You should see mention of this in both the notes and the management's discussion of analysis (see Chapter 9).

In an acquisition, the acquired company's net income is added to the new parent company's bottom line. This addition occurs even if the closing of the sale takes place at the end of the year. Many times, this addition can inflate the bottom line and make the net income look better than it actually will be when the companies are fully merged. Be sure to look closely at the impact any mergers, acquisitions, or even sales of parts of an acquired company have on net income.

Mergers and acquisitions are not always good for a company. You may see that a merger or acquisition positively impacts the bottom line for a year or two, and then the company's performance drops dramatically as the merged company sorts out various issues regarding overlapping operations and staff.

Many times, the announcement of a merger or acquisition generates excitement, causing stock prices to skyrocket temporarily before dropping back to a more realistic value. Don't get caught up in the short-term euphoria of a merger or acquisition when you're considering the purchase of stocks. Read the details in the notes to the financial statement to find out more about the true impacts of the merger or acquisition transaction.

Pension and Retirement Benefits

You may not think of pension and other retirement benefits as debt obligations, but they are. Most companies that offer pension benefits owe their employees more than they owe to bondholders and banks. Some companies offer both pensions (which are an obligation to pay retirees a certain amount for the rest of their lives after they leave the company) and other retirement benefits (which include contributions to retirement savings plans such as 401(k)s or profit-sharing plans).

When looking at the note about pension and other retirement benefits, find out which type of plan the company offers. Here are the common types:

◆ Defined benefit plan

◆ Defined contribution plan

Defined Benefit Plan

With this type of retirement plan, the company promises a retirement benefit to each of its employees and is obligated to pay that benefit. This type of benefit plan includes traditional retirement plans in which the employee gets a set monthly or annual benefit from the company after retirement.

Defined benefit plans carry obligations for the company for as long as the employee lives and sometimes for as long as both the employee and his spouse live. Determining how much that benefit will cost in the future is based on assumptions regarding how much return a company actually expects from its retirement portfolios and how long its employees and their spouses will live after retirement. As people live longer, pension obligations become much greater for companies that offer defined benefit plans.

Defined Contribution Plan

When this type of retirement plan is offered, the employer and employee both make contributions to the plan. A 401(k) is an example of a defined contribution plan. A company isn't required to pay any additional money to the employee after the employee retires and pulls her retirement funds from the company's plan.

In the notes to the financial statement, you find a calculation of the expected pension expense, the funding position of the plan, and the expectations for the future obligations of that plan, based on complicated assumptions figured by an *actuary*. Insurance companies commonly use actuaries to determine costs for life, health, and other insurance products.

def•i•ni•tion

An **actuary** is a statistician that looks at life span and other risk factors to make assumptions about an individual life span. In the retirement arena, an actuary helps a company determine its long-term pension obligations.

In the pension and retirement benefits note, you find a chart that shows the annual payments currently being made to retirees. If you see these payments increasing more rapidly each year, it may be a sign of a long-term problem for the company. Companies should provide a table that shows the current plan assets at fair value and projects the ability to meet the company's pension obligations in the future.

You need to compare a number of figures companies use when calculating their estimates for pension obligations. You should see similar assumptions used by companies in similar industries. Numbers to watch include these:

- **Discount rate**—The interest rate used to determine the present value of the projected benefit obligations

- **Rate of return on assets**—The expected long-term return the company expects to earn on the assets in the retirement investment portfolio

- **Rate of compensation increases**—The estimate the company makes related to salary increases and the impact those increases have on future pension obligations

Each of these rates requires that assumptions be made about unknown future events involving the state of the economy, interest rates, investment returns, and employee life spans. A company can do no more than make an educated guess. To be sure that a company's guesses are reasonable, all you can do is check that the company makes similar guesses to those of other companies in the same industry.

You should also look for information in the notes about whether the company's retirement savings portfolio is sufficient to meet its expected current and future pension obligations. This information is usually shown in a chart as part of the notes. If the company's retirement savings portfolio falls short, it could be a red flag that future cash-flow problems are possible.

Business Make-Up

Managing a multibillion-dollar, or even multimillion-dollar, company can be a daunting task. Can you imagine how many products are sent out to make that many sales and how many people are needed to keep the business afloat?

To be able to manage such a large operation, most major companies split up the company into manageable segments, such as departments, divisions, or operating units. This makes managing all aspects of the business, from product development to product distribution to customer satisfaction, easier.

These segments help the company designate areas of responsibility, as well as track performance of each of its product lines more easily. In the notes to the financial statements, you should find at least one note related to these segment breakdowns. In this note, you should find details about how each of a company's segments is doing, as well as about the product lines that fall under each segment.

This additional detail could include the following:

- **Target markets**—These are the key market segments that a company targets. Segments could include a breakdown by age group (teens, tots, adults), locations (north, south, east, west), or interest groups (sportsmen, hobbyists, and so on). Target markets are limited only by the creativity of the marketing team, which develops the groups of customers that it wants to win over.

- **The largest customers**—In this section, a company usually names its top customers that buy their product. For example, a manufacturer that sells a large portion of its products to major retailers such as Wal-Mart and Target usually gives some details about these relationships.

◆ **Manufacturing and other operational details**—A company gives you information about how it groups its product manufacturing and where its products are manufactured. If the company manufactures its products internationally, look for indications about problems that may have occurred during the year related to those operations. Sometimes labor or political strife can have a great impact on a company's manufacturing operations. Also, weather conditions can greatly impact manufacturing conditions. For example, if the company's manufacturing for a certain product line is in Singapore, and Singapore experienced numerous damaging storms, the company may indicate the problem and state that it had difficulty producing enough product for market.

◆ **Trade sanctions**—All companies that operate internationally must deal with trade laws that differ in every country. Some countries impose high tariffs on products coming from outside their borders, to discourage importing products into their country, giving an edge to products made at home. Sometimes countries impose sanctions on other countries for actions taken by politicians that they disagree with. For example, the United States doesn't allow trade with Cuba for political reasons, so a company that buys products from Cuba can't import them into the United States. The United States and Europe are considering imposing sanctions on China because they don't agree with certain human rights and other policies. If they do so, importing products from China will be much more expensive for companies.

If a company faces a specific marketing or manufacturing problem, you'll also find details about these problems in the note about segment breakdowns. Don't skip over this note!

How a company breaks down its management segments varies depending on the industry and management preferences. Some companies divide into regions based on geography; others designate segments based on product lines or customer target groups.

If a company operates internationally, you usually see the U.S. market segments separated from the non-U.S. segments, and sometimes you find the international portion broken into regions, such as Europe, Asia, or the Middle East.

There are no hard-and-fast rules about how to segment a business. A company bases its decisions about how to segment itself on how the company has operated historically or on the management style of the company's executives.

Significant Events

Every company faces significant challenges annually. One year a company may find out that its customers are suing it for a defective product. Another year a company may get notice from a state or local governmental that one of its manufacturing facilities is polluting the environment.

So you may find mention in the notes about significant events that are not related to external forces. Changes based on internal forces could include a decision to close a factory or combine two divisions into one.

You can look in a number of places in the notes for information on significant events. Sometimes an event has its own note, such as a note about the discontinuation of operations. Other times it is just part of a note called commitments and contingencies. Scan through the notes to find significant events that impact a company's financial position.

You're most likely to find significant events mentioned in the notes regarding topics such as these:

 ◆ **Lawsuits**—Lawsuits (which you usually find in commitments and contingencies) involve cases pending against the company. These suits can sometimes have a huge impact on a company's future. In 2007, one of the most common types of lawsuits filed by homeowners burdened by debt related to the Fair Debt Collection Practices Act. If you are looking at a financial company, stay alert for these types of lawsuits.

 ◆ **Environmental concerns**—These concerns can become significant if the company is involved in a major environmental cleanup because of discharges from one of its plants. Cleanup can cost millions of dollars. For example, Exxon paid over $1.28 billion related to damages from the Valdez Oil Spill in Alaska's Prince William Sound in 1989.

 ◆ **Restructuring**—Any time a company decides to regroup its products, close down a plant, or make some other major change to the way it does business, this is restructuring. You usually find an individual note explaining the restructuring and how that will impact the company's income during the current year and all other years in which there will be an impact from the decision to restructure.

♦ **Discontinued operations**—Sometimes a company decides not to restructure but instead to close down an operation entirely. When this happens, you're likely to find a separate note on the financial impact of the discontinued operations, which likely includes the costs of closing down facilities and laying off or relocating employees.

Many times the information included in these notes discusses not only the financial impact of an event in the current year, but also any impacts expected on financial performance in future years.

When a company discusses lawsuits and potential environmental liability cases in the notes, it commonly indicates that, in the opinion of management, the matter in question won't result in a material loss to the company. Use your own judgment after reading the details management provides. If you think the company may be facing bigger problems than the company mentioned, do your own research on the matter before investing in the company.

If a company faces a lawsuit, this matter isn't necessarily something of great concern. Given the litigious nature of society, most major corporations face lawsuits annually. But these suits do raise red flags sometimes.

Putting Up the Red Flags

Companies do like hiding their dirty laundry in the small print of the notes to the financial statements, so it's up to you to search out the hidden morsels. As you read through the notes, keep an eye out for possible red flags.

Whenever you see notes titled "restructuring," "discontinued operations," and "accounting changes," look for red flags that could mean continuing expenses for a number of years. The company will detail costs of any of these changes. Be sure to consider long-term financial impacts that could be a drain on future earnings for the company—which may mean stock prices will suffer.

Also be on the lookout for potential lawsuits that could result in huge settlements. If you see that a lawsuit has been filed against a company, search for stories in the financial press that discuss the lawsuit in greater detail than the company might include in the notes. The financial press usually covers major lawsuits filed against a company.

Significant events aren't the only things that can raise red flags. You may also see signs of trouble in the way that a company values assets or in decisions made to change accounting policies. The notes detailing the long-term obligations a company has to its retirees may also be a good spot to find some potential red flags.

The financial press often mentions the red flags that analysts spot in companies' financial reports. Read the financial press to pick up the potential problem spots and then look for the details in the financial statements and the notes to those financial statements.

Valuing Assets and Liabilities

Valuing assets and liabilities leaves room for accounting creativity. If assets are over-valued, you may be led to believe that the company owns more than it actually does. If liabilities are undervalued, you may think the company owes less than it actually does. Either way, you get a false impression about the company's financial position.

When you don't understand something, ask questions of the company's investor relations staff, who are responsible for answering investors' questions, until it presents the information in a manner that you understand. If you're confused by the presentation of asset or liability valuation, you can be sure that other financial readers are confused as well. You'll learn to recognize that the more convoluted a company's explanation is, the more likely it is that the company is hiding something.

Accounting Policies Changes

The accounting policies and methods a company uses can be just as critical as the numbers themselves. The accounting policies adopted by the company drive these numbers. Whenever a company indicates in the notes to the financial statements that it's chang-ing accounting policies, a red flag should go up. We discussed some of the critical accounting policy issues at the beginning of this chapter.

Not all changes are bad. Sometimes changes are required by the Financial Account-ing Standards Board (FASB) or the SEC. No matter what the reason for the change, be sure you understand how that change impacts your ability to compare year-to-year or quarter-to-quarter results.

If you see a change in accounting methods and there's no indication that the FASB or SEC required it, dig deeper into the reasons for the change and find out how the change impacts the valuation of assets and liabilities or the net income of the company.

You can find some explanation in the accounting policies note, but if you don't understand the explanation there, call the investor relations department and ask questions.

Money Owed to Current and Future Retirees

As noted, obligations to retirees and future retirees can be a bigger drain on a company's resources than debt obligations. The note related to pension benefits is probably one of the most difficult to understand. Look specifically at the charts that show a company's long-term payment obligations to retirees and the cash available to pay those obligations. If you find any indication that the company may have difficulty meeting these obligations mentioned in either the text of this note or the charts, this could be the sign of a major cash-flow problem in the future. Don't hesitate to call and ask questions if you don't understand the presentation.

Now that you have a better idea of what to look for in the notes to the financial statement, we'll take a closer look at what management must disclose in the management's discussion and analysis in the next chapter.

The Least You Need to Know

- The notes to the financial statements is where companies hide their dirty linen. Even if you find the information difficult to read, don't skip this.

- If you want to know how a company developed its numbers for the financial statements, your best source of detail is the notes to the financial statements.

- Keep your eyes open for indications of change when reading the notes to the financial statements. That change could impact the accounting policies, the value of assts or liabilities, the restructuring of the company, or pending legal actions.

Chapter 9

Digesting Management's Discussion and Analysis

In This Chapter

- ◆ Operations and resources
- ◆ Finding revenues
- ◆ Changing structure
- ◆ Recognizing liabilities

The management's discussion and analysis (MD&A) section gives you a brief glimpse at how management views current market conditions and what it plans to do about them. In this section, you get an overview of the resources on hand and how management plans to use them.

You also get a sobering view of the failures in the past year and how management plans to improve in the future. Always read the MD&A section carefully, because you'll find a lot of detail about how the company is doing and what management sees as its prospects for future growth. In this chapter, we review the key things you should focus on as you read the MD&A.

SEC Expectations

Luckily for you as a financial report reader, the SEC monitors the MD&A section closely to make sure that companies present all critical information about current operations, capital, and *liquidity*. In the past, this section gained a reputation for saying as little as possible and covering up as much as possible. The SEC cracked down on that several years ago, and you can now count on this section to give you a true picture of the current financial position of the company and how management plans to improve that position.

def•i•ni•tion

A company's **liquidity** is its cash position and its ability to pay its bills on a short-term or a day-to-day basis. We take a closer look at liquidity as part of our financial analysis in Chapter 11.

Management must include forward-looking statements about known market and economic trends that could impact the company's liquidity and material events. It also must include uncertainties that could impact future operating results or future financial conditions. For example, in the building industry, it's on the front pages of newspapers every day that the housing bubble has burst and sales are down dramatically. As we review the MD&A for the two builders—Company A and Company B—we'll get management's view of the current economic prospects for builders and what they are doing to minimize risks to the continuing existence of their companies.

Company Operations

You definitely want to focus on company operations as you sift through the management's commentary about income generation and expenses. Some key areas to look for include sales performance and the discussion of economic and market conditions.

Sales Performance

Both Company A and Company B reported poor sales performance in 2007 and deteriorating performance since 2005. You're probably not surprised to discover that information. One of the reasons we picked the housing industry as a good value choice is that this industry has been beaten down because of low expectations. As a value investor, you're trying to determine which company might be in the best position to minimize its risks and recover quickly when the economy improves.

For example, Company A reported that revenues fell from $6.12 billion in fiscal 2006 to $4.65 billion in 2007, and net income fell from $687.2 million in 2006 to just $35.7 million in 2007. The company also recognized $619.5 million in inventory impairments and write-offs, which are losses because land and home inventory (in various stages of completion) dropped in value.

In addition to the numbers that Company A's management reported, it was stated, "Beginning in the fourth quarter of fiscal 2005 and continuing throughout fiscal 2006 and 2007 and into the first quarter of fiscal 2008, we experienced a slowdown in new contracts signed. The value of net new contracts signed in fiscal 2007 of $3.01 billion (4,440 homes) was a decline of 32.5 percent from the value of net new contracts signed in fiscal 2006 and a decline of 57.9 percent from the value of net new contracts signed in fiscal 2005."

Company B reported a net loss in 2007 of $657.8 million versus net income of $138.9 million in 2006 and $469.1 million in 2005. The company goes on to explain that, in addition to loss of sales, it had to write off $457.8 million because of land-related charges. The managers explain, "These charges resulted from the write-off of deposit and *preacquisition costs* of $126 million related to land we no longer plan to pursue and impairments (lost value) on owned inventory of $331.8 million for the fiscal year."

def•i•ni•tion

Preacquisition costs for a builder involve the options for the purchase of land and the surveys and other work done prior to the purchase of that land. If a builder decides not to buy the land, those costs are lost.

You'll never find the type of detail given in the MD&A about sales performance in any other part of the annual report. That's one reason it's critical for you to read this section carefully—and maybe more than once. In the previous examples, you can see how the MD&A gives you a critical look at how bad the market has gotten for new homes and how severely builders are hit by current market conditions.

If you saw these numbers for a company without knowing market conditions, you definitely would think Company A is headed for bankruptcy, with a sales drop of 57.9 percent in just two years. Company B is operating at a net loss, certainly the sign of disaster. But for builders in this economy, those numbers are not surprising. The key that we'll look for as we dig deeper into the annual report is how management is dealing with the drop-off in sales and how it plans to maintain the fiscal health of the company through the current market downturn.

Economic and Market Conditions

Managers of both Company A and Company B talk about the economic conditions facing the building industry. Let's take a closer look at what each has to say.

From Company A's MD&A section:

> We believe this slowdown is attributable to a decline in consumer confidence, an overall softening of demand for new homes, an oversupply of homes available for sale, the inability of some of our home buyers to sell their current home, and the direct and indirect impact of the turmoil in the mortgage loan market. We attribute the reduction in demand to concerns on the part of prospective buyers about the direction of home prices, due in part to the constant media attention with regard to the potential of mortgage foreclosures, many home builders' advertising price reductions and increased sales incentives, and concerns by prospective buyers about being able to sell their existing homes. In addition, we believe speculators and investors are no longer helping to fuel demand.

Company B's managers came to similar conclusions about market conditions during the second half of 2006 and for 2007:

> The U.S. housing market was impacted by a lack of consumer confidence, housing affordability, large supplies of resale and new home inventories, and related pricing pressures. The results have been weakened demand for new homes, slower sales, higher cancellation rates, and increased price discounts and other sales incentives to attract home buyers.

It's no surprise that both companies see the same market conditions impacting sales performance, but let's take a closer look at how they are handling the downturn to minimize risk.

Company A writes:

> Because of the length of time that it takes to obtain the necessary approvals on a property, complete the land improvements on it, and deliver a home after a home buyer signs an agreement of sale, we are subject to many risks. We attempt to reduce certain risks by controlling land for future development through options whenever possible, thus allowing us to obtain the necessary governmental approvals before acquiring title to the land; generally commencing construction of a detached home only after executing an agreement of sale and receiving a substantial down payment from the buyer; and using subcontractors to perform

home construction and land development work on a fixed-price basis. In response to current market conditions, we have been reevaluating and renegotiating many of our optioned land positions. As a result, we have reduced our land position from a high of approximately 91,200 at April 30, 2006, to approximately 59,300 lots at October 31, 2007.

Company B writes:

We continue to operate our business with the expectation that difficult market conditions will continue to impact us for at least the near term. We have adjusted our approach to land acquisition and construction practices and continue to shorten our land pipeline, reduce production volumes, and balance home price and profitability with sales pace. We are delaying land purchases and renegotiating land prices, and have significantly reduced our total number of controlled lots owned and under option. Additionally, we are significantly reducing the number of *speculative homes* put into production. While we will continue to purchase select land positions where it makes strategic and economic sense to do so, we currently anticipate minimal investment in new land parcels in fiscal 2008.

def•i•ni•tion

> **Speculative homes** are homes built before the builder has a signed contract from a buyer who wants to buy the home.

You can see from reading these brief quotes from the MD&A of both builders that they are cutting back on land purchases to minimize their expenses and risks. Company A does not build homes for speculation, and Company B indicates it is reducing the number of homes it builds for speculation. Both indicate they are reducing their production to minimize their risks.

We are not surprised to see these cutbacks, but how are these builders positioning themselves for when the economy recovers? Let's take a look.

Company A writes:

During this slowdown, we believe our industry demographics remain strong due to the continuing regulation-induced constraints on lot supplies and the growing number of affluent households. We continue to seek a balance between our short-term goal of selling homes in a tough market and our long-term goal of maximizing the value of our communities. We believe that many of our communities are in locations that are difficult to replace and in markets where approvals are increasingly difficult to achieve. We believe that many of these communities have substantial embedded value that will be realizable in the future and that this value should not necessarily be sacrificed in the current soft market.

Losing Value

As you read the information provided by management, be sure to do a reality check. If the outsiders agree with management's view, you know the company is on the right track. But if there are significant differences between management's view and the view of outsiders, tread very carefully.

So Company A believes its unique brand and its available locations will help it recover quickly. And, as we all know, it's location, location, location, when customers are thinking about buying a home. If you see these types of claims in the MD&A, you should also research to find out what others in the financial press, as well as financial analysts, are saying about the company's future.

Now that we know their philosophy about the future of the company, let's take a closer look at their projections for income in 2008.

Company A writes:

> Given the current business climate that we are operating in and the numerous uncertainties related to sales paces, sales prices, mortgage markets, cancellations, market direction, and the potential for and size of future impairments, it is difficult to provide guidance for fiscal 2008 … we currently estimate that we will deliver between 3,500 and 5,100 homes in fiscal 2008 at an average home price of between $630,000 and $650,000 per home. We believe that, as a result of continuing incentives and slower sales per community, our cost of revenues as a percentage of revenues, before taking into account write-downs, will be higher in fiscal 2008 than in fiscal 2007.

While Company A's project is a wide range with no net income projection at all, Company B did not even try to project housing sales in 2008. Instead, Company B said this:

> Given the persistence of these difficult market conditions, improving the efficiency of our selling, general and administrative expenses will continue to be a significant area of focus. We believe these measures will help to strengthen our market position and allow us to take advantage of opportunities that will develop in the future.

If you are looking at the MD&A for a manufacturing company, some additional details you want to find about operations include the following:

- ◆ **Distribution systems**—How products are distributed.

- ◆ **Product improvements**—Changes to products that improve their performance or appearance.

- ◆ **Manufacturing capacity**—The number of manufacturing plants and their production capability. The MD&A also mentions the percentage of the company's manufacturing capacity that it is using. For example, if a company uses only 50 percent of its manufacturing capacity, that may be an indication that the company has lots of extra resources that are idle. If a company is using 100 percent of its manufacturing capacity, that may indicate that the company has maxed out its resources and may need to expand.

- ◆ **Research and development projects**—The research and development the company is doing to develop new products or improve current products.

Also look for cost information related to product manufacturing or purchase. Cost-control problems can mean that future results may not be as good as the current year's, especially if management mentions that the cost of raw materials isn't stable. Look for statements about interest expenses, major competition, inflation, or other factors that may impact the success of future operations.

Capital Resources

A company's capital resources include its assets and ability to fund its operations for the long term. In this section of the MD&A, you want to look for additional information about the following:

- ◆ Acquisitions or major expansion plans

- ◆ Any major capital expenses carried out over the past year or planned in future years

- ◆ Company debt

- ◆ Plans the company may have for taking on new debt

- ◆ Other key points about the company's cash flow

The information you'll find in this section varies depending on the industry. The discussion also may focus on items that are unique to the operation of the particular company whose reports you are reading.

Let's take a close look at key statements by Company A and Company B regarding their capital resources.

Company A indicated that it generally buys a home site each time it delivers a house, but in the current market, because of contract cancellations, it has several years' supply of home sites, so it won't be buying new sites when sales are made.

As for its borrowings, Company A said, "We have a $1.89 billion credit facility consisting of a $1.56 billion unsecured revolving credit facility and a $331.7 million term loan facility with 35 banks, which extends to March 2011." The managers go on to explain that, as of this report, the interest rate on their revolving credit facility is 0.475 percent. They also indicated that they have "no outstanding borrowings against the revolving credit facility." Management concluded, "We believe that we will be able to continue to fund our operations and meet our contractual obligations through a combination of existing cash resources and our existing sources of credit."

Company B wrote that it met its 2007 cash obligations from housing and land sales, the revolving credit facility, financial service revenues, other revenues, distributions from joint ventures, and tax refunds. The managers said, "We believe that these sources of cash are sufficient to finance our working capital requirements and other needs." Management indicated that it had $1.515 million of outstanding senior notes, with interest rates ranging from 6 percent to 8 percent. The company also has a revolving line of credit facility of $1.2 billion at varying interest rates.

For 2008, Company B said this:

> We expect to generate cash flow from operations as we limit investments in new communities and delay further investment in current communities, given the low demand for new homes. While limiting this investment, we will continue to build and deliver homes from our current communities generating a positive cash flow. We also may enter into land sale agreements or joint ventures to generate cash from our existing balance sheet.

So Company B may meet its cash needs by selling assets, such as land not developed. This is a different approach from Company A, which made a strong statement regarding the viability of its communities and how it will wait out the storm.

Revenue Recognition

In a retail store, recognizing revenue can be a relatively straightforward process: a customer buys a product off the shelf, and the revenue is recognized, or recorded, in the company's books. But things aren't that cut and dried in many complex corporate deals. For example, in the computer and hardware industry, revenue recognition can be complex because purchase contracts frequently include multiple parts, such as software, hardware, services, and training. When the revenue is actually recognized for each of these parts can vary, depending on the terms of a contract.

In the building industry, both Company A and Company B indicated that they recognize revenue when a house is completed and delivered, which means the customer bought the house after a real estate closing. In addition to selling homes, builders hold lots not yet built, upon waiting for customers who want to order a new home. Sometimes they raise additional cash revenue by selling some of this land.

We talked more about revenue-recognition issues in Chapter 8, so we won't repeat the information from the MD&A, which does match the accounting policies indicated in the notes to the financial statements. But you should always look through the revenue recognition discussion in the MD&A to see if there are any planned changes to accounting policies regarding revenue recognition.

Restructuring Charges

When a company restructures a portion of its firm—which can include shutting down factories, disbanding a major division, or enacting other major changes related to how the company operates—management discusses the impact this has had or may have in the future on the company. Costs for employee severance, facility shutdowns, and other costs related to restructuring are explained in this portion of the report. There was no discussion of any major restructuring charges for either Company A or Company B.

Impairments to Assets

The SEC expects companies to report any losses to assets in a timely manner. If an asset is damaged, is destroyed, or for any reason loses value, companies must report that loss to stockholders. Look for information about the loss of value to assets in the MD&A. Also look for information about the depreciation or amortization of these assets.

Both builders reported impairments to assets as the housing market continued to deteriorate on their statement of cash flows. Company A said its impairments of $314.8 million were primarily in Arizona; California; Florida; Nevada; and Washington, D.C. If you read the news, you'll see that these are the same markets hit the hardest during the downturn in the housing market.

Company B said, "Total inventory decreased $422 million, excluding inventory not owned, during the fiscal year 2007. This decrease excluded the decrease in consolidated inventory not owned of $130.6 million." The inventory not owned involved options on purchasing that inventory in the future. Company B went on to break down the inventory impairments: "Total inventory decreased in the Mid-Atlantic $107.5 million, Southeast $138.7 million, Southwest $40 million, Midwest $15.7 million, and West $160.2 million."

No surprises here. Both companies saw their largest impairments of inventory value in the areas of the country where the real estate market is the hardest hit.

Pension Plans

Accounting for pension plans includes many assumptions, such as the amount of interest or other gains the company expects to make on the assets held in its pension plans and the expenses a company anticipates paying out when employees retire. We talked about how to find details about pension plans in Chapter 8. If there are any significant problems with the pension plans, management will discuss them in the MD&A. Neither builder had any significant information to discuss about pension plans.

Environmental and Product Liabilities

All companies face some liability for products that fail to operate as expected or possibly could cause damage to an individual or property. In some industries, such as oil, gas, or chemical companies, an error can cause considerable environmental damage. You've probably heard stories about a chemical spill destroying a local stream or drinking water supply, or an oil spill wiping out an area's entire ecological system.

In the MD&A section, a company must acknowledge the liabilities it faces and the way it prepares financially for the possibility of taking a loss after the liability is paid. The company must estimate its potential losses and disclose the amount of money it has set aside or the insurance it has to protect against such losses.

Stock-Based Compensation

To attract and keep top executives, many companies offer stock incentives (such as shares of stock as bonuses) as part of an employee compensation package. This part of the annual report must mention details of any stock-based compensation. Many recent scandals have included disclosures of unusually high stock-based compensation programs for top executives. Keep a watchful eye (or ear) out for discussion of bonuses or other employee compensation that involves giving employees shares of stock or selling employees' shares of stock below the market value.

Allowance for Doubtful Accounts

Any company that offers credit to customers will encounter some nonpayers in the group. Management must discuss what it allows for loss on accounts that aren't paid and whether this allowance will increase or decrease from the previous year. If the allowance for doubtful accounts increases, it may indicate a problem with collections or could be a sign of significant problems in the industry as a whole.

Both builders offer mortgages as part of their sales incentive packages and then service these mortgages until they can be sold. Neither builder discussed any significant losses from their mortgage lending.

The discussion in the MD&A section of the annual report can get very technical. If you find things you don't understand, you can always call the investor relations department to ask for clarification.

Whenever you're considering an investment in a company's stock, be certain that you understand the key points being discussed in the MD&A. Anytime you find the information beyond your comprehension, don't hesitate to research further and ask a lot of questions before investing in the stock. You should always research your questions in the financial press and read analysts' reports, but don't hesitate to call the investor relations section of a company whose stock you're considering if you can't find the answers to your questions.

Now that we've dug into the reports, we turn our attention to how you analyze these reports and decide whether a stock is worth buying.

The Least You Need to Know

◆ While no company likes to air its dirty laundry, the SEC requires that they do in the management's discussion and analysis (MD&A). You'll find both good news and the dirt on how well a company is doing, so read this section very carefully.

◆ Discussion of company operations—how well the company's primary revenue-generating activity is performing—is the key information you'll find in the MD&A section.

◆ Much of the information you'll find in this section involves statistical data and explanations that may go over your head. Don't hesitate to research further or call the investor relations department to be sure you understand the key points of the MD&A before you invest.

Part

Analyzing the Fundamentals of a Company and the Market

In this part, you learn how to analyze what you found when reading the annual reports. You learn more about analysts, what they provide, and what you can trust. We also explore the basics of market behavior.

Chapter 10

Market Behavior

In This Chapter

- ◆ Bull exuberance
- ◆ Bear depression
- ◆ Market moves
- ◆ Taking control

As a value investor, it's important for you to think for yourself and not follow the crowd. But it's still important for you to understand market crowd behavior and, by understanding that behavior, know when the stock market is ripe for the picking.

In this chapter, we review the ups and downs of the market and the terminology you're likely to hear from business reporters as the market moves from one mood to another. Be careful not to get caught up in the financial press hype if you do choose to listen to it.

Can You Beat the Market?

The best answer to this question is, sometimes—but don't count on it. Generally, the market does a pretty good job of pricing stocks, but when the crowd is acting irrationally, you can find your best and worst buys.

 Losing Value

Most people get caught up in the emotional highs they feel as stocks climb and don't act to take profits before it's too late. Don't get caught up in that type of behavior.

Don't try to beat the market. Instead, focus on building the best portfolio you can. Buy stocks when they're cheap and sell them when they recover. Many value investing gurus tell you not to worry about missing the highest highs because you rarely can sell at just the right time to avoid the steep drop-off when the price of a stock plummets.

Bull Runs

Sometimes you'll hear commentators say the bulls are running. When you hear that, be very cautious. Stocks are likely overpriced.

A bull run is the best time to sell stocks you own and take your profits, but only if you're ready to sell your stake in the company. If you plan to hold a stock for years, don't feel obligated to sell it just because the bulls are running.

You'll be watching a lot of people just starting to get into a market. People who are not intelligent investors tend to get caught up in the excitement of the market and think it's safe to get their feet wet. Unfortunately, these folks buy stocks at the high and, when the bears return, sell stocks at the low when they get scared.

As a value investor, you've likely bought your stock on sale and now you're seeing some great profits. You may or may not want to sell. Run a quarterly analysis of the stock you hold, as we show you in Chapter 11, and be sure it still fits with your criteria for holding a stock.

You can set your criteria for holding a stock by reviewing the value investing strategies in Part 5. When you understand what the gurus do, you can design a strategy that works best for you based on your goals, your risk tolerance, and your financial resources.

Bear Stalls

When you hear commentators say the bears are in control and the market is stalled, it's time for some serious bargain shopping. When this mood strikes the market, most investors run for hills and sell stock at whatever price they can get. That's why, as an intelligent investor, you can find some great buys.

Be careful, though. Don't just buy a stock because you think it's cheap. Make sure you've tested the key ratios we discuss in Chapter 11 and that you've determined it's time to exit the stock based on *your* time schedule—not the time schedule of the crowd. Just because a stock is beaten down doesn't make it a good buy.

Assess the plans the management team has for the company, as well as the numbers. We show you how to scour the financial reports to get this information in Part 2.

Pendulum Swings

Your work isn't finished once you own a stock, either. You must be psychologically ready to deal with the pendulum swings of the market. Any stock you buy will go up and will go down. The trick is to not get caught up in these ups and downs, but to stick to the plan you had for the stock when you picked it.

Don't watch CNBC and the other news shows that follow the market as though it's a sports game. That will just make it harder for you to stick to your plan. You don't have to know exactly what the price of your stock is each day. Watching your stocks that closely will just make you nervous and most likely lead you to make the wrong choices.

Your best bet is to not watch the financial news on TV. Read the respected financial press, such as *The Wall Street Journal* and the *Financial Times,* to stay up on the critical news about the companies you follow and get ideas for new possible investments.

You'll find much more serious, in-depth stories in the financial press. These stories will help you make the best choices in building your portfolio.

Irrational Exuberance

When a bull run goes on for too long, it can morph into irrational exuberance. People tend to think that the market has changed and that stock will continue to go up forever. In reality, it won't—instead, a stock market bubble is gradually inflating.

Unfortunately, most people get caught in the hype and continue to buy while the bubble continues to inflate. Then that bubble bursts without warning, sending shares of stock down 50 percent and more. Asset bubbles have formed repeatedly over time, but most people can't recognize a bubble until after it bursts.

The most recent stock bubble was the Internet stock bubble, which inflated in the 1990s and burst in the early 2000s. Many people who got caught up in Internet stocks lost 50 percent to 70 percent on their portfolio—and some lost as much as 90 percent.

Losing Value

If you can't figure out how a company will generate its cash flow, walk away from it. Don't ever get caught up in promises of future earnings that have not yet materialized.

Value investors such as Warren Buffett didn't play in that market. Value investors will not buy a stock that doesn't have a proven cash flow. Internet stocks were losing money every year. Most hadn't even figured out how they would make a profit. Yet analysts recommended them based on future earnings projections. We talk more about the analysts' role in this fiasco in Chapter 12.

Unjustifiable Pessimism—Time to Find Your Best Opportunities

You'll find your best buys when the market is unjustifiably pessimistic about a sector. For example, when satellite TV was introduced in the 1980s, many analysts were speculating on the doom of the cable industry.

Well, history proved them very wrong. Cable is alive and well and thriving in the marketplace. Value investors who recognized that unjustifiable pessimism found incredible buys among the beaten-down cable company stocks. They did have to be patient and hold on to the stocks for a while until the crowd realized its mistake.

If you believe the market has beaten down a sector unjustifiably, start looking for good buys in that sector. Now, we don't mean you should find the cheapest stock; instead, find the stock of a company with financial results that meet your criteria and a solid management team.

Many times you can spot these kinds of buys by watching the new daily lows in the financial press. As you start to look at new lows, find a stock that has been beaten down for two to three years and has already taken its big fall.

Research the candidates you've found. You'll find a lot of stocks that have been beaten down justifiably—just move on. But start watching those gems in the rough as you research them further to determine whether they're a good buy for you.

Control Yourself

Patience is a virtue you must learn in order to excel as a value investor. You must think outside the box and move in a direction the crowd likely is not following.

If you want to invest intelligently according to the basics established by value investing master guru Benjamin Graham, you must control the following:

- Your brokerage costs
- Your ownership costs
- Your expectations
- Your risk
- Your tax bills
- Your own behavior

Let's take a closer look at each of these.

Your Brokerage Costs

Find yourself a good broker who doesn't charge too much to handle your stock trades. If you feel confident that you know how to handle stock trading, do it yourself with an Internet discount broker.

If you want to get additional services by placing your orders by telephone with a discount broker, you can still find a discount broker. We don't recommend full-service brokers because you don't need their research services and you certainly won't want to follow their advice—unless by some lucky break you find a broker who truly believes in value investing.

Finding Value

Looking for a good online broker? *SmartMoney* does an excellent review of online brokers every year at www.smartmoney.com/brokers.

Also, don't trade too often and waste your money jumping in and out of stocks. As you read the strategies of value investing gurus in Part 5, you'll find that most of them hold on to stocks for four to five years.

Learn to be patient and give a stock you've picked time to recover. Its price may go down after you buy the stock, so don't get discouraged. Few people can actually buy at the absolute lowest price. Most value investors choose a stock on its way down.

But don't be so patient that you end up losing all your money. Sometimes you'll make a mistake when picking a stock. Just admit your mistake, accept your losses, and move on.

Your Ownership Costs

If you decide to invest using mutual funds, be sure to buy no-load funds with very low management fees. Few funds are worth the cost if their management fees are more than 1 percent.

Remember, for a mutual fund manager to meet the returns of a stock market index, he or she must beat the index by at least the cost of the mutual fund's management fees. Management fees are a drain on all mutual funds.

Unless for some reason you've picked a particular mutual fund manager you want to follow, your best bet is to invest using an index fund. Fees for many index funds are just 0.15 to 0.35 percent. You can find good index fund choices at Vanguard (www.vanguard.com) and Fidelity (www.fidelity.com).

Your Expectations

Always be realistic about the returns you want to get out of a stock purchase. Even if you decide to follow some newsletters that specialize in value investing, don't get caught up in someone else's hype. You'll never be disappointed if you carefully assess the true value of a stock and are conservative about the cash flows you can expect from the stock purchase.

Your Risk

Keep a close eye on the amount of risk you can tolerate. Determine the asset allocation that best manages your risk tolerance. We talk more about this in Chapter 18. Periodically rebalance your portfolio so you know that you're maintaining your portfolio at a risk tolerance level that you can tolerate.

Determine how much of your portfolio you can afford to put at risk. Stock investing is a risky business. You can afford to take more risk if you have a longer time frame before you need the money.

For example, if you won't need the money for 10 years or more, you can take on the greatest amount of risk. If you plan to use the money in two years, put that money in a cash account. We talk more about types of risks in Chapter 17.

Your Tax Bills

Each time you sell a stock, you may have to pay taxes on the amount of profit you make from the transaction. If you hold a stock for less than 12 months, the taxes you pay are based on your current tax rate.

If you hold a stock for more than 12 months, your tax bill could be as little as 5 percent for capital gains, if you are in the 10 percent or 15 percent tax brackets. You'll pay 15 percent capital gains tax if your tax bracket is 25 percent or higher.

Unless you've made a terrible mistake picking a stock, you should always hold it for more than a year, to minimize the tax hit on any gain. The only exception to this rule is if you have a significant profit in a stock and you're afraid the stock could take a tumble.

Your Own Behavior

It's human nature to get excited and follow the crowd in feeling good about a stock. The crowd shows its enthusiasm when it bids the price up so high that the P/E ratio tops 20. We talk more about P/E ratios in Chapter 11. Learn to resist these feelings.

It's also human nature to get frightened when everyone is running from the stock market. Get your emotions under control and start to take a look for good buys when everyone else thinks it's time to escape.

The Least You Need to Know

- ◆ Bull markets tend to be good times to take profits on stocks you're ready to sell.
- ◆ Bear markets tend to be good times to find great buys because so many stocks are on sale.
- ◆ Get yourself under control and learn to move at your own pace, not the pace of the crowd.

Analyzing the Company's Financial Reports

In This Chapter

- ◆ Calculating cash flow
- ◆ Figuring out earnings per share
- ◆ Finding book value
- ◆ Getting the current ratio
- ◆ Checking on operations

Always do your own analysis of the numbers. We show you some key ratios and calculations that you can do to determine whether the stock you're considering meets the criteria you set.

As you review the strategies of value investing gurus in Part 5, you will find that each one uses a different type of analysis to pick stocks. In this chapter, we show you how to do the key analysis discussed in that part.

To help you learn these formulas, we take a look at two companies that build residential property. That industry was beaten down in 2007, which makes it an interesting value investing target.

We want to find out whether either of these builders meets the criteria as a good value investment. We've changed the financial statements to disguise the actual builders. You can find the financial statements for this chapter in Appendix C.

Finding Intrinsic Value

You'll see the term *intrinsic value* kicked around a lot in this book, but, unfortunately, no one formula can show you how to find this number. Each value investor reaches the decision about the intrinsic value of a company in his or her own way, using an analysis he or she has developed over the years. All value investing gurus keep the actual formula secret because it's their weapon for finding cheap stocks that make good investments.

Basically, the intrinsic value of a stock is the discounted value of the cash that can be taken out of business during its remaining life. The key lies in determining that cash value, and that's also what every key value investor decides to keep secret. The most common factors to add into this calculation are listed here:

- Sales growth rates

- Profit margins

- Market prices of assets

- Capital expenditure requirements

Let's take a closer look at how to calculate each.

Sales Growth Rates

When trying to determine the sales growth rate, you need to consider at least 5 years and preferably 10 years of data. Calculate the rate sales grew from year to year. For example, suppose a company has $10,000 in sales in 2007 and $11,000 in sales in the next year. What is the sales growth rate?

First, subtract $10,000 from $11,000 to find the dollar amount of sales growth. In this example, this is $1,000.

Next, divide $1,000 by $10,000, which equals 0.1 or 10 percent. For this company, the sales growth rate from 2007 to 2008 was 10 percent.

Both builders had a negative sales growth rate for the three years we have data. If you were considering stocks of companies in this situation, you would need to find an average growth rate for a time period when the market for housing was not as beaten down, or you would need to guesstimate a reasonable growth rate for the industry.

Finding Value

When you're trying to determine intrinsic value, you need to make assumptions about every number you use. You'll be developing cash flow numbers guessing about the future. You have only historical numbers to work with, and you must make your best guesstimate of the future growth of the company. That's why determining the intrinsic value of a company is a very inexact science and value investing gurus don't give the number they use for their assumption. Making those assumptions gets easier when you know more about the industries you follow and what's common for the industry.

Profit Margins

You want to know how much profit a company made subtracting after all expenses and costs of operations but before taxes, interest, depreciation, and amortization. On many company reports, you can find this number on the income statement, called EBITDA (earnings before interest, taxes, depreciation, and amortization). The two reports we're using as samples did not include a number for EBITDA, so let's figure it out.

Company A reported this for the year 2007:

Total Revenues	$4,646,979,000
Cost of Goods Sold	($4,125,377,000)
Selling General and Administrative Expenses	($516,729,000)
EBITDA	$4,873,000

Let's look at Company B for 2007:

Total Revenues	$4,798,921,000
Costs of Goods Sold	($4,567,383,000)
Selling General and Administrative Expenses	($539,362,000)

Financial Services	($48,321,000)
Corporate General	($85,878,000)
Other Expenses	($14,596,000)
EBITDA	($456,619,000)

So Company A had an operating profit of $4,873,000 and Company B had an operating loss of $456,619,000. Now let's figure out their profit margins. To find profit margin, divide EBITDA by total revenues.

For Company A, the calculation is this: EBITDA ÷ Total Revenues

4,873,000 ÷ 4,646,979,000 = 0.001, or less than 1%

Since Company B's EBITDA was a negative number, its growth rate was 0 percent for the year. The company took a loss of $456,619,000 from its operations.

Market Prices of Assets

Scour the notes to the financial statements (see Chapter 8) to find more detail about the assets a company holds. Then research current values for the key assets. This is where many value investors find hidden gems.

For example, a home builder may own a lot of vacant land that is being carried on the books at cost. If the builder bought the land many years ago, the actual market value of the land could be much higher than what you are seeing on the balance sheet.

Capital Expenditure Requirements

To find this number, dig into the notes to the financial statements and the management's discussion and analysis (see Chapter 9) to find plans for future expenditures and to determine what plans are already in place and how much they cost. A company with extensive plans for capital expenditures will be using a lot of the cash from operations and won't have much to pay out to shareholders.

After you've done your research, you should be able to come up with an assumption of estimated cash flow for the company. Then you'll need to calculate a discounted cash flow and figure out a reasonable price to pay for the company.

Discounted Cash Flow

Let's suppose that you've done all your research and you decide on these estimates for cash flow for the next five years:

Year 1	$10,000
Year 2	$11,000
Year 3	$12,000
Year 4	$13,000
Year 5	$15,000

Five hundred shares are outstanding. How much should you pay for this stock to get a return of 15 percent? We're using much lower numbers than you would find in the stock market, to make it easier for you to learn how to do this calculation.

This is the basic formula for discounted cash flow (DCF):

$$DCF = \frac{CF^1}{(1+r)^1} + \frac{CF^2}{(1+r)^2} + \frac{CF^{(N)}}{(1+r)^N} =$$

In this formula, *CF* stands for cash flow. CF^1 is cash flow for the first year.

R stands for the rate of return you want to get; for this example, we're using .15, or 15 percent. You can plug in any rate of return you want.

Using this formula, this is the calculation for the five-year cash flow we showed earlier:

$$\frac{10,000}{(1+.15)^1} + \frac{11,000}{(1+.15)^2} + \frac{12,000}{(1+.15)^3} + \frac{13,000}{(1+.15)^4} + \frac{15,000}{(1+.15)^5} =$$

$$\frac{10,000}{1.15} + \frac{11,000}{1.32} + \frac{12,000}{1.52} + \frac{13,000}{1.75} + \frac{15,000}{2.01} =$$

8,696 + 8,333 + 7,895 + 7,429 + 7,463 = 39,816 for five years, with an average annual cash flow of $7963.20

Now divide that by the outstanding number of shares of 500, to find that a reasonable price to pay for that stock is $15.93.

You can buy a financial calculator that lets you plug these numbers into the calculator and do the work for you. We recommend this if you plan to become a serious value investor.

Earnings Per Share

When you know the net income of a company, you can easily calculate its earnings per share. You do this by dividing the total earnings by the total number of shares. Most companies do the earnings per share calculation and print it at the bottom of the income statement.

For Company A in 2007, earnings per share were 23¢. For Company B in 2007, earnings per share were ($10.11). In other words, the company lost $10.11 per share.

Price to Earnings (P/E)

When you know the earnings per share number, you can calculate the price-to-earnings ratio, or P/E. You divide the price of the stock by the earnings per share to get the P/E ratio.

Suppose that the price of Company A's stock is $25 and that the price of Company B's stock is $10. What are their P/E ratios?

$25 ÷ $0.23 = 108.70

Company B has negative earnings, so you cannot calculate a P/E ratio.

Obviously, a P/E ratio of 108.7 means that the stock is selling more than 100 times the earnings of the company. Most value investors will not consider a stock with a P/E ratio over 15.

Price to Book

The price-to-book ratio looks at the stock market value (its stock price) versus its book value. You divide the current value (price) of the stock by the latest quarter's book value per share.

You find the book value by using the total value of assets, which you'll find at the bottom of your balance sheet. Then you subtract the total liabilities and any intangible assets.

Let's first calculate the book value for Company A in 2007:

Total Assets	$7,220,316,000
Total Liabilities	($3,685,071,000)
Total Book Value	$3,535,245,000

We find that the average number of *diluted shares* is 164,166,000.

def•i•ni•tion

Diluted shares represent the total number of shares that would be outstanding if all possible sources of conversions, such as convertible bonds and stock options, were exercised. We talk about convertible bonds in Chapter 16. Stock options are promises outstanding to employees, allowing them to purchase the stock at a set price.

To calculate the book value for a company, you first calculate the book value per share:

$3,535,245,000 ÷ 164,166,000 = $21.53

You can then calculate the price-to-book ratio:

$25 ÷ $21.53 = 1.2

In this case, the stock price just about equals the book value of the stock. Most value investors won't consider a price-to-book value over 2.5, so this ratio would look good to a value investor, provided that other ratios look good as well.

Now let's calculate the price-to-book value for Company B:

Total Assets	$4,540,548,000
Goodwill (Intangible)	($32,658,000)
Definite Life Intangibles	($4,224,000)
Total Liabilities	($3,155,017,000)
Total Book Value	$1,348,649,000

We find that the total number of shares outstanding is 63,079,000.

So to calculate the book value for company, you first calculate the book value per share:

$1,348,649,000 ÷ 63,079,000 = $21.38

You can then calculate the price-to-book ratio:

$10.00 ÷ $21.38 = 0.47

Again, the stock price just about equals the book value of the stock.

Company B is selling below its current book value, which means it's very cheap. The total assets are worth more than the price at which one could buy the stock. Some value investors would see this company as a possible takeover target since its stock price is lower than the value of its total assets.

Current Ratio

The current ratio is a good way to test whether a company can pay its bills during the next 12 months. With this ratio, you compare current assets to current liabilities. If you see a ratio of 1 or higher, that means the company can pay the bills over the next 12 months. If you see a ratio under 1, it means the company may not be able to pay its bills and could be heading to bankruptcy.

To calculate the current ratio, divide the current assets by the current liabilities.

Let's calculate the current ratio for Company A.

Current assets include these:

Cash and Cash Equivalents	$900,337,000
Inventories	$5,572,655,000
Accounts Receivables	$135,910,000
Total Current Assets	$6,608,902,000

Current liabilities include these:

Loans Payable	$696,814,000
Customer Deposits	$260,155,000
Accounts Payable	$236,877,000
Accrued Expenses	$724,229,000
Total Current Liabilities	$1,918,075,000

So the current ratio for Company A is this:

$6,608,902,000 ÷ $1,918,075,000 = 3.45

Let's calculate the current ratio for Company B.

Current assets include these:

Cash and Cash Equivalents	$12,275,000
Inventories	$3,518,334,000
Accounts Receivables	$286,221,000
Total Current Assets	$3,816,830,000

Current liabilities include these:

Total Home Building	$802,993,000
Total Financial Services	$190,730,000
Total Current Liabilities	$993,723,000

So the current ratio for Company B is this:

$3,816,830,000 ÷ $993,723,000 = 3.84

Both companies look good, but since we know that there's an incredible inventory backlog for most home builders, the fact that inventory is such a huge part of current assets may not be good. Both companies could have a hard time paying their bills if the market doesn't pick up and they're unable to get rid of the backlog in inventory.

Operating Ratios

If you want to recognize trends for the way the winds are blowing, three key turnover ratios can give you a sign about whether the company is headed into trouble. These turnover ratios are inventory turnover, accounts receivable turnover, and accounts payable turnover.

Inventory Turnover

When analyzing a company's financial statements, you want to be sure the company's products continue to be sold. Using the inventory turnover ratio, you can find out how quickly a company sells its products and you can compare that turnover ratio to the ratio of other similar companies.

If sales in the entire industry have slowed, this is likely an industry-wide problem. If you find that sales have slowed only in the company you are considering, something likely is terribly wrong with the way the company is managed or the way the company is marketing its goods. You're better off looking for another candidate if a sales slowdown is unique to the company you're considering.

Calculating inventory turnover is a three-step process.

> **Step 1:** Find the average inventory. Add the previous year's ending inventory (current year's beginning inventory) to the current year's ending inventory. Then divide by 2 to find the average inventory.

> **Step 2:** Calculate the inventory turnover ratio. Divide the cost of goods sold number on the current year's income statement by the average inventory.

> **Step 3:** Find the number of days it took to sell inventory. Divide 365 days by the inventory turnover ratio.

Let's calculate the inventory turnover for Company A:

Step 1—average inventory:

Inventory on December 31, 2006: (Beginning Inventory on January 1, 2007)	$6,095,702,000
Inventory on December 31, 2007: (Ending Inventory)	$5,572,655,000

$6,095,702,000 + 5,572,655,000 = $11,668,357,000 ÷ 2 = $5,834,178,500

Step 2—inventory turnover ratio:

Cost of Goods Sold = $4,125,377,000

$4,125,377,000 ÷ 5,834,178,500 = 0.707

Step 3—number of days it took to sell inventory:

365 ÷ 0.707 = 516

This calculation shows it will take Company A 516 days to sell its current inventory. Not a very good sign for the company, but not unexpected, given the state of the housing industry in 2007.

Let's calculate the inventory turnover for Company B:

Step 1—average inventory:

Inventory on December 31, 2006: $4,070,841,000
(Beginning Inventory on
January 1, 2007)

Inventory on December 31, 2007: $3,518,334,000
(Ending Inventory)

$4,070,841,000 + $3,518,334,000 = $5,834,178,500

Step 2—inventory turnover ratio:

Cost of Goods Sold = $4,567,383,000

$4,567,383,000 ÷ 5,834,178,500 = .783

Step 3—number of days it took to sell inventory:

365 ÷ .783 = 466

Company B would also take more than a year to sell its inventory, but it is in a slightly better position than Company A.

Accounts Receivable Turnover

Another key factor you want to test is whether a company's customers are paying on time. The accounts receivable account tracks the payment of customers who bought products from the company on credit. This does not include customers who used a credit card of another company, such as a Visa or MasterCard. The accounts tracked in accounts receivable reflect credit directly between the customer and the company.

You can find the number for accounts receivable on the balance sheet. You can test the payment record of customers by calculating the accounts receivable turnover ratio and then calculating the number of weeks it takes for customers to pay.

This is the formula for the two-step process:

> **Step 1:** Find the accounts receivable turnover ratio. Divide net sales (which you can find on the income statement) by accounts receivable to find the accounts receivable turnover ratio.

Step 2: Find the average sales credit period (the time it takes customers to pay their bills). Divide 52 weeks by the accounts receivable turnover ratio to find the average sales credit period.

Let's calculate the number of days it takes for customers to pay their bills at Company A:

Step 1—accounts receivable turnover:

Net Sales = $4,646,979,000

Accounts Receivable = $135,910,000

$4,646,979,000 ÷ $135,910,000 = 34.19

Step 2—average sales credit period:

52 ÷ 34.19 = 1.52 weeks

Let's calculate the number of days it takes for customers to pay their bills at Company B:

Step 1—accounts receivable turnover:

Net Sales = $4,798,921,000

Accounts Receivable = $286,221,000

$4,798,921,000 ÷ $286,221,000 = 16.77

Step 2—average sales credit period:

52 ÷ 16.77 = 3.1 weeks

Company A's customers pay off their accounts a bit faster than Company B's, but both companies have excellent customer payment histories.

The higher you find the company's accounts receivable turnover ratio, the faster a company's customers pay their bills. You'll find that the success of a company's accounts receivable collection usually correlates with a company's credit policies. When you see a high turnover ratio, it could be a good sign, but it also may mean that the company's credit policies are too strict and are slowing sales. If the accounts receivable turnover ratio is low, it could mean that the credit policies are too loose and the company is not doing a good job of collecting from its customers.

Accounts Payable Turnover

You also want to be sure a company is paying its bills on time. When you find that a company is having a hard time paying its bills, it's usually the first sign of serious trouble.

You can test a company's bill-paying record using the accounts payable turnover ratio. You can also check to find out how many days a company takes to pay its bills using the days in the accounts payable ratio.

Here's the formula for the three-step process:

> **Step 1:** Find the average accounts payable. First add the accounts payable totals for the current year and the previous year, and then divide that total by 2 to find the average accounts payable number.

> **Step 2:** Calculate the accounts payable turnover. Divide the cost of goods sold by the average accounts payable number to find the accounts payable turnover.

> **Step 3:** Calculate the number of days in accounts payable. Divide 365 by the accounts payable turnover.

Let's do the calculations for Company A:

Step 1—average accounts payable:

Accounts Payable on December 31, 2006 = $292,171,000

Accounts Payable on December 31, 2007 = $236,877,000

$529,048,000

You can find the accounts payable numbers in the liabilities section of the balance sheet.

$529,048,000 ÷ 2 = $264,524,000

Step 2—accounts payable turnover:

2007 Cost of Goods Sold = $4,125,377

You can find the cost of goods sold number on the income statement.

$4,125,377,000 ÷ $264,524,000 = 15.6

Step 3—days in accounts payable:

$365 \div 15.6 = 23.4$

So it takes Company A about 23 days to pay its bills.

Now let's take a look at Company B:

Step 1—average accounts payable:

Accounts Payable on December 31, 2006 = $582,393,000

Accounts Payable on December 31, 2007 =   <u>$515,422,000</u>

$1,097,815,000

$1,097,815,000 \div 2 = $548,907,500$

Step 2—accounts payable turnover:

2007 Cost of Goods Sold = $4,125,377

$4,567,383,000 \div $548,907,500 = 8.32$

Step 3—days in accounts payable

$365 \div 8.32 = 43.9$

So it takes Company B about 44 days to pay its bills. Company A has a significantly better history of paying its bills on time.

The higher the accounts payable turnover ratio number, the shorter the time is between purchase and payment of the bills. If a company has a low turnover ratio, this can indicate that it has a cash flow problem. A company that gets a reputation for paying its bills late will find it harder to get the supplies it needs.

As with any ratio, it's important to compare similar companies to see what is normal for the industry. If an industry usually pays its bills in 60 days, it's not much of a problem, even though that may look like a long time. But if a company you're looking at pays its bills in 60 days while others in the same industry pay their bills in 20 to 30 days, it can be a sign of significant trouble.

Now let's take a look at how to read between the lines of what analysts say about the companies and their numbers.

The Least You Need to Know

- Value investors develop an intrinsic value for the company, and each guru has his own way of getting there. These are closely guarded secrets developed with lots of assumptions about a company's future cash flow.

- Don't depend on analysts. Calculate your own ratios after scouring the financial reports for needed information.

- Value investors are more conservative than growth investors about what they will accept after seeing the ratios.

Listening to the Analysts Cautiously

In This Chapter

◆ Kinds of analysts

◆ Looking at ratings

◆ Listening to calls

You probably hear analysts on financial news networks recommending stocks or bonds for purchase. Each investment broker hires analysts to make recommendations about which stock or bond to buy or sell. But who are these analysts serving?

Some people realized analysts are beholden to the investment houses that pay them and decided their advice should be taken with a grain of salt after they got burned when the Internet bubble burst in 2001. Others needed a second lesson and continued to believe analysts and bond raters until the subprime mortgage mess hit the news in 2007.

Again we saw headlines about how most analysts missed the coming crisis until after it was upon us. Why do analysts keep missing asset bubbles until after it's too late? There are many answers to that, and we take a closer look at them in this chapter. We also explain why you should read reports from analysts, but just as a means to gather information from one of numerous sources. You should never follow an analyst's advice without doing your own analysis before buying a stock or bond.

Analyst Types

You probably don't know that there are different types of analysts, depending upon the type of security (stock or bond) being analyzed or the type of portfolio being managed. Whatever type of analyst you're listening to or reading, the one thing you can be certain about is that analyst isn't working for you unless you're the one paying him for the information. Analysts prepare their reports based on the needs of the person or organization paying the bill.

Buy-Side Analysts

Buy-side analysts usually work for large institutions and investment firms that manage mutual funds, pension funds, or other types of multimillion-dollar private accounts. These analysts have the responsibility to analyze stocks being considered by the firm's portfolio managers for possible purchase and placement in various portfolios managed by the firm. So the buy-side analysts are beholden to their bosses—major institutional buyers of stock. Some buy-side analysts work for mutual funds or pension funds directly. Others work for independent analyst firms hired by the mutual funds or pension funds. You rarely see this type of analyst's research available on the public market, but you will hear bits of the information gathered by these analysts as it trickles out in the financial press through statements made by mutual fund managers.

Buy-side analysts scour financial reports as well as do on-site visits to corporations they are analyzing before writing reports that help portfolio managers determine whether the stock fits the firm's portfolio-management strategy. While many analysts may be reporting that a particular stock is not worth buying, a buy-side analyst may recommend a buy to the portfolio manager they're working for. Why? Suppose the portfolio manager seeks stocks for a value portfolio made up of stocks currently beaten down by the market but with good potential to rebound. The buy-side analysts who work for this portfolio manager may recommend buying a stock that has just lost half its value.

When working for a particular portfolio manager, buy-side analysts know what particular hole in the mutual fund portfolio the portfolio manger wants to fill. So even if a buy-side analyst recommends a stock to the portfolio manger, it might not be the best stock to balance out what you need in your own portfolio.

Managers of mutual funds that focus on growth stocks will be looking at stocks that fill that niche. Managers of mutual funds that focus on foreign stocks will be looking for stocks that fit that objective.

Finding Value

One good source for independent analysts is Morningstar (www.morningstar.com), which is the one of the leading groups that rates mutual funds for individual investors. Morningstar also assigns analysts to rate stocks. In addition to individual stock ratings, you can find stories about which stocks mutual fund managers are buying and why they are buying them on Morningstar's website. Don't buy stock based on these stories. Read the financial reports yourself and do your own analysis of these reports.

Sell-Side Analysts

The types of reports you'll see most as an individual investor are from sell-side analysts. These analysts work for brokerage houses or other financial institutions that sell stocks to individual investors. When you ask the brokerage house through which you buy your stocks for a report on a particular stock, the report you get is most likely one from a sell-side analyst.

Don't trust these reports. Be sure you understand that these reports are being done to encourage the purchase of stocks, and you won't always get unbiased information. Brokerage houses want to sell stocks, and these reports are tools the company's salespeople use to help make a sale.

If you're lucky and your interest matches the interests of the stock salesperson and brokerage house, the sell-side analytical reports will be helpful. But you can never be sure who is being served with the information in those reports. As we all saw when the scandals broke after the Internet and technology stock bubble burst in the early 2000s, conflicts of interest can exist between a brokerage house's need to make money by selling stock and an individual investor's need to make money by owning stock that goes up in value.

Many brokerage houses focused on making money by selling stocks rather than meeting the goals of the investors who depended on information the brokerage house provided to put together stock portfolios that met their goals. Often sell-side analysts' glowing reports encouraged investors to buy stocks, even though the stock did not match the level of risk the individual investor wanted to take. Investors lost 50 percent or more of the money invested in stocks during the 1990s and early 2000s before the stock market crashed. Individual investors were not well served by the analysts who worked for these brokerage houses; they often hid the risks of investing in many of the stocks.

You must take the responsibility to read and analyze reports yourself. The only type of analyst upon whom you can depend is an analyst that you paid out of your own pocket to do that analysis based on your criteria for stock purchase.

Losing Value

During the late 1990s and early 2000s, sell-side analysts wrote glowing reports about the stocks or bonds that were part of investment-banking deals being sold by their brokerage house, knowing the stocks were trash. Then–New York State Attorney General Eliot Spitzer helped expose these conflicts by unearthing e-mails from superstar analysts like Henry Blodget of Merrill Lynch. Blodget wrote glowing reports about stocks being sold by his investment-banking divisions, while privately calling these stocks "dogs," "junk," and "toast." Merrill Lynch wasn't the only company exposed during Spitzer's investigation. Other firms caught in his net included Morgan Stanley Dean Witter & Co. and Credit Suisse First Boston. In fact, most brokerage houses that have an investment-banking division got caught up in these scandals.

Brokerage companies used to avoid these types of scandals and conflicts of interest by protecting themselves with what's called a "Chinese Wall." This wall kept analysts separate from the investment-banking division, which was responsible for selling new public offerings of stocks or bonds and arranging for mergers and acquisitions. When the Chinese Wall was in place, compensation for analysts wasn't dependent upon the business they helped to bring in. At some point in the past 20 years, this wall broke down and sell-side analysts became partners with the investment-banking side to help the firm make money. If a company won new investment-banking business, it rewarded analysts with fees or commissions.

The Chinese Wall for sell-side analysts was reconstructed to a certain extent after the tech stock scandals. The Securities and Exchange Commission (SEC) changed the rules in April 2002 to minimize the risks of this type of scandal happening again. The SEC endorsed the rules developed by the New York Stock Exchange and the National Association of Securities Dealers after the scandal was exposed. These new rules had the following effects:

◆ Prohibit investment-banking divisions from supervising analysts or approving their research reports.

- Ban the practice of tying analysts' compensation to specific investment-banking transactions.

- Prohibit analysts from offering favorable research to bring in investment-banking business for the firm.

- Disclose conflicts of interest in research reports and public appearances. Brokerage houses must include information about business relationships with or ownership interests in any company that's the subject of an analyst's report.

- Restrict personal trading by analysts in securities of companies they analyze or report on.

- Dictate that the firm disclose data about its historical ratings of a company and a price chart that compares its ratings to closing prices.

These rules requiring disclosure will help you quickly determine where there is a conflict of interest between you and the financial interests of the brokerage house or analyst. You can also look at the brokerage house's historical ratings for a company's stock and see how successful it has been in accurately reporting the stock's value in the past.

 Losing Value

Before you even start reading an analyst's report, look for a disclosure regarding whether the brokerage firm gets fees for investment-banking services from the company that's the subject of the report. If the brokerage firm does disclose that it gets fees, keep that in mind as you read the report. Remember, a brokerage firm makes more money from its investment banking business then it does from you. You may find useful information in that report, but do your own research to verify it.

Independent Analysts

You may think, "Well, if I can't depend on buy- or sell-side analysts, what about hiring my own?" You can hire your own, but you need to have a very sizeable portfolio for that to be affordable.

Analysts who are not paid by a brokerage house or other financial institution charge a fee to the people who want their services, but you must have a portfolio of at least $1 million or you must be able to pay about $25,000 per year. Few individual investors can afford the fees to get their own private analyst.

When you pick up an analyst's report, remember that the analyst answers first to the company or wealthy individual who paid a majority of his fees. Many independent analysts do sell the reports for a fee per report to individuals who are researching a specific company. Independent analysts sell these reports through financial websites, and you can find links to these reports as you research companies on the web. But always remember that the report you buy from the independent analyst on a particular company is one that was developed for one of the analyst's clients and not specifically for you. You may or may not have the same goals as the client who asked for the report.

After reading about analysts, you may think you don't have a chance to get good information from any analyst. Your best place to find research that isn't tainted by the investment banking business of your brokerage firm is to visit the websites of major investment research firms like Morningstar (www.morningstar.com) and Standard & Poor's (www.standardandpoors.com). You have to pay fees to access their confidential services, but they're much more reasonable than those of an independent analyst that you might hire as an individual. Depending on the information you need, their fees could be as low as $100 per year.

Bond Analysts

Bond analysts look at things in a different way than stock analysts. Their primary concern is liquidity—does the company have enough cash to pay the interest on the bond and repay its debt, as well as pay its bills? If a bond analyst issues warnings about a company whose stock you are considering, listen carefully. You certainly don't want to invest in a company that can't meet its financial obligations and may go bankrupt.

As a stock investor, your shares of stock usually become worthless after a bankruptcy, so you definitely don't want to invest in a company at risk of going bankrupt. Use bond analysts' red flags to help you find the critical information when you read and analyze financial reports yourself.

Bond analysts evaluate financial reports, management quality, the competitive environment, and overall economic conditions, but they do so with a cautious eye. If bond analysts make a mistake, they're likely to err on the side of caution. Many people believe bond analysts actually provide the best source of objective company research available to individual investors. Most of these bond analysts work for independent bond-rating agencies, as described in the next section.

Unfortunately, in 2007, bond-rating agencies lost some of their clout when they misread the subprime mortgage crisis so badly. They rated bonds related to subprime mortgages too highly, and many financial institutions are still paying the price with multibillion-dollar write-downs. Remember, even bond analysts can get caught up in a scandal when it comes to making money for their bosses.

Bond Ratings

You may not realize this, but bond ratings can have a significant impact on a company's operations and the cost of funding its operations. The rating of a company's bonds determines how much interest that company must offer to pay to sell its bonds on the public bond market. Bonds sold to the public are one way that a company raises cash for its operations. We talk more about bonds and how they work in Chapter 13.

Bonds issued by companies with a higher quality rating (not much different than your credit score in how it impacts the interest rates you can get when you want to borrow money) are considered less risky, so the interest rates the company must pay to attract individuals or companies that will buy those bonds can be lower. Companies with the lowest ratings must issue bonds that are known as junk bonds, which require companies to pay much higher interest rates to attract individuals or companies that will buy those bonds.

Remember, bonds are a type of debt for a company. The individual or company that buys a bond is loaning money to the company and expects to get paid back. The company must pay interest on the money that it is borrowing from these bondholders.

Today there are three key bond-rating agencies:

   ◆ **Standard & Poor's**—You've probably heard the name Standard and Poor's mentioned before. It's well known because of the S&P 500, which is a collection of 500 stocks that form the basis of this *stock market index*. Each year, Standard and Poor's reviews the list and tweaks it by adding some stocks and taking off others. Many mutual funds base their portfolios on this index, which is seen as one of the best indicators of stock market performance. When a stock is added to the list, its stock price usually goes up; when it's taken off the list, its stock price usually drops. You can find the list on the company's website at www.standardandpoors.com.

def•i•ni•tion

A **stock market index** is a basket of stocks whose price is closely watched for upswings and downswings in the market.

- ◆ **Moody's Investor Service**—Moody's specializes in credit ratings, research, and risk analysis. Its analysts track more than $30 trillion of debt issued in the U.S. domestic market, as well as debt issued in the international markets. In addition to its credit-rating services, Moody's publishes investor-oriented credit research, which you can access at www.moodys.com.

- ◆ **Fitch Ratings**—The youngest of the three major bond-rating services is Fitch Ratings (www.fitchratings.com). John Knowles Fitch founded Fitch Publishing Company in 1913. The company started as a publisher of financial statistics. In 1924, Fitch introduced the credit ratings scales that are very familiar today— AAA to D.

Each bond-rating company has its own alphabetical coding for rating bonds and other types of credit issues, such as commercial paper (which are shorter-term debt issues than bonds). Here's a breakdown of the bond ratings:

Bond Quality	Moody's	Standard & Poor's	Fitch
Best quality	Aaa	AAA	AAA
High quality	Aa	AA	AA
Upper medium grade	A	A	A
Medium grade	Baa	BBB	BBB
Speculative	Ba	BB	BB
Highly speculative	B	B	B
High default risk	Caa or Ca	CCC or CC	CCC, CC, or C
In default	(no rating)	D	DDD, DD, or D

Any company with bonds rated in the "highly speculative" category or lower is considered to have junk bonds. Companies in the "best quality" category have the lowest interest rates, and interest rates go up as companies' ratings drop.

Company executives feed bond analysts with critical financial data to keep a company's ratings high. Standard & Poor's (S&P) makes its bond ratings publicly available with links on its websites' home pages. You can search for information about any company's debt ratings.

Whenever a change occurs in the ratings by one of the ratings services, the service issues an extensive explanation about why the company's ratings have changed. The press releases issued by the ratings companies explaining these changes can be an excellent source of information if you're looking for opinions on the numbers you see in the financial reports. You can find these press releases on the bond-rating companies' websites, as well as in news links on financial websites, such as Yahoo! Finance (www.finance.yahoo.com).

Value Visions

Standard and Poor's founder, Henry Varnum Poor, built his financial information company on the "investor's right to know." His first attempt to provide financial information can be found in his 1860 book *History of Railroads and Canals of the United States*, where he included financial information about the railroad industry. Today Standard & Poor's is a leader in independent credit ratings, risk evaluation, and investment research. It has the largest number of credit (bond and other debts) analysts in the world, totaling more than a thousand worldwide.

Stock Ratings

Stock rating is a much different game than bond rating. Whereas bond raters tend to err on the side of caution when they rate the bonds of companies, stock raters, who are primarily sell-side analysts, seem to err on the side of optimism.

When you look at the ratings for a stock, you rarely see a sell rating. In fact, when analysts testified in Congress after the Internet stock scandal in the early 2000s, one analyst was heard saying that everybody on Wall Street knows that a hold rating (which is intended to mean you should hold the stock, but probably not buy more) really means to sell. Some firms use an accumulate rating, which you might think means to hold on to the stock or maybe even add more shares, but it really means to sell in behind-the-scenes circles on Wall Street.

Just like with bond ratings, each firm has its own terminology for rating stocks. A strong buy from one firm may be called a buy in another firm and may be on the recommended list in a third firm. You can never be sure which company is right, but after following a firm's stock ratings for a while, you can understand how its systems work and how accurate it is compared to what actually happens to the price on the stock market. Don't put much faith in the stock-analyst rating system. Following is a common breakdown of stock analysts' ratings systems.

Company A Analysts	Company B Analysts	Company C Analysts
Buy	Strong Buy	Recommended List
Outperform	Buy	Trading Buy
Neutral	Hold	Market Outperformer
Underperform	Sell	Market Performer
Avoid	None Given	Market Underperformer

From looking at this table and the differences among various companies' rankings, you can see the importance of checking out ratings from several different firms, as well as of researching what each firm means by its ratings. A stock that's rated as a "market outperformer" may sound pretty good. But in reality, it's probably not a good investment, which you can see by comparing rankings of other firms that consider it a "neutral" or "hold" stock.

We can't emphasize enough that, as you start doing independent research on a company after reading its financial reports, you must take everything you read with a grain of salt. Collect all the information you can, and then do your own analysis of the information you gather.

Analyst Calls

Companies not only send out financial reports to analysts, but they also talk with analysts regularly about the reports. Sometimes you have access to what is said by listening in to analyst calls or reading press releases.

Each time a company releases a new financial report, it usually schedules a call with analysts to discuss the results. Usually, these calls include the chief executive officer (CEO), president (if not the same as the CEO), and chief financial officer (CFO), as well as other top managers.

Luckily, today individual investors can listen in on many of these calls between companies and analysts. The calls usually start with a statement from one or more of the company representatives and then are opened to those listening to the call for questions. As an individual investor, you likely will not be able to ask any questions, but it's worth listening to the call anyway. Usually only the analysts and sometimes the financial press are allowed to ask questions.

These calls can have hundreds of listeners or only a handful. Even if you can't ask questions, you can learn a lot just by listening. The biggest advantage of listening to these calls is that analysts ask questions of the executives that help you to focus on the areas of concern in the financial reports.

The question-and-answer part of the call is usually the most revealing. During this portion of the call, you'll be able to determine just how confident senior managers are about the financial information that they're reporting. Questions from the audience usually focus on details that press releases or the annual or quarterly reports haven't revealed.

Finding Value

You can listen in on analysts' calls and find out about upcoming calls. Two websites make it easy for you to find out what is available: Vcall (www.vcall.com) and BestCalls (www.bestcalls.com).

Understanding Call Jargon

The language participants use in an analyst call is different from the language you use every day. Familiarize yourself with the most commonly used terms before you listen to your first call. Get comfortable with terms like earnings per share (EPS), EPS growth, net income, cash, and cash equivalents. We talk more about these numbers in Chapter 11.

In addition to the financial terms used throughout this book, you're likely to hear a few colorful descriptions when listening in on an analyst call. Listen for this jargon:

- **Hockey stick**—You may hear management say that company revenues came in like a hockey stick. This means that most of the revenues occurred in the final days of the quarter. In this situation, the revenue charts actually look like a hockey stick because they're flat most of the month and then shoot up in the last few days. Listen for explanations about why sales jump up at the end of a month or quarter. It may be normal for the type of business or it may be related to some outside factor, such as a storm that closed stores for part of the month.

- **Lumpy**—You may hear senior management refer to uneven sales in a given quarter as being lumpy. During some weeks, the order rates were low, and during other weeks, the order rates were high. These results make the revenue charts look lumpy. If you hear this term, listen for explanations about why sales were lumpy and whether this result is normal for the company.

◆ **Run-rate**—Sometimes you'll hear senior management use the term run-rate when talking about how to project a company's current performance over a period of time. For example, if the current quarter's revenues show a million-dollar monthly run-rate, you can expect the annual revenues to total $12 million. This type of projection may work for companies with steady earnings, but it doesn't work for companies that have primarily seasonal products. For example, if a retail company reports a run-rate for the fourth quarter, which includes holiday sales of $1 million per month, you can't expect that performance to indicate a full 12-month performance. You must be certain that you understand a company's revenue picture before counting on run-rate numbers.

Finding Value

If you hear a term you don't understand, write it down and research it after the call. You can research it on the Internet or call the investor relations department for the company that sponsored the call. Then the next time you listen in on one of these calls, you'll have a better understanding of what's being discussed.

Learn to Listen for Mood Swings

Pay close attention to how the executives handle the call and to the words they use. If management is pleased with the results, you'll usually hear very upbeat terms. They'll talk about how positive things look for the future of the company. When management is disappointed with the numbers, they'll be more apologetic and the mood of the analyst call will be low-key. Rather than talking about a rosy future, management will probably explain ways in which they can improve the disappointing results.

You'll most likely need to listen to more than one call hosted by a particular company before you start picking up the nuances and moods of the executives. Try attending as many of these calls as you can or listening to a recording of a call after it occurs. Many companies actually post recordings of their analyst calls on their websites just like they post press releases.

Take the time to read the financial reports before the call so you're at least familiar with the key points that management discusses during the call. After you've listened to a few calls for the same company, you'll find that the information management discusses becomes much clearer to you.

It's All About Earnings

All calls about a company's financial results include information about whether a company met its earnings projections or the projections of financial analysts. If a company misses its own earnings projections, the mood of the call will be downbeat and the stock price likely will drop dramatically after the call.

That doesn't mean you should buy the stock or sell shares you own, if you happen to be a shareholder. In fact, if you are listening to the call because you think you'd like to buy the stock, you might want to do so after the stock price is driven down by the bad news, but tread carefully. Be sure you understand the reason for the bad news and you analyze the company's results carefully before jumping in. The key for you as a value investor is to analyze what is being said and whether you think the company does have a good chance of turning around the bad news.

Increasing Revenues

Listen for information about the company's revenue and whether it has kept pace with its earnings growth. During an economic slowdown, revenue growth becomes very important because a company can play with the numbers to make them look better. Growth in revenues is the key to continued earnings growth in the future.

If you hear numerous questions from the analysts about revenue-growth figures, it may be a sign that they suspect a problem with the numbers or are very disappointed with the results. When you hear analysts' questions about revenue or any other issues over and over again, take a closer look at these numbers yourself after the call. Do further analysis and research before you decide to buy or sell the company's stock.

Analysts' Tone

Listen carefully to the analysts' tone as they ask their questions. Take time to assess their moods. Do they seem downbeat? Are they asking very probing questions, or are they upbeat and congratulating the executives on their performance?

When analysts are disappointed with a company's results, they dig for more information and ask for more details about the areas where they see a problem. The call's discussion focuses on past results and how management can improve future results. When analysts are happy with the results, they encourage further discussion about future results and plans.

You may find it hard to judge the mood of the analysts or the company executives when you listen to your first call, but as you listen to more calls for the same company, you'll be able to judge more easily how the mood differs from previous calls.

Testing Confidence

You can judge whether the executives are confident in their reporting by how quickly they answer the questions. When executives are comfortable and confident in the numbers, they answer questions quickly without rustling through papers. If they're very cautious with their answers and are constantly taking time to look through their papers, you can be sure they're not comfortable with the report and must carefully check themselves before answering the questions.

If you find the executives take a long time to answer a simple question or seem unsure or respond slowly, take this as a red flag. You need to do a lot more homework before making any decisions about buying or selling the stock of that company.

Future Gazing

Listen to the vision that the company's executives portray for the future. Does the vision they present inspire you, or do you think the executives didn't present a clear vision for the company's future and how they plan to get there?

If you find the executives uninspiring, a good chance exists that they're not doing a good job inspiring their employees, either. If you see a downward trend in the company, this may be one of the reasons for that trend. When company executives lack inspiration for the company's future, you have good reason to stay away from investing in that company.

Don't ever plan to buy or sell stock based only on what you hear during analyst calls. Use the calls as one more way to gather information about a stock that you're thinking of buying or for tracking stocks that you already own.

Now that you have the ammunition you need to read the reports effectively and analyze the numbers, let's take a closer look at the different ways you can invest using stocks and bonds in Part 4.

The Least You Need to Know

- Analysts don't have your best interests in mind when they do their reports unless those analysts are paid by you. Use analysts' reports to gather information, but don't depend solely upon them to make a decision.

- Get to know what bond and stock ratings really mean and how much you can trust them.

◆ You can learn a lot about a company and its executives by listening in on analysts' calls. The numbers on the pages of the financial statements mean much more when you hear the mood of the executives as they talk about them.

Part  4

Discovering How to Use Investment Vehicles for Value Investing

In this part, you review the basics of investing with bonds, stocks, and mutual funds. You also explore the use of convertibles and warrants. After introducing these basics, we review the key risks of each type of investment vehicle.

Understanding Bonds

In This Chapter

- ◆ Buying bonds
- ◆ Investment strategies
- ◆ Pricing and yield

For value investors, bonds offer a safety net of steady income and provide a good way to balance a portfolio for a steady stream of cash. Bonds basically are IOUs that the government, a company, or another entity sells to generate cash.

In this chapter, we review the types of bonds and then discuss how to invest wisely using bonds.

Investing in Bonds

You can invest in bonds by buying individual bonds, by buying bonds through bond funds, or by buying bonds through bond unit investment trusts.

Individual Bonds

You'll find a wide selection of bonds to choose from on the bond market if you want to delve in and buy them individually. You will need to work with an investment advisor to buy and sell these bonds. Most bonds are sold in the *over-the-counter (OTC) market*, but some are sold on the New York Stock Exchange.

def•i•ni•tion

The **over-the-counter (OTC) market** is made up of hundreds of securities firms and banks that trade bonds by phone or electronically.

If you want to buy a newly issued bond, your investment advisor must provide you with an offering statement or prospectus, which is the official document prepared according to federal regulations that explains the bond's terms and features, as well as the risks you face by buying this bond.

Bonds can be issued by a number of different entities:

- **U.S. government securities** —These are the safest and are backed by the government. You'll find the lowest interest rate of return on these bonds because of this safety factor.

- **Municipal bonds**—These are backed by state, county, and local governments. Watch the ratings for these. Some state and local governments are in better financial condition than others. If you buy a municipal bond from an entity in your own state, the interest will likely be free of state and local taxation. Check with your financial advisor about taxation. Since municipal bonds offer tax advantages, their rates tend to be lower than other types of bonds.

- **Mortgage bonds**—These bonds are based on mortgages. They used to be among the safest bonds, but the subprime mortgage mess tainted some of these options. For safety, when picking a mortgage bond or mortgage bond fund, be sure you are buying bonds or a portfolio of bonds backed by one of the two key government enterprises—Fannie Mae (www.fanniemae.com) or Freddie Mac (www.freddiemac.com).

- **Corporate bonds**—These are backed by the company that issued them. Their interest rates vary widely, depending on the rating (more on ratings next) that the company receives from the bond-ratings agency. Riskier corporate bonds, known as junk bonds, pay the highest interest rate, but you also face a greater risk that you may not get your money back if the company goes bankrupt.

Initially, the bond is sold at some specific amount, called its face value. In exchange for borrowing the money, the entity that issues the bond agrees to pay interest to bondholders, as well as to guarantee to repay the loan in full at some date in the future, which is called the maturity date. The time period between the initial sale of the bond and the maturity date is called the term.

The promise of periodic interest payments makes this a fixed-income investment. A bond investor who buys a bond on the day it is sold knows he can expect a certain level of income for a certain time period and get back his initial investment at the end of the time period. The risk a bond investor takes is that the entity issuing the bond may not at some time in the future be able to pay the interest or repay the full loan amount.

The interest rate to be paid on a bond can be a fixed rate or a floating rate, or can be payable at maturity. Most carry an interest rate that is fixed for the life of the bond and is set as a percentage of the principal amount (face amount). For example, suppose you could buy a bond with a face amount of $20,000, maturing in 20 years paying 5 percent interest. Every six months, you would get an interest payment of $500 during the life of a bond. When the bond matures, you would then get the face amount of the bond—$20,000. You likely won't have to pay $20,000 initially to buy the bond. Many bonds sell at a discount to their face value. We talk more about bond pricing next.

Not all bonds pay out interest during their lifetime. Some bonds pay out the interest only at maturity.

Bonds are rated by a number of agencies, including Standard & Poor's, Moody's Investor Services, and Fitch Ratings. Each rating service uses its own alphabet soup to specify the creditworthiness of a bond. The safest bonds are those issued by the U.S. Treasury or a U.S. government agency.

This excellent chart from The Bond Market Association (www.investinginbonds.com) summarizes the bond ratings from these key services.

Bond Ratings

Credit Risk	Moody's	Standard & Poor's	Fitch
Investment Grade:			
Highest quality	Aaa	AAA	AAA
High quality (very strong)	Aa	AA	AA
Upper medium grade (strong)	A	A	A
Medium grade	Baa	BBB	BBB

continues

Bond Ratings   (continued)

Credit Risk	Moody's	Standard & Poor's	Fitch
Not Investment Grade:			
Somewhat speculative	Ba	BB	BB
Speculative	B	B	B
Highly speculative	Caa	CCC	CCC
Most speculative	Ca	CC	CC
Imminent default	C	C	C
Default	None	D	D

Finding Value

To learn more about how bond rating works, visit Standard & Poor's online and go to the Research & Knowledge section of the website (www.standardandpoors.com).

Bonds that are considered investment grade receive Aaa or AAA ratings to Baa or BBB ratings from Moody's or S&P. Speculative or junk bonds ratings vary from Ba or BB to D. Companies or other entities with lower ratings must pay a higher interest rate to get buyers, so their yields will be higher, but so is the risk that investors take.

Average maturity is also a factor in bond return. Short-term bonds have an average life of one to five years. Intermediate-term bonds mature in 5 to 12 years. Long-term bonds have a life span of over 12 years.

Bonds are bought and sold throughout their life cycle, so you don't have to buy a bond when it is first issued. You can buy a bond from another individual at any time during the bond's life cycle. You still need to buy that bond through your broker because it will be traded on the OTC.

Bond prices fluctuate as economic conditions and company financial results shift. For example, if interest rates are rising, bond prices of older issues will drop if their interest rate is lower than the current rate available for new bonds. Conversely, older bond prices could rise when interest rates fall because the return on a bond paying a higher interest will be more favorable.

Bond prices usually include what's called a *markup*, which essentially pays the dealer's cost and profits. If you want to buy a bond that is not in the dealer's inventory and he has to go find an available one for you, he will likely charge additional commission fees. Each broker sets his own prices within regulatory guidelines. Prices can vary, depending on the size of the transaction, the type of bond you are purchasing, and the amount of service you need from the broker.

Finding Value

You can find the current price of bonds in many newspapers in the same area of the newspaper that you find stock quotes. The Bond Market Association (www.investinginbonds.com) offers the most recent price, as well as the historical prices. You can use its website to search for the activity of a particular bond or sort out bonds available in different categories.

Bond Mutual Funds

If you don't know much about trading in bonds, a good way to add bonds to your portfolio is to invest using bond mutual funds. These funds buy the same types of bonds that you can as an individual bond investor, but a professional portfolio manager picks the bonds to add to the mutual fund. Bond mutual funds give you the ability to own a portion of a diversified bond mix rather than try to pick just the right bond out of the hundreds of thousands of choices out there.

Bond funds are usually organized by type of fund. You'll find government bond funds, municipal bond funds, and corporate bond funds. You'll also find funds organized by length of holdings, such as short-term bond funds, intermediate-term bond funds, and long-term bond funds.

Bond funds are actively managed. The portfolio manager buys and sells bonds in response to market conditions and investor demand. Unlike buying an individual bond, you don't have to worry about terms when you a buy a bond mutual fund. The bond fund does not have a maturity at which time you must then decide what to do with the money.

But a bond's fund price changes each day as the value of bonds changes. The price of a bond mutual fund is based on the net asset value of all its holdings, so you will see that price go up and down each day. As long as you don't buy a junk bond fund, you likely won't see a drastic change in net asset value on a daily basis.

Your investment in a bond fund earns money in several different ways:

- You get a monthly distribution of interest income.

- You get a capital gains distribution (usually on an annual or quarterly basis) that reflects the gains the portfolio manager made for the fund when buying and selling bonds in the portfolio.

- You may get a capital gain or loss when you sell the bond fund. If the price of the fund goes up from the time you buy it, the difference in price is a capital gain. If it goes down, the difference in price is a capital loss.

You can buy into a bond mutual fund for as little as $1,000. Some have minimum requirements of $2,500. If you're buying a bond mutual fund for a retirement portfolio, you may be able to get started for as little as $500.

When picking a bond mutual fund, look carefully for details about management fees. These can be as low as 0.15 percent for an index bond fund or more than 1 or 2 percent for an actively managed bond fund. We talk more about mutual funds and how they work in Chapter 14.

Bond Unit Investment Trusts

A bond unit investment trust is a fixed portfolio of bond investments that can include government, municipal, mortgage-backed, or corporate bonds. The key difference between a trust and a bond fund is that the bonds for the trust are professionally chosen when the unit investment trust is set up, but then the portfolio is fixed, while a bond fund is actively managed and the portfolio changes based on market conditions.

The benefit of a unit investment trust is that you know exactly what you are buying and how much you will earn when you make the investment. Since a bond mutual fund's portfolio changes on a regular basis as the manager deems necessary, you don't have the same guaranteed income.

Since the pool of funds is not actively managed, you also won't likely have to pay a management fee, which you do have to pay for a bond mutual fund. However, you will have to pay a sales charge when you buy and sell an investment trust.

The minimum initial investment is usually between $1,000 and $5,000. You usually earn interest throughout the life of the trust and also recover principal as the bonds in the trust mature. The trust usually ends when the last bond in the trust matures.

Bond Investment Strategies

Bond investors use a number of strategies to minimize the risk of buying bonds. These include diversification, laddering, barbell, and bond swap.

Diversification

Whenever you invest, you should always consider how well your portfolio is diversified. Surely you've heard the warning not to put all your eggs in one basket. Well, that's essentially what diversification is—not putting all your eggs in one basket by mixing your investment choices to minimize the risks.

When it comes to bond diversification, you minimize the risks of your bond portfolio by holding different types of bonds. You may also hold a mix of grades. A large share of your portfolio should be in top-rated bonds, but you may want to consider buying a small portion of your portfolio in junk bonds that pay higher interest rates.

As a value investor, use the same research techniques for corporate bonds as we've discussed for stocks. Look for beaten-down companies that you believe will recover, and buy the bonds of those companies.

Laddering

Another way to diversify is to buy bonds that mature at different times. That way, you won't be stuck with the problem of having to change your entire portfolio at one time.

Since interest rates go up and down, by laddering you have to find a new investment for only a small portion of your portfolio in any one year.

For example, when you first set up your portfolio, use 25 percent of your available funds to buy bonds that mature in less than 5 years, 25 percent for bonds that mature in 5 to 10 years, 25 percent for bonds that mature in 10 to 15 years, and 25 percent for bonds that mature in more than 20 years. That way, you will never have to replace more than one fourth of your portfolio in any one year.

When the bonds that are maturing in less than five years come due, you then buy bonds that mature in 20 years or more to keep the ladder going up.

Barbell

The barbell also uses length of time to maturity. The key difference is that you buy bonds at two ends of the spectrum. Half of your bonds would be ones that mature in 1 to 5 years, and half of your bonds would be ones that mature in 20 to 30 years.

Bond Swap

When you want to make changes to the bonds you hold in your portfolio, you can use what's called a *bond swap*. You use this technique to change to bonds with a different maturity, upgrade the quality of the bonds you hold, or increase your current income by swapping to bonds that pay higher interest rates.

def•i•ni•tion

A **bond swap** is the simultaneous sale of one bond and the purchase of another.

The most common type of swap is done to save taxes. For example, if one of the bonds you hold is selling below its purchase price but you have capital gains from another transaction you want to offset, you can sell that bond at a loss. If you are considering a bond swap as part of a tax strategy, be sure to discuss this with your tax advisor first.

Pricing and Yield

When buying bonds, you should be most concerned about two things—the price you will pay and the yield (amount of money you will earn).

Price

The price you pay for a bond is based on many different factors. These include interest rates, supply and demand, credit quality, face value, and maturity. Each is described as follows:

- ◆ **Interest rates can fluctuate daily**—When interest rates go down, bond prices tend to go up. When interest rates go up, bond prices tend to go down.

- ◆ **Supply and demand**—As with anything you buy, how many bonds are available on the market and demand for those bonds impact the price. For example, suppose you find a bond with an interest rate of 8 percent and investors decide it's a good buy. Many investors will want to buy that bond, so the price will go up.

Conversely, suppose you find a bond with an interest rate of just 4 percent, while most newly issued bonds are being issued at 5 percent. That bond would have to sell for less because it would be less desirable and not as many investors would be demanding that bond. So its supply would go up and its demand would go down.

♦ **Credit quality**—We already discussed credit quality in the previous section. You will pay more for a bond with the highest credit rating. Junk bonds with ratings below B are the cheapest.

♦ **Face value**—Bonds tend to sell close to their face value when initially issued. After that, they can sell at a premium (above their face value) or a discount (below their face value).

♦ **Maturity**—How soon a bond matures also impacts its price. For example, if a bond's interest rate is low and there is a long time until it matures, the bond will be sold at a discount. Maturity greatly impacts a bond's yield.

Yield

The yield is the actual return you earn on the bond. To find the yield, you factor in both the price you pay and the interest you will receive. You should consider two types of yield—the *current yield* and the *yield to maturity*, or *yield to call*.

def•i•ni•tion

Current yield is the annual dollar amount you expect to receive in bond interest over the next 12 months.

Yield to maturity is the total return you will receive until the bond matures.

Yield to call is the total return you will receive until the bond is called. Some bonds are issued with the right to call the bond, which means the issuer can buy back the bond before it matures.

It's easy to figure out the current yield. For example, if you bought a bond at $1,000 and the interest rate is 6 percent, your current yield is $60 ($1,000 × 6%).

Yield to maturity, or yield to call, is actually more meaningful when you are trying to decide whether to buy a bond. Yield to maturity equals all the interest you receive from the time you buy the bond until maturity, plus any gain you will receive, if you bought the bond at a discount (below its face value) or at face value. If you buy a bond at a premium, there will be a loss when you sell the bond that would reduce your yield to maturity or yield to call.

Yield to call is calculated the same way as yield to maturity, but you shorten the time you will have your bond until the time it is expected to be called. When investing in bonds, be sure to ask your investment advisor for both the yield to maturity and the yield to call so you can compare apples to apples among the various bonds you are considering.

Now that you have a better understanding of the role of bonds in a value portfolio, let's take a closer look at buying and selling stocks.

The Least You Need to Know

- ◆ Bonds make a good choice to add a safety component to your investment portfolio. They are also a good choice if you need a steady income.

- ◆ You should learn four basic investment strategies—diversification, laddering, barbell, and bond swap—to minimize your bond investment risks.

- ◆ Bond prices fluctuate because of interest rates, supply and demand, credit quality, face value, and maturity.

Chapter  **14**

Focusing on Stocks

In This Chapter

- ◆ Stock basics
- ◆ Stock picks
- ◆ Understanding value
- ◆ Buying stocks

Stock investing involves taking on more risk than buying a bond or putting your money in a bank account, but your potential for gain is much greater. No insurance is available for stocks, as there is for cash investments in a bank insured through the FDIC, and there are no promises of returning the money you invest, as bondholders are promised. In fact, when you buy stocks, unless you buy them during an initial public offering, your transaction is not even with the company whose stocks you purchase. In this chapter, we review stock basics and how to buy and sell stocks.

What Is a Stock?

Stocks are certificates of ownership that entitle you to a fraction of the company that issues the stock. You actually own a tiny percentage of all the company's assets, including its buildings, inventory, furniture, and so on. Actually, there are two types of stock—common stock and preferred stock:

◆ Common stock includes voting rights, but you are last in line to claim money for your certificates of ownership if a company goes bankrupt. Most times, common stockholders lose everything they invested after a bankruptcy.

◆ Preferred stock doesn't usually come with voting rights, but its owners collect any leftover assets after the creditors have gotten their share. Also, if the company pays dividends, the preferred stock shareholders have a specific dividend guarantee that is paid first before any dividends are paid to common shareholders. If a company can't make the full dividend payment to preferred shareholders, the unpaid dividends will be tracked and paid out in some future year before common shareholders will get any dividend payments.

Many times when value investors pick a downtrodden company, they find that dividends have been suspended or lowered. If the preferred stockholders are getting less than what was promised in dividends, they will need to be repaid before common stockholders get any dividends. So when considering an investment, be sure to research the status of dividends and whether dividends are due to preferred stockholders that haven't been paid.

So far, we've been talking about stock certificates, but you probably have never seen one. In the past, actual paper certificates were handed out when stock was sold. Today most of us keep the "certificates" on deposit with our broker or bank that handles our stock transactions. If you held the certificates yourself, not only would you need to ensure their safety so they don't get lost, but you also would have to physically take them to your broker or bank to sell them. This could cause great delays in completing your sale.

Voting rights don't mean much to most stockholders today. Few have a significant enough share of a company to truly influence any key decision making. Unless you're someone like Bill Gates at Microsoft, you pretty much sit on the sidelines and watch things happen to your stock holdings.

As a value stock investor, your key responsibility is to carefully research stocks before you purchase them and determine what you think the possibilities are for a turnaround for the companies you select. There's a lot of information out there about every major company, but if you've been reading the news lately about the major financial institutions that took big losses from subprime mortgage assets that were held off the books, you can see that even major companies can hide their true value from analysts and investors alike. In fact, in some cases, regulators believe that the analysts and accountants may be too closely tied to the companies to be certain that true values are being reported to the public.

Picking Stocks

Direct stock investing takes a lot of time, but you do have the possibility of getting the highest reward if you pick correctly. You also face the greatest loss, as Enron investors found out when that multibillion-dollar company went belly up and left its investors with nothing. Before taking the plunge, take time to learn about stock investing, and maybe even practice by managing a make-believe portfolio either on paper or by using one of the free portfolio sites online.

Some excellent online resources can help you learn more about investing, with tools for practicing your own portfolio-management style. These are three of our favorites:

- Yahoo! Finance (http://finance.yahoo.com)

- Marketwatch (www.marketwatch.com)

- Dow Jones's SmartMoney University (www.smartmoney.com/university), with excellent self-directed courses that help you learn more about investing

Basically, when you're trying to decide which stock to buy, you should start by researching an industry that you think makes a good choice as a value play. For example, two key industries that were beaten down in 2007 were financial institutions and home builders. Either industry would make a good choice for bargain shopping.

Start your shopping by getting to know the industry that interests you. Read the key financial newspapers and magazines regularly to see what the analysts are saying about the industry and its major players. Four good financial websites to visit daily are listed here:

- The Wall Street Journal (www.wsj.com)

- The London Financial Times (www.ft.com)

- Investor's Business Daily (www.investors.com)

- Bloomberg's (www.bloomberg.com)

In addition, you should read these magazines regularly:

◆ *Business Week* (www.businessweek.com)

◆ *Forbes* (www.forbes.com)

◆ *Fortune* (http://money.cnn.com/magazines/fortune)

Reading these sources regularly will help you stay well informed about the industry or stocks that interest you, and you'll get ideas for other industries that have been beaten down and possibly make a good place for bargain shopping.

When you feel confident that you know the major players in an industry, pick the top three to five companies that you think are worth taking a closer look at. Get the annual reports for those companies and start the research process about the companies, as we discussed in Parts 3 and 4, to figure out which one of these companies makes a good value play.

How Is Stock Valued?

You may be wondering how a stock price is set. Well, it's pretty much a daily vote by the stock-buying public regarding what the public perceives the stock is worth. Remember, after the initial public offering (when the company offering the stock first sells it to the public), all trades are done between two individuals or financial institutions. The original company offering the stock is no longer involved in the sale.

Suppose John bought a share of stock for $10. He decides he wants to sell it for $15 a year later. Bill wants to buy the stock, but he thinks it's worth only $12. John has to decide whether he wants to take Bill's offer or wait for a better offer to come along from someone else.

Well, stock trading is not quite that simple. Basically, when you want to sell a stock, you need to contact a broker. We talk more about types of brokers shortly. The broker finds out how much the stock is selling for at the stock exchange or through various electronic trading systems. He tells you the current market price and you decide whether you want to sell or buy the stock. There are also ways you can put in an order to sell the stock based on the price you're willing to accept. We talk more about that later.

To set a price for a stock, the voting public takes a look at the daily news about the stock, as well as other economic news, and then tries to determine whether the news will help or hurt each company. For example, if the Mortgage Brokers Association announces that new mortgages are on the rise, that could be good news for the real estate industry, so real estate–related stocks may go up because more people want to buy the stock than there are available shares. As supply dries up, the stock price goes up to satisfy the demand for the stock.

Or you may hear that the CEO of a company you own is leaving the company. The market votes on whether this is good or bad news. If the market wasn't happy with the CEO's performance, as happened in early 2008 when the CEO of Citigroup was replaced, the stock price goes up because more people want to buy the stock. But if the CEO was well respected and the market perceives his leaving as a negative for the company's future, the stock price may go down because there are fewer buyers for the company's stock and the supply increases with less demand.

Basically, you can see there's no scientific basis for whether a stock will go up or down. Market winds drive stock prices.

The market rewards what it perceives to be a good stock with an increase in stock price because of higher demand for the stock. The public votes when the company's earnings are going up by agreeing to pay more for that stock to buy the shares that are available. But if a company reports a loss, the public beats the stock down.

As a value investor, if you're interested in a particular company and hear bad news, take a closer look to see if the market punished that company too severely after hearing the bad news. If you run your own analysis and believe the stock price is now a bargain, it's time to go bargain shopping.

Finding Value

The market has little patience for companies that report an earnings decline or an unexpected loss. Companies that surprise Wall Street with a bad quarterly report almost always get punished and can be ripe for the picking for a value investor. But don't jump at every beaten-down stock. Be sure your own analysis shows that the stock is worth more than the market believes it is.

Buying Stocks

You can buy stocks in one of three ways:

- ◆ Do it yourself, using an online broker or working with a brokerage house by telephone. When you do it yourself, you pick the stocks for your portfolio with no advice from a broker.

◆ Work with a broker or financial planner who will help you manage your portfolio. Fees for private money management can get high, and unless your portfolio is a large one, you'll have a hard time finding a top money manager.

◆ Invest using mutual funds. We take a closer look at how they work in the next chapter.

Types of Stock Brokers

When you want to buy stocks, you have a choice of working with a full-service broker or a discount broker.

Full-Service Brokers

A full-service broker gives you more service than a discount broker. A good broker can help you make investment choices. You pay higher commissions to buy and sell stocks through a full-service broker.

Full-service brokers include well-known firms such as Merrill Lynch, Morgan Stanley Dean Witter, and Smith Barney. They also provide you with extensive research on individual stocks, but remember, the information is from sell-side analysts (see Chapter 12), so you can't depend solely on this information when you're trying to make buying or selling decisions.

Full-service brokers also offer estate-planning services and tax advice. Your broker will help you set up your financial—based on your assets, income, and goals—and advise you based on this profile. Of course, you will pay for these services.

If you're sure you know exactly which investments you want to buy and don't need to pay for the services of a full-service broker, you may want to consider using a discount broker. But if you want to buy individual stocks and lack the time or experience needed to do the research yourself, don't try to go it alone. To find a good broker, ask your friends or colleagues you trust for financial advice to recommend a good broker.

If you do decide to use a full-service broker, make sure you get a commission schedule that spells out the fees you'll have to pay. You also want to find out how your broker is paid, especially if he'll get higher commissions for selling certain financial products. By knowing how he'll get paid, you'll have an idea of what he may want to steer you toward. Be careful whenever he recommends a product you know he earns extra commission on when he sells it. He may try to push you into something you don't need.

Some brokerage houses offer two options to pay for trades. One is to pay a commission per trade. The second is to pay a certain percentage of your portfolio. As a value investor, you aren't likely to do heavy trading. You'll more likely take the time to research beaten-down stocks and then buy and hold them for a while, so a commission per trade will likely be more cost-effective for you. People who choose a percentage fee structure usually like to trade more frequently.

Discount and Online Brokers

If you'll probably be making most of your investment decisions on your own, you won't want to pay commissions to a full-service broker. You can buy and sell your stocks more cheaply using a discount broker. Four well-known discount brokerage firms are Charles Schwab, Fidelity Investments, E*Trade, and TD Ameritrade.

Schwab and Fidelity offer some of the services of full-service brokers, so their trading fees are higher. TD Ameritrade and E*Trade offer primarily online trading and the lowest per-trade costs. While you may find the low cost tempting to trade on your own online, you must be very familiar with the technical side of making trades to do it yourself.

Finding Value

Each year, SmartMoney does a survey of online brokers. For the most up-to-date information about how well online brokers serve their customers, go to www.smartmoney.com/brokers.

If you're new to stock trading and want to make your own decisions about which stocks to buy, we recommend that you start with Charles Schwab or Fidelity Investments and take time to learn more about the mechanics of trading before you start to do your own online trades.

Get to Know Buy/Sell Orders

If you trade on your own, you must know exactly the type of buy or sell order you want to use. You can choose from a variety of buy or sell orders. Each one gives you a different level of control over the stock transaction. Some of the orders restrict the transaction by price. Others control it by timing.

Whether you are dealing with an Internet-based broker or an actual human being, you'll want to know these terms to trade a stock:

- ◆ Market order
- ◆ Limit order

- ◆ Stop-loss order
- ◆ Good till canceled
- ◆ Day order

Market Order

Market orders are the simplest, cheapest, and quickest way to place a stock buy or sell order. When you place a market order, whether you are placing the order online or by telephone, you tell your broker to buy or sell the stock immediately at the prevailing price, whatever that may be. You may or may not get the price you last saw listed online. When the market is volatile, you will probably get a price close to the one you are seeing online, but there are no guarantees for a specific price when you place a market order. Market orders will likely be the cheapest types of orders to place.

Limit Orders

Limit orders tell your broker to buy or sell a stock at a particular price. You set the price at which you want to buy and sell based on the research you've done. The purchase or sale will not happen unless you get your price.

Finding Value

If there is a significant difference and the price of the stock you are considering is not moving up and down wildly, you may want to save the money and place a market order.

Limit orders give you control over your entry or exit point by fixing the price. As a value investor, you definitely want this type of control, but be sure you know what the commission is on limit orders versus market orders. Limit orders require more time of the broker and usually have higher fees.

Stop-Loss Orders

When you place a stop-loss order, you tell your broker the price at which you want to sell a stock, to avoid taking a big loss if the stock drops below a price you set. As a value investor, it's good to set a stop-loss order point below the current market price so that if the stock falls to this price point, your broker will sell the stock. That way, if you made a mistake when bargain shopping and chose a company that doesn't recover, you won't lose all the money you have invested in the stock.

If the stock stays level or rises, the stop-loss order will not be implemented and you'll still have the stock. Stop-loss orders are cheap insurance that protects you from a big loss.

Good Till Canceled

When you place a good till canceled (GTC) order, you tell your broker to keep the order active until you cancel it. You use this order with any other order types, to specify a time frame for the order. Some brokers have time limits on how long they will allow you to have a GTC order in place.

Day Order

Most of your stock orders will be day orders. Any order in which you do not specify good till canceled is assumed to be a day order—good for only the day you placed the order. If the stock was not bought and sold as you instructed, you must place the order again the next day.

For example, suppose you placed a stop-loss order to sell a stock if it drops below $10, and the lowest price was $11. The stock would not have been sold. If you still want the stop-loss order in place and you used a day order, you would need to place the order again the next day.

The Least You Need to Know

◆ Two types of stocks exist. One gives you voting rights; the other guarantees dividends.

◆ Get to know an industry first and then look at the companies in that industry that look like they're selling at a bargain.

◆ You can buy stocks on the cheap through a discount broker or get more personal service from a full-service broker.

◆ Get to know the various types of orders you can place to buy or sell stock. A market order is the simplest, but a limit order or stop-loss order might be better to use in certain circumstances.

Using Mutual Funds

In This Chapter

♦ Mutual fund basics

♦ Exploring types

♦ Picking funds

♦ Understanding fees

Mutual funds pool the money of hundreds of investors to build a portfolio that can include cash, stocks, and bonds, depending on the objectives the portfolio manager has chosen. If you're just starting out as an investor, mutual funds offer a great alternative for investing your money as you learn more about investing directly in stocks and bonds.

In this chapter, we discuss how mutual funds work, the various types of funds on the market, how you research funds, and how you buy funds.

Why Mutual Funds?

Mutual funds allow you to instantly buy into a diversified portfolio and slowly build your asset base while you learn more about investing and ultimately decide whether you want to go it alone or continue working with a professional money manager.

Mutual fund investing is very popular today and a much safer way to take advantage of the higher returns available with stock investing. More than 70 million people invest through mutual funds, with over $11.742 trillion held in mutual fund accounts at the end of February 2008, according to the Investment Company Institute. You can also choose from over 8,000 mutual funds, so picking funds can be a real chore. But if you take the time to pick the right funds, you won't need as much time to monitor your investment as you would for a portfolio built with individual stocks.

When you buy a mutual fund, you're buying not only the value of the investments the fund holds, but also the expertise of the portfolio manager. Mutual funds are run according to a set of objectives clearly stated in the mutual fund prospectus, which is a legal document you should review before purchasing any fund. These documents not only include the stated objectives, but also give you a history of the fund's performance and the fund's top holdings as of a specific date. In addition to the prospectus, you should review the quarterly or semiannual reports that give you the most up-to-date information you can find on most funds. Some funds report their portfolios more frequently online. Various investor groups also have called for more frequent reporting.

Basically, the objectives state the fund goal, the types of investments that can be included in the portfolio, and the country or countries in which the fund can invest. These pooled portfolios help the small investor reduce the risks and volatility of investing directly in stocks or bonds of individual companies. Portfolio managers use two styles of investing—active money management and indexing. Indexing is a mathematical model based on tracking the results of various indexes, such as the popular Standard & Poor's 500, which is a grouping of 500 of the top growth companies.

As an individual investor, what you actually own is a pro rata share of the portfolio. You receive distributions in the form of dividends, interest, and/or capital gains, based on that pro rata share. You can build your portfolio even more quickly by automatically reinvesting these distributions.

Exploring Fund Types

Choosing a mutual fund can be a daunting exercise. You can choose from over 8,000 mutual funds, in four distinct groups: equity funds, fixed-income funds, balanced funds, and money market funds. Equity funds, which account for about 50 percent of the total dollars invested in mutual funds, invest primarily in shares of common stock. Money market funds, which are the next-largest portion of the mutual fund pie, account for approximately 30 percent of mutual fund assets. They invest in short-term debt securities of the U.S. government, banks, and corporations, as well as U.S. Treasury bills.

Fixed-income funds, which make up about 13 percent of total mutual fund assets, invest primarily in bonds and preferred stocks. These funds can be either taxable, which include corporate and long-term government bonds, or tax-free, which include municipal bonds. Tax-free bond funds are free from taxes on interest earned but can be taxed on capital gains.

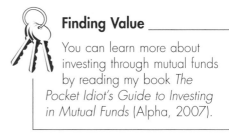

Finding Value

You can learn more about investing through mutual funds by reading my book *The Pocket Idiot's Guide to Investing in Mutual Funds* (Alpha, 2007).

The smallest piece of the pie is in balanced or hybrid funds, which total about 5 percent of the mutual fund universe. These funds invest in a combination of both stocks and bonds.

Choices get even more confusing when you start looking at the objectives of funds. Stock funds mix their assets under varying criteria, based on the risk of the stock holdings. When you start researching stock funds, you'll find categories such as aggressive growth funds, growth funds, and growth and income funds. We take a brief look at the kinds of companies you can expect to find in each of these different types.

Aggressive Growth Funds

Aggressive growth funds are definitely the most volatile type of equity mutual funds and not the type of fund you'll likely choose as a value investor. You will usually find these at both ends of the performance line—the top 10 performers of the year and the 10 worst performers. Their goal is to find assets that will give them maximum capital growth by picking stocks in companies the manager believes has good potential for rapid growth and capital appreciation.

When you invest in this type of fund, be ready for a wild ride. These funds have wide swings up and down, and low stability of principal. You definitely must have a strong stomach for this type of investment, and a lot of patience. If not, you could end up selling out of the fund at its worst point, when your mutual fund has lost a lot of money and you're too nervous to wait for a rebound. The types of companies you'll usually find in these funds are small emerging growth companies. You also may find a concentration of one or more industry sectors. Some will use speculative strategies, such as short-selling or options, to leverage their results.

Growth Funds

You may want a fund that has good growth potential but is not as risky as the aggressive growth funds. For this alternative, seek out growth funds, which are less volatile. As a value investor, you probably want to avoid these funds as well; however, you may want to balance out your portfolio with a percentage of growth mutual funds because growth stocks tend to shine when value stock mutual funds do poorly.

In these types of funds, you will find managers who invest in common stocks seeking growth rather than current income. Their portfolio holdings are more conservative than aggressive growth funds because the portfolio will be built using well-established companies within industries with long-term growth potential rather than small, emerging companies.

You can't expect to get much income from these funds. Growth companies usually reinvest their profits and pay low or no dividends. Therefore, these funds are not suitable if you're seeking current income. Although their potential for a drop in principal value is less than with aggressive growth funds, their volatility may not be right for you if you can't assume risk to your principal. By taking some risk of a short-term drop in principal, however, many growth funds have sustained strong long-term performance records.

Value Funds (Growth and Income Funds)

Your favorite as a value investor will be growth and income funds, also known as value funds. These have stated objectives that seek both long-term growth and current income. In these portfolios, you will find stocks of well-established companies and most likely significant dividend payments. Value fund managers use dividend yields to offset the volatility that can be found in pure growth funds. Dividends are a stable component of this type of funds' total return, while capital returns can fluctuate widely.

A number of different investing styles make up the value or growth and income fund universe. Some managers concentrate their portfolios in growth and income stocks, or put together a combination of growth stocks, stocks that pay high dividends, preferred stocks, convertible securities, or fixed-income securities such as corporate bonds and money market instruments. Others may look for the beaten-down companies that they think have a good chance of recovery. Still others may be a bit more aggressive and use what is called hedging strategies by investing in growth stocks and then buy and sell covered call options to generate the income side of the portfolio instead of depending on dividends.

Without a doubt, as long as you've picked a good manager, this style of mutual fund management is the least volatile of equity mutual funds.

Bond or Fixed-Income Funds

These types of funds can invest in bonds and preferred stocks. They can also be taxable, when their assets are held in corporate or government bonds, or tax-free, if their assets are in municipal bonds. Even tax-free bond funds may experience capital gains. While the interest earned is tax-free, capital gains are generated when municipal bonds are sold at a profit prior to their maturity date.

As with stock funds, you should select a bond mutual fund instead of investing directly in bonds if you want greater diversity in the types of bonds held in the portfolio. These funds also offer more liquidity; in many cases, you can get your money by writing a check, if the service is offered.

When picking a bond fund, research the types of bonds in a portfolio, the creditworthiness of the bonds, and their average maturity date. As we discussed earlier, all these factors determine the safety of a bond.

Bond ratings vary by credit rating agency. In addition to their individual bond ratings, Standard & Poor's uses a similar rating system for bond funds. To give you an idea of how these ratings work, here's a brief description from Standard & Poor's about its rating criteria.

> **AAAf** —The fund's portfolio holdings provide extremely strong protection against losses from credit defaults.
>
> **AAf** —The fund's portfolio holdings provide very strong protection against losses from credit defaults.
>
> **Af** —The fund's portfolio holdings provide strong protection against losses from credit defaults.
>
> **BBBf** —The fund's portfolio holdings provide adequate protection against losses from credit defaults.

BBf —The fund's portfolio holdings provide uncertain protection against losses from credit defaults.

Bf —The fund's portfolio holdings exhibit vulnerability to losses from credit defaults.

CCCf—The fund's portfolio holdings make it extremely vulnerable to losses from credit defaults.

Money Market Funds

The safest of all mutual funds is the money market fund, but these also offer the least potential for the growth of your money. Money market fund holdings can include short-term debt securities of the U.S. government, banks, and corporations, as well as U.S. Treasury bills. These funds have no potential for capital appreciation.

Money market mutual funds have a constant share price of $1. The interest rate they earn, not the share price, fluctuates. They frequently earn more interest than an insured bank account, but you don't have the safety that insurance offers. You may find a better interest rate with a long-term certificate of deposit (CD), but the advantage of mutual funds is that they are more liquid. CDs usually limit your access to the money during the term of your investment, while money market mutual funds allow you to write a check on the money at any time. However, some money market funds limit the number of free checks you can write each month and charge a fee if you exceed that minimum.

You can choose from three types of money market funds: general money market funds, funds that invest only in U.S. government instruments, and tax-exempt money market funds. General money market funds usually invest in a combination of commercial paper and U.S. government securities. The U.S. government funds invest in money market instruments whose principal and interest is backed by the U.S. government or its agencies. The cost of this guarantee is slightly lower yields than general money market funds.

Tax-exempt money market funds invest in short-term municipal bonds that are exempt from federal income taxes. These types of funds usually offer the lowest return among money market mutual funds because of the tax-free advantage. When deciding whether to use a tax-exempt money market fund or a taxable one, you'll need to compare the after-tax yields for both taxable and nontaxable funds to find out which is best for you.

Hybrid and Balanced Funds

While most of these mutual fund types hold cash assets at some time, if you don't want to worry about how to mix your portfolio among stock funds, bond funds, and money market funds, you can invest in funds whose objectives are to do this balancing act for you. These are called hybrid or balanced funds.

These funds are usually the least volatile of funds that include stocks and bonds. Their objective is not to achieve the highest possible return, but to provide stability and some income. You will never find a balanced fund in the top 10 funds of the year, but you also won't find it at the bottom of the pack, unless you've selected an incompetent manager. Usually the stated objectives specify a specific balance between stocks and bonds, such as 60 percent stocks and 40 percent bonds or cash.

International Funds

You may want to add an international flavor to your mix. You can find international funds within all of these mutual fund types. You basically can choose from two types of international mutual funds—world/global funds or foreign funds. The key difference is whether they invest in U.S. stocks or bonds as well as foreign funds. Purely foreign funds do not invest in U.S. stocks. A world or global fund may be less volatile, but if you choose to add an international component to your portfolio using these funds, be sure there's not a significant overlap with your domestic stock funds.

Researching Your Choices

As you can see, you have a lot of different types of funds to choose from, so how do you make your selection? One of the best sources on the Internet for mutual funds is Morningstar (www.morningstar.com). At its website, you will find detailed information about most of the mutual funds available. You'll also find stories about mutual fund managers.

As you start to research your choices, you can narrow the options considerably using the fund screener (http://screen.morningstar.com/FundSelector.html). Using this fund screener you can choose the following:

◆ **Fund type**—You can pick the fund group, Morningstar Category, and manager tenure (five years or more is good). As a value investor, you can choose from three categories: large value, midcap value, or small value. These relate to the size of the companies. Large value refers to large companies with a market value of $5 billion or more, midcap refers to medium-size companies with a market value of $1 billion to $5 billion, and small value refers to companies with a market value of $250 million to $1 billion.

◆ **Cost and purchase**—Pick how much you want to purchase initially; this can range from as little as $500 up to $10,000. You can choose a load (commission must be paid) or no-load fund (no commission must be paid). Finally, you select an expense ratio you will accept. We recommend that you set this to 1 percent or lower. Expenses can quickly eat up your gains.

◆ **Ratings and risk**—Morningstar has its own ratings system, called the star system. We recommend you look for funds rated with four or five stars to find the best funds in the category in which you are searching. You can also choose your risk level—high, above average, average, below average, or low.

◆ **Returns**—In this section, you set a criteria for the returns you want. We recommend you look at long-term returns of three years and five years at greater than or equal to the category average.

◆ **Portfolio**—You can select different criteria for stock and bond funds to narrow your choices further. For example, for stock funds, you can pick a total asset size for the portfolio. For bond funds, you can pick an average credit quality.

After you pick your criteria, click the button to show the results; you'll get a list of mutual funds that meet the criteria you set. Then pick the funds that interest you and score the results.

When you get to the Score Your Results page, you can set a priority for the various criteria you select. The funds then will be scored based on the priority you set.

Once you've prioritized the funds you want to look at, click the button to show the details, to get more details on the funds that best meet your criteria. You can then click on the funds that interest you and see more information about each individual fund.

Buying Mutual Funds—Loads vs. No Loads

You can buy mutual funds directly from a mutual fund company or through a broker. As long as you feel confident that you can choose your own funds, we recommend that you buy no-load mutual funds, which means that you won't have to pay a commission to a broker to buy those funds.

Load mutual funds require you to pay a commission that usually ranges from 3 percent to 6 percent of the amount of money you want to invest. For example, if you plan to invest $10,000 and you must pay a 6 percent commission, $600 will be subtracted up front before you even buy the mutual funds. That means you start at a disadvantage, with only $9,400 invested versus the $10,000 you would have invested with a no-load fund.

Minimizing Fees

All mutual funds charge fees to pay a professional mutual fund manager for his skills in managing the fund. These fees pay the manager and his research staff and cover the costs of doing business, such as transaction fees for trading stocks, shareholder account administration, and other administrative duties.

Keep a close watch on the fees the mutual funds charge for operating the funds. Whatever you pay for mutual fund management reduces the possible gain you can make on the fund.

You'll find the lowest fees on index mutual funds. These funds are managed using a computerized program based on a set of criteria determined by the portfolio manager. Since they don't require as much time of the manager or his staff as an actively managed fund, they cost less to operate. You can find index funds with fees as low as 0.15 percent.

Actively managed mutual funds could have fees as high as 2 percent or 3 percent. Look for funds with management fees below 1 percent so you can be sure you're getting the most out of your investment.

In the next chapter, we take a look at two other alternatives you can use to build your investment portfolio—convertibles and warrants.

The Least You Need to Know

- Mutual funds are a great alterative if you're new to investing or you just don't have the time to manage your own stock and bond portfolio. They also offer you a well-diversified portfolio even if you have only a small amount to invest.

- Picking among the over 8,000 mutual funds on the market can be a daunting task, so take advantage of the screening tools available on the Internet.

- Minimize the fees and commissions you must pay to invest through mutual funds. Focus on no-load mutual fund options with very low management fees.

Chapter 16

Discovering Convertibles and Warrants

In This Chapter

- ◆ Exploring convertibles
- ◆ Finding the zone
- ◆ Checking out warrants

If you're a conservative investor and aren't quite ready to dive into the stock market, you may want to get your toes wet with convertibles. You'll get a payout similar to a bond, but you'll have the option to convert your holding to stock at some point in the future.

In this chapter, we look at how convertibles work. We also take a quick peek at warrants, but we don't recommend them for the value investor.

What Are Convertibles?

A convertible bond is a type of security issued by a company that you can convert to stock at a set price and time during the life cycle of the security.

Buying stocks always means that you will be taking a risk of losing money. However, convertibles give you a chance to make profits closer to those offered by the stock market, but with less risk because there is a guaranteed return.

Convertibles give you the protection of a bond or preferred stock, plus you have the opportunity to participate in any substantial value increase of the stock. The advantage for companies that issue convertibles is that the company can raise capital with an ongoing expense that will be lower than what they would have to pay out to holders of a traditional bond. If the company's stock does go up, the company may never have to pay back the principal of the loan when the investor converts the bond into common stock.

Convertibles do tend to act more like stocks than bonds. Their average return is about 80 percent of what you could expect had you purchased common stock, but you have the safety of a steady income stream. Some people have dubbed convertibles "stocks for chickens." But if you're nervous about investing in stocks, don't worry what people call you if you want to get your feet wet.

def•i•ni•tion

When you **redeem** a bond or convertible security, you turn in the security and are paid the principal value of that security plus any interest due.

Most convertibles have a 7- to 10-year term until they must be converted or *redeemed*. Only about half of them are investment grade, which means about half of them are issued by companies in trouble. As a value investor, you're likely to see convertible issues for many of the companies you're researching.

Not all convertibles are the same. The three most common are these:

◆ Convertible preferred stock

◆ Zero-coupon convertible

◆ Mandatory convertible

Convertible Preferred Stock

These are shares of stock that include a steady income stream at a set percentage, just like a bond. The big difference from a bond is that these can be converted to common stock with full voting privileges.

But unlike a bond, you aren't guaranteed that income each year. If the company doesn't do well, it can decide not to pay the preferred stock dividends. The company must track any unpaid preferred stock dividends and pay them in the future when it's able to start paying dividends again.

When the company does have the money to make dividend payments in the future, it must pay all the dividends owed to preferred stockholders before the company can pay common stockholders. This is true even if there are several years of unpaid preferred stock dividends due to preferred stockholders.

Zero-Coupon Convertibles

These are zero-coupon bonds that can be converted into stock at a set time and at a set price. This type of bond can appreciate in value when the stock price of the issuing company increases.

A zero-coupon bond accrues interest through the life of the bond. You are not paid that interest until the bond is due to be paid in full.

Mandatory Convertibles

A mandatory convertible bond is a bond that must be either converted to stock by a specific date or redeemed. You are paid interest on that bond based on the terms set at the time the bond is issued.

Convertible Pros and Cons

Let's take a look at the investing opportunity convertible issues offer you. Suppose Company ABC issues one million convertible preferred shares of stock at $100 per share. These shares pay a dividend of 5 percent, as long as Company ABC earns enough profit to pay those dividends. If not, Company ABC must keep track of unpaid dividends to preferred shareholders.

So suppose you bought 100 shares of this convertible preferred stock for $10,000. When the company closes its books after the first year of ownership, you are due a 5 percent dividend, or $5 per share, which would total $500.

Suppose Company ABC had a loss for the year, so it couldn't pay the dividend. In that scenario, you won't get any money. So if you're counting on bond income to meet your monthly bills, don't even think about using convertible preferred stock.

If you owned a traditional bond with a return of 5 percent, the company would have to pay that interest or *default* on the bond. But that's one key advantage to companies that issue convertible preferred stock: the company can put off making the dividend payment. This feature makes it easier for the company to use convertible preferred stock if it knows it will have trouble making the interest payments on a bond. So research a company carefully before you buy a convertible security, to be sure the company has enough cash flow to pay dividends.

def•i•ni•tion

A **default** involves the failure of a company to make required debt payments. Companies in default on their debt payments often file for bankruptcy to buy time to restructure their financial situation. Some come out of bankruptcy by getting lenders to agree to different terms for debt repayment; others go out of business.

When you own preferred stock, you may have to wait several years to get your dividend payment—and if the company goes into bankruptcy, you may never be paid or you may be paid only a few cents for every dollar due you. The key advantage preferred stockholders have over common stockholders is that they will be paid dividends first if any money is left over after the creditors are paid. But traditional bondholders are paid before preferred stockholders.

If the stock does recover, a preferred stockholder can decide to convert preferred stock shares to common stock when the preferred stock issue reaches its reset date. At the reset date, the company either buys back the preferred shares or converts the holdings to common stock at a set price.

Converting Shares for Profit

Now let's look at what happens if the stock price goes up and you decide you want to convert the preferred stock you own to common stock. This conversion is based on the conversion ratio, which is set at the time you initially purchase the convertible security.

In this example, assume the conversion ratio is 7.5. This means that you can trade in the preferred stock for 7.5 shares of Company ABC common stock.

So how do you figure out at what stock price you should consider converting the preferred stock shares to common stock shares? You do that by calculating the conversion price. This price is equal to the purchase price of the preferred shares divided by the conversion ratio. To calculate the conversion price, use this formula: Purchase Price ÷ Conversion Ratio.

$100 ÷ 7.5 = $13.33

So based on this calculation, Company ABC would have to be trading higher than $13.33 for you to gain from the transaction.

For example, suppose the stock is selling for $15. You decide to convert your 100 preferred shares to common stock. That means you'll have 750 shares of common stock in Company ABC. You calculate the number of common shares you can get by multiplying 7.5 times the number of preferred shares you have (7.5 × 100 in this example).

If the stock is selling for $15 per share, that means your 750 shares will be worth $11,250. You originally paid $10,000 for the 100 shares of preferred stock, so if you sell those shares of common stock, you will have a profit of $1,250.

But suppose Company ABC was selling for only $12 per share. If you converted the preferred stock to common stock, your 750 shares would be worth only $9,000. In this scenario, you'd take a $1,000 loss if you converted the preferred shares to common stock. So instead of converting the shares, you would let the company buy back the shares at the reset date.

Conversion Premium

The stock price doesn't always go up the way you hope, and you may decide you'd like to get rid of the preferred shares and do something else with the money rather than wait around until the reset date or until the stock price is high enough for a conversion to be worthwhile. You can sell the preferred shares on the secondary market.

The market price for convertible preferred shares is determined by their conversion premium, which is the difference between the parity value of the preferred stock and the value of the preferred shares if they're converted. The parity value of the preferred stock is the amount you originally paid for it. In this example, it would be $100 per share for Company ABC.

To calculate the conversion premium, assume Company ABC is selling for $11.50, so the current value of the preferred stock if converted to common stock is $86.25 ($11.50 × 7.5); this is $13.75 per share less than what you paid for the preferred stock. Remember, you paid $100 for the preferred stock with a conversion ratio of 7.5.

So how do you find the conversion premium? Given the fact that Company ABC is trading at just $11.50 and the conversion price is $86.25, the conversion premium is calculated using this formula: (Preferred Stock Price – Conversion Price) ÷ Premium = Conversion.

($100 – 86.25) ÷ 100 = 13.75%

The lower the premium, the more likely it is that the convertible's market price will follow the common stock value up and down. As the premium moves higher, the convertible will act more like a bond because it is less likely that the common stock price will go up enough to make conversion a profitable choice.

As the premium moves higher, interest rates can impact the value of the convertible preferred shares. The price of convertible preferred shares normally falls as interest rates go up because the fixed dividend looks less attractive—investors can get higher interest rates on other investments. But if interest rates fall, the value of the convertibles goes up because their fixed dividend rate then looks more attractive than interest rates on bonds or other fixed-rate investments available for sale.

Getting in the Zone

When you're trading in convertibles, you need to learn the language of trading zones for convertibles:

- Distressed debt
- Busted convertible
- Hybrid zone
- Equity zone

When reading about convertibles, you'll probably hear analysts mention these four zones of convertibles.

Distressed Debt

When a convertible is in this region, the company is likely facing a default event. This means the company won't be able to pay its creditors or the preferred shareholders.

Unless your research shows that the analysts are completely wrong about the company, don't waste any money buying these convertibles. You'll probably lose it.

Busted Convertible

When a convertible is in this zone, it's likely acting like a bond and is very sensitive to interest rate change. You can look at convertibles in this range like you would a bond. Take a risk with convertible preferred stock in this zone only if you feel confident that new leadership of the company will be able to drive this company to profitability.

Hybrid Zone

When a convertible is sitting between the stock and pure bond zones, this is your best time to buy a convertible if you believe the company is on the road to recovery. When the company does recover, the stock price will go up and you likely will be able to convert the shares and make a profit.

While you are waiting for the company to recover, either you will collect the guaranteed quarterly dividends or the amount due you will be building up in an IOU-type account. When the company does recover, these past due dividends will be paid out to preferred stockholders before common stockholders get any dividends.

Equity Zone

As the convertible price gets closer to the stock price, it falls into the equity zone. The convertible is less likely to be impacted by interest rate changes. This is the least risky zone in which to buy shares of convertible preferred stock.

If you're gun-shy about investing in stocks, convertible preferred stocks give you a good way to get into the game, with a less risky investment and a steady cash flow from the dividends.

Unless you have at least $100,000 to risk in the market, don't try to play on your own. You can buy low-cost mutual funds that specialize in building portfolios of convertible securities. The two leading low-cost mutual fund companies, Vanguard and Fidelity, both offer mutual funds that focus on convertible securities.

Finding Value

You may think convertibles could be a good option if you're squeamish about the stock market, but the big disadvantage is that they sell for so much more per share. You must have a lot more cash to be able to build a diversified preferred stock portfolio. Most advisors recommend that you have at least $100,000 in cash to build a diversified convertible preferred stock portfolio before you start to play in this market.

Assessing Warrants

While convertibles are a way to get your feet wet in the stock market, warrants give you a way to get into options. Basically, a warrant gives the holder the right but not the obligation to buy an underlying security at a certain price and quantity at a particular point in time.

We don't recommend that you even consider trading using warrants, but if you do decide to do so, be sure you understand the risks you're taking. Spend a lot of time researching warrants, how they work, and their inherent risks.

> **Value Visions** _____
>
> Value investing guru Benjamin Graham had little use for warrants. He said as early as 1970, "Let us mince no words at the outset. We consider the recent development of stock-option warrants as a near fraud, an existing menace, and a potential disaster. They have created huge aggregate dollar 'values' out of thin air."

Buying Convertibles

Most major business newspapers quote convertible prices and their terms daily. You will need to work with a broker if you plan to buy and sell these products.

Before you start trading, be sure you understand the terms and how you get into and out of a convertible security investment. We have room for only a brief introduction into this very complicated world of convertibles and warrants.

> **Finding Value** _____
>
> For further research on the topic of convertibles, we recommend _Global Convertible Investing: The Gabelli Way,_ by Hart Woodson III and A. Hart Woodson (Wiley, 2001). This book gives you in-depth knowledge about the process of convertibles, what they are, how to value and price them, how to identify convertibles with potential, and how to profit from them.

Now that we've given you an overview about all the different types of investment vehicles you can use to build a portfolio, let's take a look in the next chapter at the risks you face when using each type of investment.

The Least You Need to Know

- The three most common convertible security types include convertible preferred stock, convertible zero-coupon bonds, and mandatory convertibles.

- Convertible preferred stock gives you a way to get your feet wet in the stock market if you're concerned about risk and need a regular income from guaranteed dividends.

- Warrants are much riskier than convertibles and require that you understand how options work.

17

Exploring Risks

In This Chapter

♦ Exploring types

♦ Understanding time

♦ Managing your risk

You can't avoid risk when you invest. Even if you decide to play it safe by putting all your money into an insured savings account, you're still taking a risk. That risk is that your money won't grow fast enough to beat inflation, so you end up running out of money in the long run.

In this chapter, we explore the various types of risks you take every day as an investor. We also look at how time impacts your risk taking.

Types of Risks

You may not realize it, but there are many different types of risk. Not all investments are impacted by each type of risk, but possible risks include these:

♦ Inflation risk

♦ Opportunity risk

♦ Reinvestment risk

- ◆ Concentration risk

- ◆ Interest rate risk

- ◆ Credit or default risk

- ◆ Marketability risk

- ◆ Currency translation risk

Inflation Risk

Inflation risk usually impacts people who are afraid to take risk. These folks risk the possibility that their money will not be worth as much in the future.

Losing Value _____

Don't be afraid of risk. You will face some kind of risk no matter what you do with your money. Fear of risk can sometimes paralyze your investing. You end up watching your money lose value solely because you missed investment opportunities and let the money sit in a safe savings account, earning less interest than the inflation rate.

You know that the costs of the basics increase every year—energy, housing, clothing, medical care, and food. By investing solely through guaranteed investment alternatives, you will not be able to keep pace with inflation.

If you are building your portfolio so you'll have enough money for retirement, you'll most likely run out of funds in retirement—unless, of course, you are already a multimillionaire.

Opportunity Risk

Opportunity risk looks at your trade-offs. Each time you make an investment, you risk the possibility of missing out on a better use for your money elsewhere.

You can choose a stock or stock fund that ends up with a large loss. In this scenario, you've not only lost your initial investment, but you've lost the possibility of earning interest had you invested that money in bonds or in a cash-based opportunity.

Bonds and cash-investment vehicles have the opposite problem. If you invest in long-term bonds and certificates of deposit, you are most likely to face this situation from a different perspective. For example, if you deposit funds in a long-term CD earning 3 percent interest and interest rates rise to 6 percent, you are stuck earning the lower rate or you'll have to pay a penalty to get out early.

Long-term bonds can be even riskier because you'll take some loss on principal to sell the bond if interest rates are higher than the rate your bond is earning. The value of long-term bonds goes down when interest rates go up. You'll lose principal if you try to sell.

But if you hold on to the fixed-rate investments rather than buy a stock you believe has great potential, you take the opportunity risk of missing out on a great investment. So opportunity risk is essentially the risk of missing out on another opportunity for investing your money.

Reinvestment Risk

Reinvestment risk primarily affects fixed-income investments. When a CD's term ends or a bond matures, you have to find another investment alternative for the money.

The alternatives available may not be as good at the time you must reinvest. This can be of great concern to conservative investors because they are more likely to have most of their funds tied up in fixed-income investment vehicles.

Concentration Risk

Concentration risk becomes a factor if you put all your eggs in one basket. Some investors like to jump on whatever stocks are hot without carefully diversifying their portfolio. When that hot investment type is no longer in favor, a portfolio can drop dramatically if your investments are too concentrated in one or two investment vehicles.

Generally, financial advisors recommend that you hold no more than 4 percent of your portfolio in any one investment. That means you must diversify your portfolio with a least 25 different stock investment options.

Finding Value _____

You may think that managing 25 stocks sounds like too many options. That number can be reduced significantly if you diversify using mutual funds, which already offer you a diversified portfolio. Generally, if you decide to invest using mutual funds, you can diversify your portfolio well by owning 5 to 10 mutual funds.

Interest Rate Risk

Interest rate risk is related primarily to cash and bond investments. Bonds are impacted the most when interest rates rise, because their prices fall.

Stocks can also be affected depending on the market reaction to rising or falling rates. When the Fed lowers rates, stocks tend to rally. When the Fed raises rates, stocks tend to fall.

Also, company profits can be severely impacted if they carry a lot of debt and interest rates are rising. Consumers tend to slow spending when rates are rising, which can also impact sales and business profits.

As a value investor, if you are looking at companies with a lot of debt, be sure you consider the impact of interest rate risk. The recovery of a company with a lot of debt will be greatly impacted when interest rates rise.

Credit or Default Risk

Credit or default risk is the risk that the borrower won't repay an obligation. You face this risk primarily if you invest largely using bonds. In most cases, unless you are investing in junk bonds, you probably don't have to worry about this kind of risk.

A bond mutual fund with a high yield may look very attractive to you, but remember, the reason for that higher yield is the risks being assumed because of the low-quality assets that are held by that bond fund.

When considering a fixed-income investment, such as a bond or bond fund, that is offering an interest rate higher than that available generally on the market, do a lot of research before jumping in. In most cases, when you see a higher interest rate, it's because you are taking a greater risk that the company behind that bond will default and not pay back the debt.

Marketability Risk

Marketability risk relates to the liquidity of an investment. You may not be able to sell your investment when you want to do so. This can be true as a value investor if you choose common stocks, preferred stocks, or bonds that are not traded broadly on the market.

You are more likely to face this risk when trying to sell real estate than stock. But the stock of a small company that is not heavily traded can sometimes be hard to sell.

Currency Translation Risk

Currency translation risk is a risk you will experience only if you are buying investments outside the country in which you live. This risk relates to the fluctuation of currency exchanges. Each country's currency value fluctuates daily against the currency of other countries.

If you want to sell a foreign asset when the value of the U.S. dollar is down, you could lose additional money just based on that drop. In international investing, you face both market risk and the risk that the value of the dollar will drop against the currency of the countries where assets are held. Most investors face this risk if they invest in international mutual funds.

Finding Value _____

If you want to learn more about foreign currency trading, you can read Lita Epstein's book, which she wrote with trader Gary Tilkin, *The Complete Idiot's Guide to Foreign Currency Trading* (Alpha Books, 2007).

Fear of risk keeps many people away from investing entirely. They just can't face the possibility that something could happen that could result in the loss of part or all of their investment. Even the slightest probability of that happening persuades them to keep everything in the bank.

You can't avoid risk, but you can minimize it. Also, time heals many risk problems, as long as you have the patience to wait out the storm.

Let's first take a look at how time can heal risk wounds. Then we introduce you to how you can manage risk.

How Time Impacts Your Investing Choices

Time can be your best friend when investing, or it can be your biggest enemy. If you have 10 or more years before you need the money, you can take a lot of risk because you have plenty of time for that investment to recover from any market shock. If you need the money in two years, you don't want to take any unnecessary risk because you don't have time to wait for a market turnaround.

For a short-term horizon, your primary concern should be preservation of principal. The last thing you want to face is selling an asset when it is in a loss position just because you need the money.

Don't think we're telling you that you'll never lose money when investing. Sometimes you have to accept your losses and move on if you made a bad investment choice. But you don't want to be forced to do this just because you don't have the time to wait for better market conditions.

Losing Value

Think carefully about whether you have the temperament to ride out an investing storm if you want to be a value investor. You could face a long period of time before an investment recovers. If you don't have the patience or are afraid to take the risk to ride out the storm, you will end up selling an investment too soon and taking losses.

Even if you do have the time to wait, it's important to know whether you will have the patience to ride out an investing storm. Many investors who got caught up in the technology stock bubble sold out at the bottom after investing at the top when technology stocks were high. That type of impatience can be more devastating to a portfolio than waiting for a turnaround if you then decide to put everything in safe and insured asset types. Inflation risk then becomes a big factor in your investing future.

No doubt, you will face ups and downs when investing in stocks and bonds. You have to learn how to have enough patience to ride out a storm, provided that you believe the investment is still a good choice and will recover after the economy improves. Economic cycles are a fact of life, and you will see numerous periods of inflation and recession throughout your lifetime.

A good way to learn that patience is to not watch the market fluctuations daily and make yourself sick. Pick investments carefully and feel confident in your choices and how they fit into your investing style. Then make changes if the choice no longer fits your plans for your portfolio. You also want to start shifting to safer investments as you get closer to needing the money.

You may need to switch if a company you thought was on the road to recovery no longer looks good to you.

Another reason to switch may be that a mutual fund changes its management strategy and no longer fulfills a particular niche in your portfolio. When management changes, you may want to reassess your holding that fund.

But if the stock or fund drops in value because that type of stock or fund is down across the board, you probably want to hold on to it, as long as you think your initial reasons for selecting the investment are still valid.

Market Timing vs. Buy-and-Hold Investing

Some investors try to improve their investing odds by timing the market, but, in reality, those who have been most successful in value investing believe the buy-and-hold strategy works the best. In fact, billionaire investor Warren Buffett goes one step further. He recommends buying good companies and holding them "forever."

> **Value Visions**
>
> In a quote from the owner's manual for Berkshire Hathaway stock, chairman and CEO Warren E. Buffett writes: "As owners of, say, Coca-Cola or Gillette shares, we think of Berkshire as being a non-managing partner in two extraordinary businesses, in which we measure our success by the long-term progress of the companies rather than by the month-to-month movements of their stocks. In fact, we would not care in the least if several years went by in which there was no trading, or quotation of prices, in the stocks of those companies. If we have good long-term expectations, short-term price changes are meaningless for us except to the extent they offer us an opportunity to increase our ownership at an attractive price."

You probably are not as astute at picking stocks as Buffett. So the idea that you hold a company forever may not work for you. Knowing when to sell your stocks or mutual funds requires regular monitoring of the quarterly reports you receive either from an individual company or from a mutual fund company, depending on the type of investment you select.

As a value investor, if you believe your initial assessment of the company's potential for recovery and growth is still valid, don't be afraid to take the time to wait for that recovery. Trying to perfectly time when to get in and out of an investment can be a fool's game that you don't want to get caught playing.

Manage Risk, Don't Avoid It

The key to any good investment strategy is to manage risk, not to avoid it. You can't avoid risk, no matter what you do, but you can minimize it. In Part 5 of this book, we introduce you to the investing strategies that legendary value investors used to manage risk and build their portfolios.

To minimize your fear of risks and learn how to manage it, look inside yourself and work on your investing emotions, minimize any tendency to procrastinate, and keep from being paralyzed by analysis.

Emotions

One of the biggest mistakes investors make is falling in love with a stock. You spend so much time researching the stock that you just can't let it go, even if the company clearly shows no sign of recovery.

Yes, a stock purchase can almost become like your child that you want to nurture and grow, but remember, you have no real control over what happens inside any company unless you have a controlling interest and own more than 50 percent of all outstanding shares. That's not likely as an outside investor.

So admit your research mistakes and be willing to sell a stock if you no longer think the company will recover. Don't let your emotions for the stock lead you to make poor investing choices. Treat your portfolio management like any other business decisions. It's a business, not a family that you're nurturing.

Procrastination

If you tend to be someone who procrastinates, avoid it all costs when you are investing in stocks. Read and analyze your quarterly reports when they arrive so you can determine whether the company's financial results are still performing as you expect.

People who tend to procrastinate and put the financial reports in a big pile that they'll get to eventually tend to just toss those reports when they next decide it's time to clean up the room. Don't get into that habit if you plan to be a value investor.

Paralysis of Analysis

As we showed you in Chapter 11, you need to complete a lot of analysis to determine whether a stock makes a good choice for your value portfolio. Don't get caught up in the paralysis of analysis and be afraid to buy stock. At some point, you do need to make a decision if you want to be a stock investor.

Now that you know the risks of investing, let's move on to Part 5, where we take a closer look at how value-investing gurus manage those risks.

The Least You Need to Know

- ◆ Get to know the types of risks you face as a value investor, but don't be afraid of them.

- ◆ No investor can avoid risk, but you can learn how to manage it.

- ◆ Time can heal many investment woes, as long as you have the patience to wait out an investment storm.

Part

Value Investing Strategies

In this part, we explore various investing strategies value investors use. We introduce you to the favorite strategies of some key legends, such as Warren Buffett, Mario Gabelli, Glenn Greenberg, Michael Price, and Walter and Edwin Schloss.

Chapter 18

Asset Allocation

In This Chapter

- ◆ Keys to asset allocation
- ◆ Gauging risk tolerance
- ◆ Mixing assets
- ◆ Exploring Warren Buffett's style

The best way to minimize the risk of your portfolio is to carefully balance your assets among various investment vehicles. Many people think that seeking out the top-performing stocks and mutual funds is the key to successful investing. They are wrong.

Study after study has shown that individual investment choices account for only 5 to 10 percent of a portfolio's success, while 90 to 95 percent can be attributed to the way the portfolio is allocated among stocks, bonds, and money market instruments.

In this chapter, we review the basics of asset allocation and then take a closer look at one of the world's best value investors who excels at allocating capital, Warren Buffett.

Five Factors of Asset Allocation

When you plan to allocate your assets, you must consider five key factors: your investment goal, your time horizon, your risk tolerance, your financial resources, and your investment mix.

◆ Your investment goal is based on why you want to build your portfolio. Is it to have a nest egg for retirement, pay for your children's college expenses, go back to school for a higher-level degree, start a new business? To be successful, you must determine why you want to invest and how much you need.

◆ Your time horizon relates to when you will need the money. You must know how much time you have until you'll need the money before you can decide what investment vehicles you can consider using. For example, if you'll need the money in two years, you don't want to consider a stock investment because the risks are too high that your principal may not be there. Cash and cash equivalents (certificates of deposit or money market accounts) are best for short-term horizons. Stock portfolios are best if you don't need the money for at least 10 years or more.

◆ Your risk tolerance relates to how much risk you can comfortably accept. We give you a risk-tolerance test in the next section to help you determine that.

◆ Your financial resources relate to how much money you have to invest.

◆ Your investment mix relates to how you will allocate what you have to invest.

We take a closer look at investment risk next.

Testing Your Risk Tolerance

In Chapter 17, we discussed different types of risks, but do you know your risk tolerance? To try to figure that out, here are some questions you should ask yourself:

◆ Do market fluctuations keep you awake at night?

◆ Are you unfamiliar with investing?

◆ Do you consider yourself more a saver than an investor?

◆ Are you fearful of losing 25 percent of your assets in a few days or weeks?

If you answered "yes" to these questions, you are likely to be a "conservative" investor. You're not comfortable with taking risks, and you seek safe investments. Stock investment may not be right for you, but you may want to consider mutual fund investing if you want to get your toes wet in the stock market.

- ◆ Are you comfortable with the ups and downs of the securities markets?
- ◆ Are you knowledgeable about investing and the securities markets?
- ◆ Are you investing for a long-term goal?
- ◆ Can you withstand considerable short-term losses?

If you answered "yes" to these questions, you are likely to be an "aggressive" investor. You will be more willing to take a risk that could mean a short-term loss in your stock holdings. You will be comfortable as a stock investor, but you should still seek to minimize the risks you take.

If your answers were mixed between the two groups of questions, you are probably a "moderate" investor. While you can consider stock investing, you probably are better off starting as a mutual fund investor until you are more comfortable making your own stock selections.

Assessing Your Financial Resources

Once you've got a handle on your risk tolerance, it's time to look at your financial resources. The amount of money you have to invest will be a big factor in the risks you want to take.

A small investor just doesn't have the funds to properly diversify a portfolio. In that case, a well-diversified mutual fund is your best bet for getting started. Once your portfolio has grown large enough, you may want to take some risk by selecting a more aggressive mutual fund or picking individual stocks.

Getting Ready to Mix Your Assets

Historically, the rate of return for large-company stocks has averaged 11.3 percent between 1925 and 2000. During that same period, bonds averaged 5.1 percent return and cash savings averaged 3 percent return. Rates of return are even higher for small company stocks, but they are also much more volatile.

Let's take a look at a sample portfolio. A portfolio balanced for growth would likely have 60 percent stock, 20 percent bonds, and 20 percent cash. Using these returns as the average, the portfolio would likely earn 8.4 percent before taxes and inflation. This is what is called a weighted average.

Let us show you how it works:

> 60% stock at 11.3%
>
> $11.3 \times .60 = 6.78\%$
>
> 20% bonds at 5.1%
>
> $5.1 \times .20 = 1.02\%$
>
> 20% cash at 3%
>
> $3.0 \times .20 = .60\%$
>
> Total = 8.40%

You can group your portfolio into these types of baskets and get a weighted average of the return you might expect from the portfolio. If you have mutual funds, they should calculate what percentage of stock, bonds, and cash are held within the fund. You can use those percentages when you want to compare this in your portfolio.

Use this information to decide how balanced your portfolio really is and whether that balance matches your savings goals and your risk tolerance. What chance does your current asset allocation have of meeting your goals?

If your gap is huge and you know you can't meet your goals with the current estimated level of return, you must decide whether you can tolerate more risk and try to improve your portfolio's growth potential or revise your goals to a level that more realistically matches what your portfolio can achieve.

Market Timing vs. Buy-and-Hold Investing

Market timers believe that they can buy low and sell high. The problem is that few can accurately time the market. In fact, one study done at the University of Michigan for the period from December 31, 1981, to August 25, 1987, showed that stocks returned an average of 26.3 percent annually. During that period, there were 10 days when the largest price advances occurred. If you missed those 10 days, your annual return would have been only 18.3 percent, or a loss of one third of the market's return. Take out the 20 biggest days, and the annual return would have been 13.1 percent, or a 50.2 percent loss of the market's return.

Managing Your Portfolio

Many of us may wish we could do the research, pick our investments, and put our entire portfolio on autopilot. Wouldn't it be nice if investing were that simple? Unfortunately, it's not. Even if you choose to build your portfolio using index mutual funds, which are the simplest way to invest, you still need to monitor what is happening with your investment choices, as well as watch to be sure your asset allocation is remaining within your level of risk tolerance.

Monitoring Your Investments

You may think the business press is covering the stock market almost as though it's a sports game—reporting ups and downs with action words that make you want to take action yourself. Don't get caught up in all the hype and respond too quickly to a bad day. Investing is for the long term. Any change to your portfolio should be done with careful consideration of why you initially picked the investment and what has changed that is making you want to reconsider your choice.

A good practice is to plan annual reviews of your investment portfolio, at which time you check your asset-allocation balance and review the performance of your portfolio's choices. If the performance of any of your assets is negative, that doesn't automatically mean you need to pick something else. You should research how other similar assets have done and whether your choice is performing badly compared to the asset type.

For example, if you held growth funds at the time the Internet bubble burst, you certainly saw negative returns, but so did everyone else who owned growth funds. What you needed to check at the end of 2000 was how badly your funds were hurt and how their negative performance compared to others in the same fund category. A good place to find average returns by fund category is Morningstar (www.morningstr.com). The same is true for any stock choices. You must compare your picks to others in the same industry.

You also want to check your asset allocation. For example, if you decided based on your risk tolerance that you were comfortable with a balance of 60 percent stocks, 30 percent bonds, and 10 percent cash, you need to run the numbers to be certain you are still in that ballpark. If it has been a stellar year for growth stocks, you'll find this balance to be way out of whack, and your portfolio actually has a much greater exposure to growth stocks than you intended. Other times, when stocks are down, your bond or cash balance might be high.

Adjusting Your Portfolio

You can adjust your portfolio in one of these three ways or possibly by combining two:

- ◆ Invest a lump sum of any new investments into the type of assets that are below your intended allocation targets.

- ◆ Reallocate your assets by selling the types that exceed their target allocation and buying the types that are low. If you choose this method, be sure to check with your tax advisor about tax consequences.

- ◆ Change your plans for next year and allocate contributions to your portfolio, to increase your investment in the types of assets that are low and decrease the portion that goes toward the assets that are high.

 Losing Value

Make changes to your portfolio outside of your annual review only if you find out about a significant change in a mutual fund or stock that is in your portfolio. Obviously, if you held Enron stock before its collapse and saw its dramatic decline, you would have minimized losses by selling as soon as you realized it was going to fall. In that case, the fall was so swift that you might not have reacted in time anyway. Investors lost billions of dollars during that catastrophic fall.

What Changes to Watch For

If you have a lot of individual stocks in your portfolio, you will need to monitor them much more closely than if you invest using mutual funds. If you invest in stocks, you need to keep up on company news and watch company reports, as well as reports from analysts and others.

Mutual fund investors need to monitor significant changes in fund managers or fund-management strategy. Also, they need to be certain that the fund is actually investing your money based on the portfolio-management strategy indicated in the prospectus.

You will receive at least semiannual statements and, in most cases, quarterly statements from your mutual fund companies, to show the top portfolio holdings and performance results. Don't just take a quick look and throw them away. Spend some time reviewing the types of stocks and bonds included in the portfolio, and maybe research some of the companies yourself, if you don't recognize them.

If you have some questions about investment strategy, do some additional digging to find out what others are saying about the fund. One great website to find out more about management changes and other problem alarms is FundAlarm.com. You can sign up for a free monthly e-mail that lets you know when the site is updated with mutual fund changes.

If you find out there is a major management change for one of your mutual fund picks, there is still no reason to panic. Unlike a stock that is hit with bad news and can drop dramatically in a day, mutual funds take longer to show the effects of a manager change.

Even if the manager plans to make a major shift in mutual fund strategy, it usually takes months, or sometimes even years, to buy and sell assets strategically. Just because a fund changes managers does not automatically mean you should sell it.

Research the new manager's performance. Most likely, he or she managed at least one other fund before taking over yours. Websites like FundAlarm.com and Morningstar.com do cover manager changes and frequently give you a good deal of information about whether the change is good or bad for the fund.

Following Warren Buffett

Warren Buffett, known by many admirers as the sage of Omaha, is the quintessential capital allocator and premier modern-day value investor. He's the chairman of Berkshire Hathaway and has been in that position since 1977, when the stock was selling at $120 share. In March 2008, Berkshire Hathaway's stock sold for $129,500. Wouldn't you like to own 100 shares of that stock?

Many of his devoted followers did buy shares of stock in Berkshire Hathaway in the late 1970s and 1980s, and many of those who stuck with that investment are million-aires today. Just to give you an idea of how Warren Buffett runs his company, here are some of his key principles from his owner's manual for stockholders:

♦ Shareholders are owner-partners. Charlie Munger (vice chairman of Berkshire Hathaway) and I are managing partners who view the company "as a conduit through which our shareholders own the assets." Buffett tells people who want to buy his shares, "I hope you do not think of yourself as merely owning a piece of paper whose price wiggles around daily and that is a candidate for sale when some economic or political event makes you nervous."

♦ We eat our own cooking—99 percent of Buffett's net worth is based on Berkshire Hathaway, and he tells shareholders many of his relatives are also shareholders. Munger has 90 percent of his net assets in the company.

Value Visions

Buffett tells shareholders, "Charlie and I feel totally comfortable with this eggs-in-one-basket situation because Berkshire itself owns a wide variety of truly extraordinary businesses. Indeed, we believe that Berkshire is close to being unique in the quality and diversity of the businesses in which it owns either a controlling interest or a minority inter-est of significance."

♦ The long-term economic goal is to maximize the average annual rate of gain in the intrinsic business value on a per-share basis. When Buffett took over the company in 1965, the earnings per share were $22.54. In 2008, the earnings per share were $8,547.95.

♦ Buffett prefers to reach his goals through "directly owning a diversified group of businesses that generate cash and consistently earn above-average returns on capital." He determines the capital allocation for new investments on the "price and availability of businesses and the need for insurance capital" in any given year. Some years he decides available businesses are too costly to buy, and he hoards cash for better opportunities in the future. This was particularly true in 1999 just before the Internet crash, when he held cash and missed the run-up in stock values that year. Buffett had lots of cash to spend after the crash when companies were cheap.

♦ Buffett uses debt sparingly, and if he does borrow money, he using long-term debt on a fixed rate. Much of the cash he has to spend on new businesses comes from deferred taxes and the cash in his insurance businesses' *float*.

def•i•ni•tion

Insurance businesses carry a large cash **float**, which is made up of premiums paid based on possible future losses. Buffett wisely invests this cash float to build the cash that may be needed to pay claims in the future, as well as to earn additional capital gains for Berkshire Hathaway. This large cash float helps him avoid having to borrow money to cover the company's capital allocation decisions (buy companies entirely or minority stakes in other companies).

♦ Buffett doesn't look for paychecks or plush offices, and he tells his shareholders that he and Munger are "interested only in acquisitions that we believe will raise the per-share intrinsic value of Berkshire's stock." We talk more about intrinsic value next.

♦ Buffett doesn't sell any good businesses he owns "as long as we feel good about their managers and labor relations." Sometimes a business performs subpar, which he calls a capital allocation mistake, and he'll work with the management team to improve the financial results.

♦ He promises his shareholders no accounting trickery and promises full disclosure of company results, even if it means giving shareholders bad news.

♦ Buffett does not discuss his investing activities beyond what is legally required. He tells shareholders, "Good investment ideas are rare, valuable, and subject to competitive appropriation, just as good product or business acquisition ideas are. Therefore, we normally will not talk about our investment ideas."

 Finding Value

You can read the full owner's manual and Buffett's annual reports at www.berkshirehathaway.com, which we recommend you do. You'll learn a lot about how Buffett invests by reading his annual reports.

Understanding Intrinsic Value

Buffett's core investment measure is finding the intrinsic value of a company and being certain the price he pays for the company is justified by that intrinsic value. The definition of intrinsic value is the discounted value of the cash that can be taken out of a business during its remaining life.

The key secret there is that the way to calculate intrinsic value is not precise. It's based on a lot of assumptions, and those assumptions can be easily adjusted based on anticipated interest rate.

Buffett never gives investors the intrinsic value he has calculated for a company, but he will give details in his annual reports relating to the facts that he and Munger used to determine the intrinsic value of a company.

Buffett believes Berkshire Hathaway's book value far understates its intrinsic value because many of the businesses Berkshire Hathaway controls are worth much more than their carrying value.

Now that you have a good understanding of asset allocation and Warren Buffett's capital allocation style, let's take a closer look at contrarian investing and value investor Paul Sonkin.

The Least You Need to Know

- You must understand five factors to properly use asset allocation—your investment goal, your time horizon, your risk tolerance, your financial resources, and your investment mix.

- Don't take on more risk than you can tolerate, or you'll make bad investment choices, selling stock low when you get nervous and buying it high when you think it is safe.

- Warren Buffett believes in buying a stock and holding it forever. He practices careful capital allocation to diversify his holdings in well-run businesses and watch them grow, always being sure to buy a business when the price is not too high.

Contrarian Investing

In This Chapter

- ◆ Getting down to basics
- ◆ Introduction to the dogs
- ◆ Reading investor sentiment
- ◆ Small company options

All value investors are contrarian investors, looking for those diamonds in the rough that no one else wants to touch. But not all contrarian investors are value investors.

In this chapter, we explore the basics of contrarian investing and discover the simplest way to be a contrarian investor by following the dogs of the Dow. Then we discuss a simple tool for gauging investor sentiment and finally introduce the basic strategy used by one of the gurus of contrarian investing—value style.

Basics of Contrarian Investing

Any investor who seeks to profit from investing by following a strategy that differs from conventional wisdom because he believes that the conventional wisdom is wrong can be considered a contrarian investor.

Contrarian investors look at key ratios like price-to-earnings (P/E) and price-to-book. (We talk more about how to calculate these ratios and what they mean in Chapter 11.)

The key difference is that value investors not only look at these key ratios, but they do a lot more research to find the intrinsic value of the firm. (We show you how to do that in Chapter 11.) While a contrarian investor may decide to jump on the band-wagon of a stock that has tumbled dramatically, the value investor digs a lot deeper into the financial status of the company and looks at the company's management team and what plans are in the works to turn the company around.

Some key factors are common to contrarian investors:

- A contrarian investor believes that the crowd tends to misprice securities by overreacting to bad news. This can lead to a stock price that overstates the company's risk and understates its likelihood of returning to profitability. Finding these distressed stocks and then selling them when the company recovers is a common strategy for value investors.

- Contrarian investors see overly optimistic crowds as a key sign to stay away from buying a stock because these situations tend to drive the price too high and the stock will eventually fall—and fall hard. Contrarian investors avoid these sharp drops, like we saw when the Internet bubble burst in the early 2000s, because they just do not play in those types of markets.

- Contrarian investors don't necessarily have a negative view of the overall stock market or believe that the crowd is always wrong. Instead, they seek opportunities to buy low and sell high because the crowd is doing exactly the opposite of what the contrarian investors thinks needs to be done.

- Contrarian investors are more likely to find good buy candidates when the market sentiment is primarily negative and the market is generally in decline. However, they don't look for buys only in down markets. Good buys can be found in any type of market, but there are likely to be more good buys in a down market.

- When contrarian investors buy stocks, they seek a margin of safety. They find this in a stock that's selling at a discount to its intrinsic value.

- Contrarian investors tend to believe that investors as a group follow the herd and weigh recent trends too heavily when predicting the future. For example, they tend to believe that a poorly performing stock will remain bad and a strong performer will remain good. The crowd frequently makes wrong long-term assumptions, and that's when contrarian investors can find the best buys.

Finding Value

Since the market crowd tends to act like a herd and expects bad news for a company to stay bad and good news to stay good, you can find some real gems when the market generally believes the bad news about a company. Take a closer look at that company and find out whether the crowd is overreacting and beating down the stock price too far.

Following the Dogs

If you're new to investing and want to get started using contrarian investment theories, one easy way to start is to follow the Dogs of the *Dow*. This strategy believes you should look at the list of the 30 stocks of the Dow at the end of any given year and buy the 10 stocks with the highest dividend yield. These will be stocks that the market has beaten down but that are still paying significant dividends.

How successful has this strategy been? If you had followed this strategy since 1973, you would have gotten a 17.7 percent annual average return. The return on the Dow was only 11.9 percent in that same period. This chart shows you how the Dogs of the Dow have performed in the last 10 years:

def•i•ni•tion

The Dow Jones Industrial Average (the **Dow** or **DJIA**) is an index made up of 30 stocks, primarily industrials. This indicator is one way to quickly check the general direction of the stock market. The 30 stocks are chosen by the editors of *The Wall Street Journal* (which is published by Dow Jones & Company).

Year	Percentage Gain/(Loss)
1996	Up 28.6%
1997	Up 22.2%
1998	Up 10.7%
1999	Up 4%
2000	Up 6.4%
2001	Down 4.9%
2002	Down 8.9%
2003	Up 28.7%

continues

Year	Percentage Gain/(Loss)
2004	Up 4.4%
2005	Down 5.1%
2006	Up 30.3%

Finding Value

When you consider a Dogs of the Dow strategy, it's a safety strategy, not one that will get you the highest return in a bull market. You can find out more about the Dogs of the Dow online at www.dogsofthedow.com.

During the stock crash of 2000–2002, the Dogs of the Dow were down, as was the entire stock market, but it did outperform the Dow, the S&P 500, and the Nasdaq. In 2003, even though the bear market was in full swing, the Dogs of the Dow gained 28.7 percent. During a boom market like 1999 and 2000, before the Internet bubble burst, the Dogs of the Dow lagged behind the bull market. That, too, will always be common.

You can invest using the Dogs of the Dow strategy using Dog Steps or Small Dog Steps. Each has its pros and cons. Let's take a look at the differences.

Dog Steps

If you want to follow the simplest route to invest in the Dogs of the Dow, you start by looking at the Dow on its last day of the year. Luckily, you can get a chart that shows the key information at the Dogs of the Dow website (www.dogsofthedow.com), to make it even simpler. After the stock market closes on the last day of the year, select the 10 Dow stocks that have the highest dividend yield.

Once you've made that list, contact your broker and buy an equal dollar amount in each of these 10 high-yield stocks. Hold these stocks for one year. Then at the end of the next year, look for the 10 high-yield stocks for the second year.

You'll find some of the stocks you own still on the list. Sell those that are no longer on the list and buy those that are new to the list. To make things even easier for you, you can get on a free e-mail newsletter list that notifies you when the list is ready at the end of each year.

Small Dog Steps

You may want to take on a bit more risk and buy only the Small Dogs of the Dow. The Small Dogs of the Dow have traditionally outperformed even the Dow.

To invest in the Small Dogs of the Dow, on the last day of any given year, select the 10 highest-yielding stocks, as you would if you were planning to invest in the Dogs of the Dow. Then pick the five Dogs that have the lowest stock price. These are called the Small Dogs of the Dow. Some people refer to these stocks as the Puppies of the Dow or the Flying Five.

Once you've identified the five stocks you want to buy, contact your broker and invest an equal dollar amount in each of these stocks. Hold these stocks for one year. Just to give you an idea of how well this strategy works, if you had continued this approach since 1973, you would have gotten an average annual return of 20.9 percent.

Here are the winning Dogs for 2008:

Symbol	Company	Price	Yield	Small Dog
C	Citigroup	29.44	7.34%	Yes
PFE	Pfizer	22.73	5.63%	Yes
GM	General Motors	24.89	4.02%	Yes
MO	Altria	75.58	3.97%	No
VZ	Verizon	43.69	3.94%	No
T	AT&T	41.56	3.85%	No
DD	DuPont	44.09	3.72%	No
JPM	JP Morgan Chase	43.65	3.48%	No
GE	General Electric	37.07	3.35%	Yes
HD	Home Depot	26.94	3.34%	Yes

You may also be interested in seeing the Dogs for 2007 so you can see how much overlap there can be year to year:

Symbol	Company	Price	Yield	Small Dog
PFE	Pfizer	25.90	4.48%	Yes
VZ	Verizon	37.24	4.35%	Yes
MO	Altria	85.82	4.01%	No
T	AT&T	35.75	3.97%	Yes
C	Citigroup	55.70	3.52%	No
MRK	Merck	43.60	3.49%	No
GM	General Motors	30.72	3.26%	Yes

continues

Symbol	Company	Price	Yield	Small Dog
DD	DuPont	48.71	3.04%	No
GE	General Electric	37.21	3.01%	Yes
JPM	JP Morgan Chase	48.30	2.82%	No

One of the hardest-hit Dogs of the Dow in 2007 was Citigroup. Of course, the mortgage mess hitting most banks was the culprit for this fall.

You can see that Citigroup, which was a Dog of the Dow in 2007 with a stock price of $55.70 and a yield of 3.52 percent, looked even better in 2008 as a first-time purchase, with a stock price of $29.44 and a yield of 7.34 percent. Had you bought it at the beginning of 2006, you would have had a considerable loss in principal, but as long as you hold on to the stock, you won't lock in that loss.

Finding Value

All of us watched in horror as the stock market took its biggest two-week drop since 1929 in September of 2008. The Dow Industrial Average started the month at 11,516.92 and by September 17 fell to 10,609.66—a drop of 907.26 or 7.8 percent in just two weeks. The other indexes fell by similar percentages.

As many investors bailed out of the stock market to safer quarters, value investors scooped up the bargains. For example, during this period I bought one financial stock for just $10—a stock that sold for more than $50 dollars in February of 2008. Yes, I'll have to hold it for a couple years, but it's a bank that makes most of its money on traditional banking services, so I believe it's been unjustifiably beaten down.

Other value investors also went bargain shopping, picking up good bets in many sectors beaten down by a panicked market. Wise value investors moved into cash as the market climbed and were ready for the bargain shopping as the market crashed.

Using the VIX for Investor Sentiment

You may be wondering how you can be sure you're reading investor sentiment correctly. One of the most powerful tools for contrarian investors is the *VIX* index.

The VIX Index was first introduced in a paper written by Professor Robert E. Whaley of Duke University. In 2003, the methodology for calculating this index was improved and it was officially introduced as the VIX Index.

In March 2004, investors started trading based on the index on the CBOE Futures Exchange. While we definitely don't recommend that you trade futures as a value investor, you can get a quick reading on investor sentiment by watching this index, which is also known as a fear index.

When the number for this index is low, investor sentiment tends to be optimistic or confident about the future and stock prices tend to be going up. When the VIX is high, the fear factor is strong and investor confidence is low.

To use this index, compare the VIX to the major stock indexes, such as the Dow or the S&P 500. You'll see that peaks in this index generally give you good buying opportunities.

def•i•ni•tion

The Chicago Board of Options Exchange Volatility Index (VIX) measures market expectations and their near-term volatility by looking at S&P 500 stock index option prices. Since its introduction in 1993, VIX has been considered by many to be the world's premier barometer of investor sentiment and market volatility.

Keeping It Small

Not all contrarian investors seek to invest in large, blue-chip stocks. One of the leading contrarian investor gurus is Paul D. Sonkin, who prefers small companies—the smaller, the better.

Sonkin believes analysts don't watch small companies as closely, which gives you a great opportunity to find diamonds in the rough. He likes small companies because there aren't as many players in the field and there's less competition for the gems he finds, which usually means better prices.

For Sonkin, a gem is a company with a lot of cash and a P/E ratio of 20 or higher, which, to most, doesn't look like a good buy. But Sonkin believes that if the company has a hoard of net cash, which means cash after all the loans have been subtracted, you've found a good gem that you can buy at a great price.

Sonkin uses a special measuring device to find these companies, called a capitalization ratio. We show you how to calculate this in Chapter 11. He uses this ratio to find what you should consider paying to own all the after-tax operating earnings of the company. For Sonkin, this capitalization ratio is his screening test to see if it's worth spending more time researching the company.

Sonkin looks for buys by looking at a list of companies that hit a new low. He then researches the company to see if it meets his criteria as a good buy. If he believes bad news is overblown and the company has been beaten down unnecessarily, the stock goes to his watch list.

Sonkin prefers small companies for these reasons:

- They have better growth prospects.

- They can be more nimble and better positioned to take advantage of new opportunities.

- Fewer analysts watch them, so not much news about the company is available and the noise of the stock market and the crowd is less likely to impact the stock price.

- They are easier to understand because their financial statements are less complex.

Large companies can have 5 to 15 different businesses and their financial statements are consolidated, so you really can't assess the true value of any one of these businesses. That makes it very difficult to find the true value of the company.

Small companies usually focus on one business. They most likely are in a niche market with fewer competitors. Frequently, they have a few major customers, so it's easier to analyze their potential.

An analyst such as Sonkin can easily make calls to find out details he needs to make a decision. Unless you have a lot to invest, you likely can't get the access to a small company like Sonkin can get.

Some value investors believe in having a small, concentrated portfolio of just 10 to 20 stocks. We look at that concentrated strategy in Chapter 23, but Sonkin definitely believes in managing a portfolio with a large number of companies. He divides his portfolio into two segments:

- General Portfolio Operations, which is made up of traditional value stocks of small companies that have been beaten down and are out of favor on Wall Street. Sonkin finds these stocks on the new lows list each day. He screens them for companies that are cheap relative to the amount of money they have in the bank. He usually holds these stocks for one or more years, to give the company time to regain favor in the market.

♦ Arbitrage Situations, which are small stocks that Sonkin has identified as companies that are anticipated to experience an event that will change the stock price. This could include an expected takeover, a spin-off, a company liquidation, a corporate restructuring, or some other event that he identifies as a good opportunity. With these stocks, he expects a high return with a low level of risk. Sonkin usually holds these stocks for a short period of time.

Now that you've taken a closer look at contrarian investing, let's move on to another common strategy—defensive investing.

The Least You Need to Know

♦ All value investors are contrarian investors, but not all contrarian investors are value investors. Know the difference and take the time to be a true value investor.

♦ Until you feel confident in your investing style, one of the best ways to get your feet wet as a value investor is to use the Dogs of the Dow strategy.

♦ You need to find a way to identify good buys. The VIX index can help identify the timing. Sonkin's new lows strategy can help you find the hardest-hit stocks.

Chapter 20

Defensive Investing

In This Chapter

- ◆ Testing your risk meter
- ◆ Allocating your assets
- ◆ Bond choices
- ◆ Stock picks
- ◆ Cash options

Defensive investors tend to seek safety over return, but not if they follow the lead of Benjamin Graham, the granddaddy of value investing. He did not believe it was necessary to give up earning a decent return on your investments, as long as you invested wisely.

In this chapter, we review Graham's style of defensive investing. We start by looking at risk tolerance and time constraints. Then we review the basics of allocating your portfolio based on your tolerance and constraints. Following that, we introduce you to basic asset-purchase strategies for a defensive portfolio.

Recognizing Your Risk Tolerance and Time Constraints

Graham believed that an individual's risk tolerance and the amount of time and effort one was willing to put into managing a portfolio were the two key factors to determining whether an investor could succeed in Graham's style of defensive investing. He believed that an investor had to know his or her risk tolerance and to identify his or her time constraints before deciding what type of investment portfolio to build.

Value Visions

Benjamin Graham believed: "The role of return sought should be dependent … on the amount of intelligent effort the investor is willing and able to bring to bear on his task. The minimum return goes to our passive investor, who wants both safety and freedom from concern. The maximum return would be realized by the alert and enterprising investor who exercises maximum intelligence and skill." This is a quote from Benjamin Graham's classic book *The Intelligent Investor* (Collins Business Essentials, 2006).

Risk Test

Before we dive into a discussion about how to allocate your portfolio defensively, let's look at how you can judge your risk tolerance. In the 2006 revised edition of Graham's book *The Intelligent Investor*, Jason Zweig identified this list of questions you should ask yourself to test your risk tolerance and time constraints:

- Are you single or married?

- If married, what does your spouse or partner do for a living?

- Do you or will you have children?

- If you do have children, when will the tuition bills hit home?

- Will you inherit money?

- Will you be financially responsible for aging, ailing parents?

- What factors might hurt your career? For example, if you work for a home builder, economic conditions could put you out of a job. If you're self-employed, your income may not be as dependable as it is for someone with a guaranteed paycheck.

- If you are self-employed, how long do businesses similar to yours survive?

◆ Do you need your investments to supplement your cash income? If so, bonds work better than stocks. Stocks for which dividends are consistently paid may work, but the money is not guaranteed.

◆ Given your salary and your spending needs, how much money can you afford to lose on your investments?

As you sort through these questions, your ability to take on risk will become clear. If you are in a steady job in which you can count on an income and you already have a sizable amount of money saved, you can take on more risk than someone who is self-employed and may occasionally have to draw from the portfolio to make ends meet. If you don't have children or your children have already completed college, you will be able to take on more risk than someone who will need funds for college tuition in a few years.

Think carefully about your current, near-term, and long-term financial needs as you make a decision about the type of portfolio you want to build. The biggest mistake you can make is to take on too much risk and be forced to cash in your portfolio in a down market.

Sorting Out Your Money Needs

As you think about your money needs, group them into three categories: 2 to 5 years, 5 to 10 years, and 10 years and more. Anything you need in the next two years should always be in cash or cash equivalents.

Generally, if you want to invest in stocks and take on significant risk, you should have at least a 10-year horizon before you need that money. That way, you'll never be caught needing to sell stocks when they're in a loss position just because you need the cash. Sometimes you will take a loss on stocks. Everyone makes mistakes, but don't set yourself up for failure just because you didn't plan your cash needs correctly.

Funds that you need within a two-year period should always be in cash or a cash equivalent. We talk more about cash equivalents shortly.

Bonds are good for funds you need in two to five years. Funds you'll need in 5 to 10 years will likely be a mix of stocks and bonds. If you know you'll need the money in less than 10 years, you'll want stock in solid, blue-chip companies whose prices don't jump up and down dramatically on a monthly basis.

Of course, any stock can take a tumble when bad news about the company is released. For example, most financial stock prices have been cut in half since the mortgage mess began to unfold in 2007. Prior to that mess, financial stocks were considered a relatively safe haven for a steady stock price and steady dividends.

Learn Patience

You can never count on stocks for short-term needs. As long as you have at least 5 to 10 years and you've chosen a solid company, there's a good chance you won't have to take a loss on a stock. But you must be patient and willing to wait for the market to turn around for that stock.

Losing Value

While value investors need to learn patience, you should never hang tough if you believe you made a mistake and the company is performing much worse than you expected, or if you no longer believe in the company's management team. Take your hit and get out before things get even worse.

Yes, patience is a virtue you must have as a value investor. To get a good bargain, you need the patience to wait for a stock to recover, as well as the risk tolerance that allows you to hang tough even if the stock has been beaten down.

How do you know if the company is still on the right track? That comes with research and what Graham calls intelligent investing.

To be an intelligent investor, you must have the time and knowledge to carefully pick your stocks and then monitor your portfolio. So if your time constraints won't allow you the time you'll need for the research, you may need to be a passive rather than active investor. In the next section, we look at how these differences impact the type of portfolio you want to build as a defensive value investor.

You also need to know how you will react when the market takes a nosedive and drops 10 percent to 15 percent. Are you the type of investor who will run for the hills and sell off all your stock? If so, you do not have the risk tolerance to be an active investor; you need to develop a more passive portfolio with steady returns. A down market is the time an active defensive investor looks for good buys.

Another question you must ask is, what will you do when the market is going up 10 percent to 15 percent or more? If you think you're the type of investor that will jump on the bandwagon, you don't have the discipline to win as a value investor. When the market goes up that dramatically, stocks are usually overpriced. Active defensive investors might sell some winning holdings, but they would not likely buy any stock during this type of market unless they believe they've found a good beaten-down stock that the crowd missed.

Are You an Intelligent Investor?

Graham believed someone could be an intelligent investor in two ways:

◆ **Active or enterprising investors**—These types of investors have a lot of time to spend on building and managing their portfolios and also have a high risk tolerance. They must continually research, select, and monitor a dynamic mix of stocks, bonds, or mutual funds.

◆ **Passive or defensive investors**—These types of investors don't have a lot of time to spend on a portfolio or can't tolerate much risk. They must create a permanent portfolio that runs on autopilot and requires no further effort. This type of passive portfolio won't be very exciting, but it will get you steady returns over your lifetime.

Defensive Portfolio Asset Allocation

Graham also identified three basic asset-allocation mixes, depending on your risk tolerance and time constraints:

◆ Investors who are passive investors with a low risk tolerance should hold a mix of 25 percent stocks and 75 percent bonds. You should always have at least 25 percent of your portfolio in stocks, to keep up with inflation and have some growth in your portfolio.

◆ Average investors should hold a mix of 50 percent stock and 50 percent bonds. This mix tends to give steady returns over a long period of time, without too much risk for most average investors.

◆ Active or enterprising investors should hold a mix of 75 percent stocks and 25 percent bonds when they believe that the market is undervalued and that they can find some good buys. They should hold a mix of 75 percent bonds and 25 stocks when they believe that the market is too hot to touch and most stocks are selling above their intrinsic value.

Graham believed most investors should stick with a 50/50 portfolio because they will more likely hold firm in a down market and have the patience to wait for the market winds to shift if at least half of their portfolio is making money through regular dividends.

> **Value Visions**
>
> Graham believed: "We are convinced that our 50–50 version of this approach makes good sense for the defensive investor. It is extremely simple; it aims unquestionably in the right direction; it gives the follower the feeling that he is at least making some moves in response to market developments; most important of all, it will restrain him from being drawn more and more heavily into common stocks as the market rises to more and more dangerous highs."

So how do you keep your portfolio balanced as stocks and bonds go up and down in price? That's when asset allocation balancing goes into effect. Generally, it's a good idea to review the balance of your portfolio twice a year. We talk more about asset allocation and how you can balance your portfolio in Chapter 18.

You may be thinking that you can tolerate a lot of risk and, therefore, can manage a 100 percent stock portfolio because you plan to be an active and enterprising investor. You definitely should not consider a 100 percent stock portfolio unless these apply to you:

♦ You have enough money set aside to support your family for at least a year.

♦ You plan to invest steadily for at least 20 years in the future.

♦ You survived the bear market that started in 2000 after the Internet stocks crashed and did not cash out and take a huge loss.

♦ You bought more stocks during the bear market that started in 2000 and continued through 2003.

Few people can meet these criteria. Holding at least 25 percent of your investment portfolio in bonds or cash and cash equivalents is a must for most investors.

Bond Portion of Your Portfolio

You have a lot of different types of bonds to choose from. Graham had his favorites and thought others were not worth considering. In this section, we take a closer look at the pros and cons of key bond types for the defensive investor. For more information on bonds and how they work, read Chapter 13.

Taxable or Tax-Free

Unless you're in the lowest tax bracket, Graham believed you should buy only tax-free municipal bonds outside of a retirement portfolio. If you don't, you'll find the taxman taking too much of your dividend income.

Taxable bonds, and their higher returns, are a good choice inside a tax-deferred retirement savings vehicle, such as your employer-sponsored retirement savings—401(k) or 403(b), or individual retirement account (IRA).

Short-Term or Long-Term?

Bonds and interest rates move in opposite directions. When interest rates rise, bond prices fall; when interest rates fall, bond prices tend to rise. In the long term, you are better off holding a long-term bond: it will outperform a short-term one. Also consider buying intermediate-term bonds, which tend to be more stable.

Bond Mutual Funds

Your other option is to build the bond portion of your portfolio using mutual funds. That way, you can let a good bond portfolio manager make these difficult portfolio balance choices for you. Remember, though, bond mutual funds don't have huge profit margins. To make the most of your investment, it's best to choose a bond index fund with low management costs. You can find out more about mutual funds and how they work in Chapter 15.

Stock Portion of Your Portfolio

Selecting stocks for your portfolio is a much more difficult task, so we've devoted an entire chapter to this subject for the value investor. Read Chapter 21 for more information on stock-selection strategies.

Cash and Cash Equivalents

Many people think cash has no place in an investment portfolio, but you definitely won't find that to be the case with defensive investors. Graham believed in using cash or cash equivalents as tools for managing your portfolio.

You definitely will find the market to be too hot to touch at times. You may want to sell some of your winners in a market that has been driven too high and take your profits, but you might not know where to put those profits. Often a cash equivalent is your best choice until the market cools down.

Holding a large chunk of your portfolio in cash instead of investing it during a bull market that's ready to fall makes a lot of sense. That why, when the market corrects, you'll have the ready cash to make some good buys as stock prices tumble.

Let's take a look at some of Graham's favorite cash equivalents:

- Treasury securities
- Mortgage securities

Treasury Securities

The U.S. government guarantees these securities, so they carry no credit risks. The U.S. government has never defaulted on debt and would be more likely to just print more money rather than hurt that safety record.

You can find Treasury bills that mature in 4, 13, or 26 weeks. These T-bills have a very short life span and rarely move significantly in value as interest rates change.

Interest income from Treasury securities is taxable on your federal income tax return, but most states allow you to collect that income tax-free. More than $3.5 trillion is held in U.S. Treasury securities, so it's a huge market with a lot of different places to park some cash safely.

Finding Value

You can buy U.S. Treasury securities directly from the government at www.treasurydirect. gov/tdhome.htm. If you don't want to buy individual securities, you can also choose to buy mutual funds that specialize in Treasury securities. Be sure to look at the details of the portfolio, though, to be sure the fund is investing only in government-backed securities.

You can buy these types of Treasury securities:

- Treasury bills are short-term government securities with maturities ranging from a few days to 26 weeks. Bills are sold at a discount from their face value.

- Treasury notes are government securities that are issued with maturities of 2, 5, and 10 years and pay interest every six months.

- Treasury bonds have a term of 30 years and pay interest every six months.

- ◆ Treasury inflation-protected securities (TIPS) are marketable securities whose principal is adjusted by changes in the Consumer Price Index.

- ◆ I savings bonds are low-risk bonds that earn interest while protecting you from inflation.

- ◆ EE/E savings bonds are a secure savings product that pays interest based on current market rates for up to 30 years.

Mortgage Securities

You can get higher interest rates but still get a high degree of safety by buying mutual funds that specialize in mortgage securities, packaged by the Federal National Mortgage Association (Fannie Mae) or the Government National Mortgage Association (Ginnie Mae). These Treasury-backed securities are government-backed bonds, so you don't have to worry about losing your money.

But don't buy these securities directly. Portfolios of these types of bonds require good asset allocation to avoid a huge hit when interest rates change. Instead, buy these securities using an index mutual fund; this is safer and requires a lot less work to manage the portfolio.

Other Investment Vehicles

Other investment vehicles that you can consider for your defensive investing portfolio include preferred stocks or convertibles. We cover these alternatives in detail in Chapter 16, but Graham was not a big fan of either.

He believed preferred shares were the worst of both worlds. They are less secure than bonds because they have only a secondary claim if a company goes bankrupt. Preferred stocks also have less profit potential because a company can call them (buy them back) when interest rates drop or their credit rating improves. A company usually calls preferred shares when the dividends they are paying are higher than the interest rates they can get if they take a loan to buy back the preferred shares.

Graham didn't think preferred stocks made sense for individual investors, but he did think they were a good idea for corporate investors. Corporate investors have to pay much higher tax rates on interest earned than they do on dividends, so preferred stocks often are the better choice for them.

Now that we've reviewed the basics of defensive investing, let's take a closer look at how you pick stocks defensively.

The Least You Need to Know

♦ You must take stock of your risk tolerance and time constraints before you can even think about becoming a defensive investor—that's true for any investor.

♦ Most average defensive investors should build their portfolios with 50 percent stocks and 50 percent bonds.

♦ Carefully portion out your portfolio based on when you need the money. Funds needed in the next two years should be in cash or cash equivalents. Money invested in stocks should be money that you don't need for at least 10 years.

Chapter 21

Stock Investing—Value Style

In This Chapter

- Stock choices
- Growth versus value
- Do it yourself or get help
- Selection rules

Many defensive investors fear stocks because they've seen them drop like a stone, devastating all portfolios in their path. Yes, stock investing can be risky, but you can minimize that risk by carefully building a solid portfolio of stocks using techniques developed by the guru of value investing, Benjamin Graham.

In this chapter, we review stock investing basics for the defensive investor, which includes most, if not all, value investors. First, we make the case for stocks. Then we look at whether growth stocks have any role in a value portfolio. Next, we discuss whether you should invest on your own or with help. Finally, we explore Graham's rules for stock selection.

Why Stocks?

As you watched the stock market take a nosedive as the mortgage mess unfolded in 2007, did you wonder whether you should ever trust investments in the stock market again? If you also followed the bear market that started in the early 2000s after the Internet stocks crashed, you're probably pretty skittish about even thinking about buying stocks.

Well, stocks do have a place in every portfolio. As we discussed in Chapter 20, even the most conservative investors would be wise to maintain at least 25 percent of their portfolio in stocks.

When we discuss percentage of stock holdings in this chapter, we're talking specifically about the amount of money you have set aside for stock investing. For example, if you have a portfolio of $100,000 and you set aside $25,000 for stocks, then when we discuss using 10 percent of your stock portfolio for stocks, that would be $2,500 (10 percent of the $25,000 you have set aside for stocks).

So why are stocks that important to a balanced portfolio?

- They offer critical protection against the erosion that inflation can have on both bond investments and cash savings.

- Stocks offer you a much higher return, so you can grow your portfolio significantly above the inflation rate and have a nice nest egg for your retirement or other long-term savings goals.

But you can lose the benefit of buying stocks by paying too much for the stock. This usually happens when investors feel that it is safe to get into a bull market because it appears as though stocks are going up and will be going up forever. Guess again. They never go up forever—every stock eventually goes up and down in price.

For value investors, a bull market can be the most dangerous time to buy stock. The fact that everyone else is buying stocks does not signal a good time to buy. The stock market will fall again. The key is to buy stocks on sale and sell them when people are paying full price.

The best time to find sale prices is during a bear market, when no one else is buying. Then sell them during a bull market, when you've made a nice profit, or hold on to stocks you like to build a long-term portfolio. Any stock you've picked could be worth keeping if it's a solid company with a strong possibility of continued growth.

Now don't get me wrong—you can find good buys in a bull market. But you must tread more carefully and be sure you're not just getting caught up in all the hype of the market. The biggest mistake you can make as a stock investor is to buy high and sell low. In Chapter 11, we show you how to analyze a stock to be sure you're not paying too much for it.

Graham believes you should follow these guidelines for the stock component of your stock portfolio:

- Diversify your portfolio with at least 10 stocks and no more than 30 stocks. Since you must continually research the stocks you hold, few individuals have the time to research more than 10 stocks, so be careful about how many stocks you add to the stock portion of your portfolio.

- Select companies that are large, well known, and well financed (which means not too much debt). We talk more about debt ratios in Chapter 11.

- Make sure each company has a long history of dividend payments.

Role of Growth Stocks

Should you consider only solid, blue-chip companies that are already making a good, steady income? These are the types of companies that pay a steady dividend every quarter.

By all means, dividend-paying companies should be the core of any good value portfolio, but don't write off *growth stocks* completely. Growth stocks may have a role in any portfolio, provided that you have the risk tolerance to accept the lows as well as the highs and not sell as soon as the stock drops a few dollars.

Dividend-paying companies are companies that have been around a long time, have developed their core products, and earn significant profits each year. While they do reinvest some of their profits in future growth, they also have enough to share those profits with investors.

def•i•ni•tion

Growth stocks are stocks in companies that focus primarily on growing the company. They rarely pay dividends and instead reinvest all profits in future growth. Companies start paying out dividends to their investors only when they no longer have good ideas for investing all the money they make into plans for future growth.

Stocks of companies primarily in growth mode don't have enough extra profit to pay dividends. Investors in these stocks expect to get their payback for choosing this investment from the anticipated rise in the stock price as the company grows.

While Graham did see the potential in growth stocks, he basically considered them too dangerous for defensive investors. He believed the average investor wasn't likely to find such growth gems.

Value Visions _____

Benjamin Graham wrote in his book *The Intelligent Investor* (Collins Business Essentials, 2006 edition), "[W]e regard growth stocks as a whole as too uncertain and risky a vehicle for the defensive investor. Of course, wonders can be accomplished with the right individual selections, bought at the right levels, and later sold after a huge rise and before the probable decline."

Some value investors do focus on small companies with strong growth potential. We focus on one such guru, Paul Sonkin, in Chapter 19.

On Your Own or with Help?

You may be wondering whether you should invest on your own or with the help of a broker. That depends on your knowledge of the stock market and the basics of investing.

If you're comfortable with the mechanics of investing, you understand how to place a stock order, and you believe you have the resources you need to research stocks, go for it. Find yourself a discount broker or buy stocks directly from the companies you choose, to save brokerage fees.

Finding Value _____

You can find stocks that are sold directly to investors, bypassing brokers, on many different websites. Two good ones to check out include Drip Central (www.dripcentral.com) and ING Direct's Sharebuilder (www.sharebuilder.com).

Many large companies today have a direct purchase plan. The big problem to watch out for when buying direct is the fees per purchase. A discount brokerage house may offer better options for trading. Direct purchase plans are good if you're starting out very small. Once your portfolio is large enough, you can probably trade stocks more cheaply with a discount broker.

If you buy in small amounts directly from a company, be sure to keep good records of each purchase. You will need to prove your costs when you sell the stock in the future. If you don't keep good records, you could end up paying more than necessary for *capital gains*.

def•i•ni•tion

Capital gains are profits you make when you sell a stock. For example, if you buy stock for $10 a share and sell it for $15 a share, the $5 of profit you make is capital gain.

People who are new to stock trading definitely shouldn't try to trade stock on their own. While it may cost you more, get some help from a discount broker, a financial planner, or a full-service broker.

You've worked too hard to earn that money—don't be a fool and lose it quickly just because you didn't understand the basics. Once you're feeling more comfortable with your stock trading skills, you can consider saving money and trading on your own.

You may not enjoy researching and picking stocks. There's nothing wrong with that. You can do very well as a defensive investor by hiring someone else to manage your portfolio.

If you're just starting out, the best way to build a stock portfolio with professional help is to buy mutual funds. We talk more about how they work in Chapter 15. People who already have a sizable portfolio can find a professional portfolio manager, but you will need at least $250,000 to get individual help from a portfolio manager.

When selecting a manager, take the time to interview the candidates and find out what style of investing they prefer. Be sure they match your desire to be a defensive or value investor. If not, you'll be very unhappy with the results.

Graham's Stock-Selection Rules

Graham would have no problems with your building a portfolio that includes every stock in the Dow Jones Industrial Average. That would be 30 stocks of steady companies that pay dividends regularly. In Chapter 19, on contrarian investing, we talk about the Dogs of the Dow, another simple value investing strategy.

But if you want to start picking stocks on your own, Graham had several key rules you would be wise to follow regarding the size of your portfolio, the financial condition of the companies you choose, and their ratios. Let's take a closer at these rules.

Adequate Size of the Company

Graham excluded all small companies as possible candidates for the defensive investor. In fact, he believed that most defensive investors should steer clear of companies with less than $100 million in sales (this translates to more than $500 million in today's market).

In the 2006 updates to the book, Jason Zweig clarified what would be Graham's minimal size company for defensive investors in today's market. He said investors should steer clear of companies with a total market value of less than $2 billion. That leaves you with more than 400 companies in the Standard & Poor's Index of the 500 top companies, which is certainly enough to choose from.

If you're just starting out and have only a small amount to invest in your portfolio, buy an index mutual fund from one of the discount mutual funds companies, such as Vanguard or Fidelity, as you start to build your portfolio. When you have enough invested to manage your own portfolio of at least 10 stocks, you can consider managing your own portfolio.

You can get started more slowly. For example, once you have $10,000 in your mutual fund portfolio, consider buying one stock with 10 or 20 percent of that money to get started. Keep your balance at 80 percent in index mutual funds and 20 percent individual stocks until you have at least 10 stocks in your individual portfolio.

At that point, you can cash in your mutual funds and maintain your own stock portfolio, if you choose, but don't feel bad if you like the idea of having your portfolio professionally managed. Many people don't have the time or the skills to manage a stock portfolio.

If you do choose to build your portfolio with mutual funds, you may want to add funds with different focuses, to balance out your portfolio. Focuses could include contrarian investing, value stocks, or small stocks. You also may consider a small portion of your portfolio in a specific industry, such as energy.

Financial Condition

Graham believed you should buy only companies with current assets that are twice their current liabilities. This makes a 2:1 current ratio. We show you how to calculate that in Chapter 11. When companies have a current ratio that is twice their current liabilities, they have enough of a cushion to survive any economic downturn.

> ### Value Visions
>
> In his 2006 commentary on Graham's *The Intelligent Investor* (Collins Business Essentials, 2006), Jason Zweig wrote: "If you build a diversified basket of stocks whose current assets are at least double their current liabilities and whose long-term debt does not exceed working capital, you should end up with a group of conservatively financed companies with plenty of staying power."

You won't find a lot of companies with this financial condition. There are probably only about 100 companies out there, but that's still enough for you to find at least 10 good choices.

Earning Stability

Graham believed any company you pick should have some earnings in each of the past 10 years. You won't find that difficult to spot. In fact, in a study done by Morgan Stanley, 86 percent of all companies in the S&P 500 had positive earnings in every one of the 10 years between 1993 and 2002.

When you consider that 2000, 2001, and 2002 were bear market years, you can see that this won't be a difficult test for you to use. Even in a tough bear market, conservatively financed companies can survive financially.

You can usually find this information quickly when you look at the financial summary in a company's annual report. Most companies will give you a 10-year history; you just need to check to be sure their earnings were positive in each of the 10 years.

Dividend Record

Graham believed you should consider only companies that paid dividends without interruptions for the past 20 years. That rules out all growth companies. If you do decide to add one or two growth companies, you will be ignoring this key rule from Graham.

But, again, you won't find it hard to select stocks with this rule. More than 350 of the Standard & Poor's 500 have paid dividends for at least 20 years now.

Finding Value _____

You can quickly check a company's dividend-paying record on many different financial websites. One of the easiest to use is http://finance.yahoo.com. Search for the company you are researching. When you get to that company's summary page, click on Historical Prices. Then select Dividends Only; you will get a summary report of how often and how much the company paid in dividends over the years.

Earnings Growth

Graham believed that a company's earnings should grow at least one third per share earnings in the past 10 years. That's not a hard test to beat. That 33 percent growth translates into just a 3 percent average annual increase in earnings. While a company may have some bad years, you definitely don't want to consider any company that doesn't grow at least an average of 3 percent per year. Bond investment earnings would be better than that.

As part of your research, you should collect numerous annual reports. You will be able to find the earnings growth rate for the current year and three previous years in each report. So for example, if you have the 2007 annual report, you'll also have earnings results for 2006 and 2005. If you then ask for a copy of the 2004 annual report, you'll get 2003 and 2002, so you'll also need the 2001 annual report to find a full 10-year history.

Most companies provide older reports as a file you can download from the investor section of the company's website. If you can't find older reports there, you can always find them at the Securities and Exchange Commission website (www.sec.gov).

P/E Ratios

Graham believed that a company should have a price-to-earnings (P/E) ratio of no more than 15 times the average earnings for the past three years. As you start looking at ratios, you'll see that many companies have much higher P/E ratios. As a defensive investor, you'll want to stay away from them. You'll find plenty to choose from that meet Graham's standards.

We show you how to calculate a P/E ratio in Chapter 11. You will find several kinds of P/E ratios, such as a forward P/E, in reports by analysts. Don't get caught up in these attempts to make things look better. Keep it simple and use the P/E ratio formula we show you how to calculate.

The big problem with forward P/Es is that they use projected earnings, and no one can be sure whether those projected earnings are correct. Analysts' projections are frequently not accurate.

Price-to-Book Ratios

Graham believed the current price of a stock should be no more than 1.5 times the book value of the stock that the company last reported. But this formula doesn't work well for companies that have a lot of intangible assets, such as copyrights, patents, or goodwill and other assets that would not be included in a price-to-book ratio calculation. We show you how to do a price-to-book ratio calculation in Chapter 11.

To adjust for today's marketplace, a more likely figure to use would be price-to-book ratios of under 2.5, according to Jason Zweig in the 2006 addition of *The Intelligent Investor*. Zweig found 273 companies that met these criteria when he updated that book.

Graham also suggested that if a company had a P/E ratio of less than 15, you can multiply that by its price-to-book ratio. If the calculation comes out to less than 22.5, Graham thought that was a company worth investigating further.

Now that we know the rules Graham used when picking stocks, let's take a closer look at how Mario Gabelli developed his unique method of valuing companies, called Private Market Value.

The Least You Need to Know

- Stocks must be in every portfolio, to maintain enough growth to beat inflation.

- Growth stocks are too risky for most defensive investors.

- Get to know Benjamin Graham's key rules for picking stocks as a defensive investor, to put together a solid portfolio.

22

Using Gabelli's Style—Private Market Value

In This Chapter

- ◆ Defining PMV
- ◆ Getting control
- ◆ Analyzing the numbers
- ◆ Finding the catalyst

Can you match Mario Gabelli by using the techniques he developed called private market value? Probably not, but you can use his known strategies to improve your stock-picking skills.

Gabelli's Asset AAA mutual fund, which is managed using these value investing strategies, kept this fund in the top quartile of similar mutual funds (midcap blend) for the past 15 years. He has other mutual funds he manages for investors as well—but you must have at least $1 million to get him to manage an individual portfolio for you.

In this chapter, we take a closer look at Gabelli's style and how you can imitate what he does. You may not be able to copy him exactly because he talks only vaguely about his analytical tools when he speaks around the country. Still, you can learn a lot from Gabelli's style about how to investigate companies whose stocks you are considering buying.

What Is Private Market Value?

Gabelli tells people who want to buy one of his value mutual funds that Private Market Value is the value he believes "informed investors would be willing to pay for the company."

Gabelli also believes that each investor has an equal say in what the price should be for a stock. When investors trade stocks, there must be a buyer and a seller for each stock. The seller usually believes he has done the best he can with that holding and thinks it's time to move on. The buyer usually believes that there's money to be made and is willing the pay the price for the possibility of future gains. So who's right?

Unless someone has a crystal ball and can tell exactly which way the stock will move, only time will tell. The only thing you know for sure is that the stock will either go up or go down over the next six months—and it might go up, go down and again go up or down, or go up and go down again, depending upon how volatile the company's stock is.

In the marketplace every day, the last trade determines the crowd's perception that day of the value of the stock. In a perfect world, the market price should be a good reflection of the intrinsic value of the company, but the world of stocks is not perfect.

Gabelli, like other value investors, looks for stocks that he believes have an intrinsic value that's higher than what the market believes. What makes his search unique are the three pieces he adds to the puzzle to create the concept of Private Market Value:

- Premium control
- Gaps in the GAAP
- A change catalyst

In this chapter, we delve into what each of these means to Gabelli and his team, and how you can use his strategies to improve your own investment choices.

Importance of Premium for Control

As an individual investor, you won't likely have enough money to take control of a stock. But a premium comes along with that kind of power, as Gabelli has when he buys a large percentage of stock in a company for the various funds and individual stock portfolios he manages.

Essentially, this "premium for control" gives Gabelli, or any investor who has the money to buy it, the ability to fire incompetent managers, sell assets that aren't producing revenue at needed levels, consolidate operations with another firm (this is true when two companies merge, after either a total buyout or a friendly merger), restructure the balance sheet, and do whatever else the person in control thinks needs to be done to turn the company around and improve profitability.

Since a major investor can do more to impact the turnaround of the stock, he may be willing to pay more for the stock than its intrinsic value if that additional money will buy him enough shares to gain that premium for control. This premium for control drives many hostile takeovers of companies.

You've probably heard offers of $10 to $20 more per share than the stock is currently trading for. Why are knowledgeable investors making such offers for large blocks of shares or possibly a total takeover? It's because they believe the stock actually has an intrinsic value that is worth more, as long as they can use that premium being offered to get control.

If you held a stock and someone wanted to pay $20 more than the current market price, would you sell it? Probably. That's how hostile takeovers work. The board won't agree to sell the company, so the group of investors that wants to buy it does so by buying stock on the open market directly.

Remember, stock sold on the open market is traded between buyers and sellers without any involvement of the company whose stock is being traded. The only exceptions to this rule are when the stocks are initially offered for sale or the company decides to buy back stocks and take them off the market.

Finding Value _____

Just like Gabelli, you can watch for situations in which you think the stock has been beaten down but you see a major player making moves to buy that stock. You can watch for major purchases of a stock at http://finance.yahoo.com. Search for the stock you want to research. When you get to its summary page, click on "Major Holders" in the left column. You can also watch "Insider Trades" to find out which major players in the company are buying and selling.

Analyzing Your Options

Gabelli's analytical tools are closely guarded, but he has discussed some basics over the years. We can't give you exact formulas, but we can give you clues to what he looks for when he does his analysis.

def•i•ni•tion

GAAP stands for "generally accepted accounting principles." These are the rules companies must follow when they report their numbers to the general public.

Like many value investors, Gabelli looks for gaps in the *GAAP*. Because these rules require companies to report certain items that don't show the true value of the company, a knowledgeable investor can find hidden value in a company's balance sheet.

Let's take a closer look at two key types of gaps that you can see by reading through the lines of financial statements:

◆ Assets on a balance sheet are shown at their original cost rather than their current value. For example, suppose a company you're considering bought property and built its factory on that property 25 years ago. You can be certain that the land is worth a lot more than it was 25 years ago. The value of the actual factory may or may not be higher, depending on whether the technology is still usable or it needs major upgrades to be competitive.

◆ Operating income of one key division in the company may actually be a lot higher, but you can't see that on the income statement because the company is writing off losses for some divisions that a good manager would shut down. These tie directly into the issue of the premium for control.

When looking for stock to buy, Gabelli seeks to find gems that appear undervalued on paper but truly would have a much higher value if they were taken over by another company or investor group that knew how to clean up the financial mess and turn the company around. Gabelli finds these gems in industries he knows very well. To spot these gems as well, you have to know the workings of the industry and the types of profits to expect in various divisions.

Gabelli focuses primarily on the media and communications arenas, which he knows best. This includes telephone companies, cable and broadcast television companies, radio operators, and magazine and newspaper publishers. The common tie for these businesses is subscribers who must pay to get their services.

So you have the two pieces of information you need to calculate the revenue of these types of companies:

- The number of subscribers in an operating statistic. The companies must report this to get advertisers to want to advertise.

- The subscription prices that subscribers must pay.

With these two pieces of information, you can calculate the revenue these companies are generating from subscribers. You can also get information about their advertising revenue and build your own gross revenue estimate.

You can use this data to then calculate how much money a knowledgeable investor would be willing to pay per subscriber for the company. For example, suppose you know that a newspaper was just bought out for $1 million and it had 100,000 subscribers. That means a knowledgeable investor is willing to pay a price of $10 per subscriber.

This becomes your starting point for finding those hidden gems. You can then look at other similar companies and see if their stock price is at or below their intrinsic value by comparing similar statistics.

You can do this with any industry that has operating statistics that are publicly available and for which you have a good working knowledge of the industry. Some examples include these:

- Hotel industry—the number of hotel rooms

- Broadcasting—the population reached by a broadcaster

- Retailing—the number of square feet a commercial retailer manages

Finding Value _____

Yes, a lot of digging is involved. If you don't think you're ready to handle this on your own, you can buy shares in one of Gabelli's mutual funds and let him do it for you. The big disadvantage of Gabelli's mutual funds is that their management fees are high, but that premium may be worth it to you, given the success he has had with Private Market Value. To look at Gabelli's mutual fund options, go to www.gabelli.com/indiv.

Seeking the Catalysts for Change

The third key factor Gabelli looks at when picking a stock for his portfolios is environmental catalysts. We're not just talking about the impact on the environment because of global warming; other key environmental catalysts operate as well:

- Social

- Political

- Laws and Regulations

- Technological

> **Value Visions**
>
> Mario Gabelli tells his mutual fund shareholders in the prospectus for his funds, "We look for a catalyst—something happening in the company or industry that may create value."

Often these environmental catalysts overlap to bring about major global changes that can drive business opportunities in new and profitable directions. The key for the value investor is to spot a potential catalyst before the rest of the market.

For example, a major change catalyst for China and the global economy as well was the change in political and social beliefs that opened China to outsiders. Politically, China had been a closed society that did not want to allow the influences of the Western world to impact its hold on the communist nation.

Social and Political Changes

The key catalyst for change here was the Chinese taking back Hong Kong in 1997. Hong Kong had been a dependent territory of Great Britain since 1892. Britain had a 99-year lease on the territory.

During that lease period, Hong Kong's economy flourished and it became a strong global economic competitor. When China took it back, the rest of its people wanted a piece of the economic action. China could no longer hold back the Western influence and slowly started to negotiate with corporations to operate within mainland China. The rest is now history, and China's stock market is booming.

At the time of this writing, in early 2008, many believe that China's stock market is near the top of a stock bubble that may soon burst. So we don't recommend that you buy Chinese stock, but there may still be opportunities for solid European and

American companies that see the growth potential in China. You can jump on their bandwagon by investing in the stocks of companies that you believe are building a strong presence in the future Chinese marketplace.

Finding Value

You can see how this type of change played out if you review what has happened since the Berlin Wall game down in 1989. Major companies like Coca-Cola and General Electric expanded rapidly by taking advantage of the new market opportunities. Research who benefited from this change catalyst and how they benefited to get ideas that might help you analyze potential companies that will benefit from the changes in the Chinese marketplace.

Changes in Laws and Regulations

Changes in laws and government regulations are another good example of a change catalyst impacted by governmental moves. Almost all changes in laws positively impact one industry and negatively impact another. As a value investor, you must get to know the standing laws and regulations for the industries you focus on and carefully watch changes to those laws and regulations.

If you spot a law change or regulation change that you think will have a major economic impact, carefully look at which companies will be hurt and which companies will be helped by that change. Look for some good buys in companies that will be helped by the change.

A classic change by governmental action was the break-up of AT&T because of a 1974 antitrust action by the U.S. Justice Department. Think about what has happened to that industry since the breakup.

Many of the Baby Bells that were formed have since merged, and AT&T is almost back together again. Had you bought stock in the stronger Baby Bells soon after the breakup, you'd be a major stockholder today in one of the few companies left controlling the U.S. communications industry.

Technology Catalyst

Advances in technology can be a major catalyst for change that can shut down some companies that don't adapt quickly enough and drive other companies to success. The two major catalysts many of us have seen during our lifetimes are the space race and the Internet boom.

Think about how these two technological developments have impacted companies across the board. Entirely new technologies were developed that are now successful companies. For example, Tempur-Pedic, which developed a unique mattress as an innovation for space travel, is now a major seller of upscale mattresses for the general public.

Finding Value

Today NASA seeks new technological developments and even sponsors innovation with its Innovative Partnership Program. You may be able to find some ideas for technological catalysts at its website, www.ip.nasa.gov.

The Internet has changed the way nearly every business operates. You'll find many opportunities by looking at how this new technology continues to change our global business environment.

Now that you have an idea of how Gabelli works his stock-picking magic, let's take a look at someone who believes in portfolio concentration rather than diversification as the way to build a portfolio—Glenn Greenberg.

The Least You Need to Know

◆ Look for stocks that you believe are trading below their intrinsic value and are ripe for picking by a takeover specialist, who, with a premium for control, could turn the company around.

◆ Find industries that must provide their operating statistics publicly, to help you find a company's true revenue-generating capabilities.

◆ Keep your eyes open for a change catalyst that could have a major impact on the future growth or demise of companies you're considering.

Chapter 23

Concentrate Your Portfolio

In This Chapter

- Portfolio concentration
- Choosing companies
- Determining the right price
- Seeking value
- Careful monitoring

Putting all your assets in one basket, essentially concentrating your portfolio on just a few stocks, doesn't work for most people. It takes on a lot of risk and requires that you have a lot of confidence in knowing how to pick the right companies.

Most value investors look to diversify their portfolios and rarely put more than 4 percent of their assets in one particular company. But some value investors believe that concentration in just a few companies makes sense because they then will have the time and effort they need to find just the right companies, do their homework, and do an extensive job monitoring the companies they've chosen.

In this chapter, we take a closer look at one value investing guru, Glenn Greenberg, whose claim to fame is concentrating his portfolio. We review how he picks stocks and what he does once he buys them.

Why Concentrate?

Many value investors believe it's dangerous to concentrate, so why do some believe concentration is the only way to go? Most value investors who choose to concentrate do so because they believe that one needs to spend a lot of time researching a company to get to know it well enough to want to buy shares in that company and then continue to do that level of research to monitor the stocks. To have enough time to maintain that level of research, value investors who believe in concentrating their portfolios like to hold just 10 stocks or fewer.

Let's take a look at one of the proponents of concentration and explore why he chooses to concentrate. Glenn Greenberg, who started Chieftain Capital in 1984, earned a phenomenal record for his clients over a long period of time. For the first 17 years, he achieved a compounded growth rate of 25 percent per year, minus advisory fees, for his clients. During that same time period, the average investor who used an S&P 500 index mutual fund earned an average annual growth rate of 16 percent.

Finding Value

If you think concentration may be a tactic you'd like to use to build a portfolio, we recommend you start by building up the assets in your portfolio using well-diversified mutual funds. Then gradually start adding individual stocks. When you think you're ready to concentrate, you'll have the money sitting there that you'll need for buying individual stocks.

Greenberg doesn't necessarily believe the prevailing wisdom on Wall Street, although sometimes he does. He needs to understand why he holds every stock, not just why Wall Street analysts think it's a good buy. He researches any stock he buys very deeply both before and after the stock purchase. We talk more about his research techniques later.

He won't even begin to buy shares of a stock until he feels comfortable enough in the stock he's choosing that he'll put 5 percent of his portfolio in that stock. Many portfolio managers buy a small number of shares as they start to research and watch stocks, and then sell off those that don't pan out.

Greenberg doesn't believe in the strategy of buying a bunch of stocks to diversify and then maybe adding to the stocks that look good. For the stocks he really likes, he builds his holdings to as high as 20 percent.

So how does Greenberg go about concentrating his portfolio? These are the keys to concentrating a portfolio:

- ◆ Buy good companies.
- ◆ Find great buys.

- ◆ Value companies right.
- ◆ Stay informed.

Let's take a closer look at how Greenberg carries out these tasks. You'll find a lot of clues for how you might be able to use his strategy to build your own portfolio. We definitely don't think you should consider concentrating your portfolio until you feel very confident in your ability to pick stocks.

Buy Good Companies

Of course, everyone knows it's important to buy good companies when picking stocks. But what does that really mean? For Greenberg, it means this:

◆ Look for companies that can't be easily challenged by new entrants. For example, to start a new telephone company, you would have to either gain the rights to a particular service area (not likely—companies rarely give up their rights, and rights are usually gained by taking over a company that has them) or build a multibillion-dollar wireless service. Other good industries that have significant barriers to entry include oil companies, utility companies, and railroads.

◆ Companies that have earnings that are growing.

◆ Companies that aren't vulnerable to new technologies that could hurt their competitive edge.

◆ Companies that pay dividends regularly or regularly repurchase their shares. When a company repurchases shares, the earnings are then divided among fewer shareholders, so the earnings per share go up.

When Greenberg picks a stock, he expects to own it for four to five years. So when he picks stocks for his portfolio …

◆ He doesn't necessarily buy cheap stocks. Instead, he focuses on whether he will get the return he expects after he buys a stock at its current price.

◆ He looks for high profit margins.

◆ He looks for companies that have proven they act with the best interests of their shareholders in mind. He doesn't buy shares of a company with any plans to influence managers. He does his homework and buys only companies whose management team is already acting in the best interest of their shareholders.

◆ He likes a *duopoly* but avoids a *monopoly*.

def•i•ni•tion

A **duopoly** occurs when two companies dominate a business sector that has a high barrier to entry, but coexist without competing directly with each other. For example, Fannie Mae and Freddie Mac, both major power players in the mortgage market, serve different niches. A **monopoly** occurs when only one company serves a particular market segment. For example, Microsoft has been charged with using its computer operating system monopoly unfairly to crush competitors.

Why does Greenberg avoid monopolies? He believes monopolies face a lot more government scrutiny then duopolies. Microsoft, which is constantly facing courtrooms in the United States and globally, is a good example of what happens to a monopoly power. Microsoft spends billions each year either defending its position in the world or paying fines when it's charged with taking advantage of its monopoly power.

Find Great Buys

Let's take a look at how Greenberg goes about finding these great buys. He doesn't look for beaten-down companies, as many value investors do. Instead, he looks for companies that are selling at low enough prices with a good cash flow to give him the return he wants. His strict stock-picking criteria narrows his candidates to very large companies with a good cash payout in the form of dividends to shareholders, as well as a potential for share price growth (capital gains). With his strict method of valuation, he's usually left with about 300 companies from which to choose, and few of those make the grade. That's why he believes concentration in 10 companies is the only way he can give his clients the results he wants to attain.

So what makes a great buy? Greenberg looks for change catalysts that tend to beat down an industry unjustifiably. This could include a change in government regulations or the introduction of new technologies.

Change in Governmental Regulations

Sometimes governmental regulations can initiate a major change in how an industry behaves and can act as a catalyst for industry consolidation. Let's look at how governmental regulation change in the mortgage industry gave Greenberg an opportunity for his portfolio.

When the savings and loan industry first started to show signs of trouble in the 1980s, Congress tried to help without shelling out tax dollars. Congress voted to allow savings and loans to sell to the public their shares of the Federal Home Loan Mortgage Company (Freddie Mac), which is one of the two government-sponsored mortgage enterprises, to raise cash.

Before this regulatory change, only shares of Fannie Mae, the other major government-sponsored mortgage enterprise, could be sold to the public. This move drove the price of Freddie Mac down because there were so many shares to be sold at the same time. Greenberg jumped on this opportunity because the company met his criteria:

♦ Freddie Mac was a duopoly.

♦ Freddie Mac paid a good dividend.

♦ Freddie Mac had a good management team.

♦ Freddie Mac was on sale because the change in government regulations triggered a fire sale of the company's stock.

When the government passes new regulations that impact an entire industry, look outside the box and try to figure out who the winners and losers will be. Look for a company whose stock is selling below what you think should be its intrinsic value, and ride out the storm.

New Products Impact Negatively on Stock Price

Sometimes Greenberg recognizes that the general public and Wall Street analysts both make a mistake about the impact a new technology will have on an industry. He watches as the shares of stock within the industry are dubbed a dying industry and get beaten down unjustifiably.

While the crowd runs from companies in the supposedly dying industry, Greenberg begins his research for opportunities. The introduction of satellite TV and its expected impact on cable TV is an example of a situation in which the general public and many analysts overreacted and dubbed cable TV a dying industry.

Greenberg bought a couple of cable outlets at the time because he thought the crowd was wrong. He was right. They were wrong. He made steady profits for his clients for many years.

Don't always assume the crowd is correct about changes in an industry. Determine for yourself what you think the impact of a new technology will be on an industry you follow. Sort out the winners and losers, and then find a good company among the winners.

Value Companies Right

Greenberg uses a complicated form of discounted cash flow to value the companies he is considering. We show you how to do a discounted cash flow computation in Chapter 11.

Since Greenberg's primary test for a company is that it will produce a good cash flow that will allow him to get the returns he seeks, he doesn't worry as much about asset values as other value investors do. Instead, he scours the financial statements to determine the amount of cash that flows into and out of the company each year. By discounting that cash flow back to the present-day value based on a rate of return he wants, he can determine how much he should pay per share for the stock.

To pull together this cash flow value, he looks at the following factors:

- Sales growth rates
- Profit margins
- Market prices of assets
- Capital *expenditure* requirements

def•i•ni•tion

Capital **expenditures** are funds a company uses to acquire or upgrade assets. For example, if a company has an older factory that needs to be modernized, the funds that will be spent on that modernization would be a capital expenditure.

To analyze a company's cash flow, you must understand how the company operates and how it generates its cash flow. Greenberg's researchers take the time to learn these details before they can even think of running a discounted cash flow analysis.

Stay Informed

After Greenberg buys a stock for his portfolio, his hard work begins. He and his researchers continue to do in-depth analysis every quarter when they receive the quarterly reports from the company, to be sure the stock is performing as expected.

If the company is not performing as expected, Greenberg may decide to sell the holding. In most cases, however, he and his staff have done a good job of picking and add to a holding. When he finds a really good pick, he holds as much as 20 percent of his portfolio in one stock.

Concentrating a portfolio is risky. Unless you feel very confident that you have the skills for this type of research and stock selection, we don't recommend that you follow this strategy.

Let's take a look at strategies for buying stocks cheap in the next chapter.

The Least You Need to Know

- Concentrating your portfolio can be very risky. While some value investors have been successful using this strategy, don't try it until you trust your stock-picking skills.

- Develop criteria for picking good companies and stick to it. Don't worry about what the crowd thinks if you believe you've done your homework to prove yourself right.

- When you've got a good stock and you believe it has a solid future, if you want to concentrate your portfolio, don't be afraid to hold a large stake in that stock.

24

Focusing on the Cheap

In This Chapter

- ◆ Finding the right price
- ◆ Where to look for opportunities
- ◆ Buying and selling tips
- ◆ Monitoring your holdings

Most value investors' first priority is to buy stocks cheap and hold them until the market realizes what a bargain they are. This type of strategy takes a lot of patience and discipline, often requiring decisions to buy a stock that most of the market is selling.

In this chapter, we focus on three value investing gurus who have two distinct strategies for buying stocks cheap. We explore how they find their choices and how they manage their portfolios.

Pricing Stocks with Price

Michael Price doesn't look for a stock that will soar when the market is hot and then fall like a stone and lose half its value when the crowd loses interest. He prefers to look for less volatile companies that might not soar in a bull market but won't do too bad during the down markets. He believes that if you focus on lower risk, higher returns will follow because you won't always be trying to climb out of a hole when a stock holding drops like a stone.

Price manages portfolios for his clients using four basic principles:

- **Discipline**—He never deviates from his valuation standards and never gets caught up in the prevailing winds of the market. Before he even starts to build a portfolio, he determines the balance for that portfolio and then doesn't deviate, no matter what is happening in the stock market.

- **Patience**—He waits to buy the stock at the value he deems appropriate. He won't pursue the stock—he patiently waits for the stock price to drop to or below what he believes is its intrinsic value.

- **Focus**—He never lets himself get distracted by global predictions or forecasts. He believes it is much easier to understand a stock than to understand what's happening economically.

- **Homework**—He always does his homework on a stock before buying it. Only the buyer or the seller can be right about price, and the one likely to be right is the one who has done a better job of figuring out its true value.

Price uses these key factors to build his portfolio with a focus on finding buys in one of three areas—cheap stocks, arbitrage, and bankruptcies. Let's take a closer look at how he puts these principles to work in each of the three areas.

Finding Value

One of the best times to look for bargains is after a major one-day drop in the market, like the 504-point drop in the Dow on September 21, 2008. While many people run for the hills, that's when you should go bargain shopping.

In order to do this wisely, you should research and keep a list of potential stocks you'd like to own that you've already fully researched. Then, when the market goes into panic and people run away, you'll be ready to scoop up the best bargains.

Valuing Stocks

To find cheap stocks, you must have a strategy for setting a value for each stock. Price does this by keeping a database of mergers and acquisitions. Many people are involved in determining the price when a merger or acquisition takes place, and the investment bankers trying to put together the deal must publicly disclose a lot of the details about a company's assets, debts, and operations.

Price collects these merger and acquisition public documents and then enters the key information about the variables involved in setting the price. This gives him excellent information about what a knowledgeable buyer is willing to pay for a company.

When Price and his staff enter the details from these merger documents, they break down the detail by division. Most major companies have numerous divisions. Each operates in a different segment of the market. To use this pricing detail and to compare apples to apples when pricing a stock, you must be able to put together a value for a company based on a similar mix of market segments. No two companies have exactly the same mix of businesses, but by collecting the information by business segments, Price can value any company with any mix of divisions.

In addition to keeping track of the price at which companies are being sold, Price looks at more traditional ways of pricing stocks:

- Market price of the assets shown on the balance sheet

- Cash flow

- Book value

But he uses these more traditional methods of valuation as a check for the price he developed using his database of merger and acquisition transactions.

Finding Cheap Stocks

When it comes to looking for cheap stocks to consider, Price's first stop is always the newspaper. He follows the deals in the works and looks for the stocks that are hitting new lows. He also follows earnings reports that talk about companies that missed their earnings expectations or may be in trouble financially.

To be considered a cheap stock in Price's eyes, the stock must be selling for 40 percent below what Price determines is the stock's intrinsic value. While he waits for his potential candidates to drop that low, he continues to research the company and its management team. Price also looks at the debt structure, to be sure the balance sheet doesn't show too much debt.

Picking an Arbitrage Position

The arbitrage portion of Price's portfolio is made up of merger and acquisition deals already announced on the market. He sees these types of investments as a more profitable place to put his cash than traditional money market funds.

Usually there are about 300 deals in various stages of completion in the market at any one time. If Price picks the deals correctly, the profit can be between 10 and 20 percent in a short period of time. This can be a risky strategy at times because there is always the chance the deal will not go through or will take longer to complete than anticipated and will lower the actual return on the investment.

Jumping on arbitrage deals requires a lot of research to know whether the deal is really solid and whether the stockholders likely will support the merger or acquisition. If you see a lot of stories about stockholder groups or a board member who opposes a deal, don't jump on that bandwagon. Or if you find out about a hostile takeover attempt, such as the attempt by Microsoft in early 2008 to take over Yahoo!, don't get caught up in the hype. It's not worth the potential losses.

Losing Value

Be careful not to get caught up in the excitement for a deal that really is not secure. For example, amid market rumors that Microsoft would buy Yahoo! in early 2008, investors gobbled up Yahoo! stock. When the deal fell through, Yahoo! shares tumbled from a high of $29.03 in early March to a low of $25.93 on May 9. That translates to a loss of 10.7 percent in just about two months.

Banking on Bankruptcies

While most value investors stay away from bankruptcies, Price believes bottom-fishing in this arena, if done carefully and with a lot of knowledge, can be a great way to buy stocks or bonds cheap. You must know what you're doing and understand the bankruptcy process completely to carry this out successfully. Bankruptcy has four stages:

♦ **Before the filing**—In this stage, companies negotiate with creditors to try to restructure debt. To take advantage of a deal at this stage of the process, you must have a lot of cash to help the company out of its problems. If Price believes he can get a portion of ownership cheap enough in what he thinks is a good company, he has the cash from the portfolio he manages for his clients to jump on the deal. Unless you have a large hoard of cash, your best bet is to stay away from a company at this stage of bankruptcy. Otherwise, you'll be wishing and hoping someone comes along with the cash needed to prevent a bankruptcy and just watch the money you spent on buying the shares of stock drop to nothing when the company actually files bankruptcy.

◆ **The actual filing of the bankruptcy**—Immediately after the filing, some holders of bonds must sell the bonds they hold because of the rules of the portfolios in which they hold the assets. Both banks and mutual funds can be in this position. There's always a fire sale after a bankruptcy filing, so if you know what you're doing and you believe the company will successfully restructure its debt and come out of bankruptcy, you may want to take advantage of the cheap prices. Price usually looks to buy *senior debt* at this stage because these debts will have to be paid first as part of any restructuring. But he keeps his eye on *junior debt* prices, which could go low enough to make it worth taking the risk.

def•i•ni•tion

> **Senior debt** is debt (bonds or loans) that must be paid first. **Junior debt** is paid only if enough money is left over after the senior debt holders have been satisfied. For example, when you take a first mortgage on your home, that is considered senior debt. If you then take out a second mortgage or equity line, that is considered junior debt. If you can't pay the bills and the mortgage holders foreclose, the first mortgage holder must be paid in full before the second mortgage holder gets any money.

◆ **Reorganization plan**—The company filing bankruptcy offers a plan to reorganize its debt, usually with lower interest rates and sometimes even a reduction in the principal of the debts on the books. The company then negotiates with creditors to see what they will accept. During this stage, Price watches the price of each type of debt and tries to figure out which debt will give him the best return after negotiations. Each debt class has the right to block any deal unless two thirds of the debtors agree to the reorganization plan. Any debt holder who holds one third of one type of debt or more can block any reorganization agreement. So in this stage, Price seeks to get that level of control so he can block a reorganization deal. Unless you, too, have the money to get that level of control, stay away from buying any bonds or stocks during this stage.

◆ **Emergence from bankruptcy or liquidation**—Either the company successfully restructures its debt or it must sell whatever assets are available and pay
what it can to creditors. If the company must liquidate, the game is over and
you'll likely get pennies on the dollar, if anything. If the company emerges from
bankruptcy, it begins to operate again. In most cases, the company emerges
from bankruptcy much stronger because it has cleaned out its debt problem.
Also during a bankruptcy, a company doesn't have to pay interest or taxes, so
usually it emerges with cash on hand. It also may have generated cash by selling
off assets as part of the reorganization plan to satisfy creditors.

When a company emerges from bankruptcy, it can be a great time to buy stock
cheap. But be certain you've done your homework.

Finding Value _____

You can find out a lot about the inner workings of a company during a bankruptcy
because the bankruptcy court requires regular filings about a company's financial
position and you can access that information on the Internet. For more about bankruptcies, go to the website of the U.S. Bankruptcy Courts (www.uscourts.gov/
bankruptcycourts.html).

Exploring Stocks with Value's Hermits—Walter and Edwin Schloss

While most value investors talk with analysts, meet with the management team, and
gather information in whatever way they can, Walter and Edwin Schloss do none of
that, so they operate almost as hermits in the field of value investing.

They get their information about a company by reading publicly filed annual reports
and other filings required by the Securities and Exchange Commission. They pick
their possible candidates by looking at the financial reports of companies whose
stocks have taken a significant fall.

Each day they scrutinize the new lows list for new research possibilities. They particularly like stocks that are at their two- and three-year lows.

When they find a stock that looks promising, they buy a small amount even before
they've completed their research. They believe the only way someone can truly get to
know a stock is to own it.

Valuing Stocks

The Schlosses look closely at assets to find good buys. They believe that if you can buy a company for less than the value of its assets, even if there aren't earnings at the time, the company is worth looking at more closely. Either the company will return to profitability or it will be taken over by someone who can do so. They usually hold a stock for about four years.

The Schlosses generally do not consider a stock for which they must pay more than three times book value. We show you how to calculate book value in Chapter 11. The industries that are the most promising for their style of investing are food, defense, and manufacturing. All of these industries tend to carry significant assets and will sell for more than book value even when their stocks are down.

After buying their first shares in a company, the Schlosses start to investigate the company more completely. They don't just look at the financial statements, but they also scour the notes to the financial statements (read Chapter 8), looking for the following:

- Off-sheet liabilities, such as leases that are detailed in the notes but are not shown on the balance sheet.

- Capital spending, to be sure not a lot of future spending is needed to upgrade old factories. If so, the assets may be worth less than initially determined by looking at the balance sheet. You can find out more about capital spending plans in management's discussion and analysis (read Chapter 9).

- Accumulate depreciation, to judge the age of the existing plants. If a plant is almost fully depreciated, it's likely an older plant that needs major renovation or one that doesn't have modern equipment.

The Schlosses look to buy cheap and hold a company until it has recovered. Sometimes during a bull market, their definition of "cheap" can be a little more flexible if they think they've found a good candidate for their portfolio.

Timing the Buy and Sell

The Schlosses believe, as do we, that no one can accurately predict the top or bottom for a stock or any price in between.

Most value investors tend to buy stocks on the way down. The Schlosses tend to buy a small amount at first and then add to their holdings as the stock drifts downward, but they do hope that they have bought after any major dive down in price. That's why they look for stocks that have taken a significant fall, as well as hit their two- or three-year lows.

They also don't talk about the stocks they're considering with anyone. Since the stocks they look at are beaten down, analysts and others are not paying attention to them. But if word gets out that they are buying shares of a stock, others will jump on it and drive up the price too high for them.

The key for them is to not buy too many shares on their initial purchase of a stock so they have room to buy more shares as the price drifts down. Most value investors tend to buy too soon and sell too soon. They tend to buy before the stock has hit bottom and sell once the stock recovers. The Schlosses seek to get the return on the stock they wanted and won't ride a stock to its new highs. This means they often miss out on profits, but they also miss out on a huge fall when the stock corrects. Safety is very critical to value investors.

The Schlosses carefully look at the results in every quarterly report for a stock they own, but they don't watch the day-to-day ups and downs of their stocks. They also don't panic if a company misses its earnings projections by a few cents.

But they do watch for actions by the management team. For example, if a company whose stock they hold decides to merge or to acquire another company and they disagree with management's decision, they may decide to sell the stock.

Once the Schlosses pick a stock, they start researching other companies in the same industry. If they find one they think is a better choice, they may decide to sell their holdings and buy the other stock.

Diversification Without Limits

The Schlosses do believe in diversification, but they are flexible with their limits on how much of one company's stock they will hold. They tend to hold about 100 stocks in the portfolios they manage, but about 20 stocks make up about 60 percent of that portfolio. The stocks in which they hold the greater percentages are stocks they liked and decided to add to their holdings. The other 40 percent of their holdings consists of stocks they're researching further. Remember, the Schlosses believe you can get to know a stock only after you buy it.

We've given you a good overview of the various strategies that some top value investing gurus employ. Pick and choose from these strategies and develop your own unique style. But always keep one thing in mind—buy low and sell high. Don't get caught up in the winds of the market and ride the train up a cliff only to find yourself quickly at the bottom with a huge loss from which you must recover.

The Least You Need to Know

◆ The key principles Michael Price follows to maintain his value investing strategies are discipline, patience, focus, and homework.

◆ You can find good buys in all markets, but some of the best places to look are the daily new lows, pending merger or acquisition deals, and bankruptcies.

◆ As a value investor, you need to think out of the box and not follow the crowd. While you may not want to follow the hermit ways of the Schlosses, you should definitely learn to do your own research and make decisions based on that research.

Glossary

accounts receivable   The account that tracks credit extended to customers. The amount shown in this account on the balance sheet summarizes all these customer accounts.

accrual accounting   A method of accounting commonly used by business that recognizes revenue when it's earned, not necessarily when the money is collected. It also recognizes expenses when they are incurred, not necessarily after they have been paid for.

accumulated depreciation   The total amount depreciated against tangible assets over the life span of the assets shown on the balance sheet.

actuary   A statistician who looks at life span and other risk factors to make assumptions about an individual life span. In the retirement arena, an actuary helps a company determine its long-term pension obligations.

amortization   A method that permits a company to spread out the expenses of a project over a number of years rather than take off the full cost in the first year.

audit   The examination and verification of a company's financial and accounting records. Certified public accountants (CPAs) perform audits for major corporations. Auditors don't look at every piece of paper related to financial transactions, but instead review a sampling of the materials involved and count the cash on hand.

bear market   A market in which most stocks are going down in price.

bond   A long-term liability to be paid back over a number of years.

bond swap   The simultaneous sale of one bond and the purchase of another.

bull market   A market in which most stocks are going up in price.

capital expenditures   Include money spent to buy or upgrade a company's assets. This can include, for example, the purchase of a new building or another company's stock, or it can be a major improvement to buildings already owned.

capital gains   Profits you make when you sell a stock. For example, if you buy stock for $10 a share and sell it for $15 a share, the $5 of profit you make is capital gain.

capital improvements   Upgrades to assets held by the company. For example, if the company buys a new building or rents new space, any renovation done to get that new property ready for use is a capital improvement.

cost of goods sold   Summarizes what it costs to manufacture or purchase the goods that a business sells to its customers.

current yield   The annual dollar amount you expect to receive in bond interest over the next 12 months.

default   Involves the failure of a company to make required debt payments. Companies in default on their debt payments often file for bankruptcy to buy time to restructure their financial situation. Some come out of bankruptcy by getting lenders to agree to different terms for debt repayment; others go out of business.

depreciation   A method used to show that an asset is gradually being used up. For example, suppose that a truck the company owns must be replaced every five years because it's essentially used up—it needs more repair than is worth doing. During the time a company uses that truck, is subtracts a portion of the asset's value using depreciation, to show that the asset is no longer as valuable as it was when it was first bought.

dividends   Certain portion per share paid to common stockholders from profits. A company's board of directors declares the amount of the dividend to be paid. Dividends are usually paid on a quarterly basis.

duopoly   Occurs when two companies dominate a business sector that has a high barrier to entry, but coexist without competing directly with each other. For example, Fannie Mae and Freddie Mac, both major power players in the mortgage market, serve different niches.

errors and omissions insurance   Protects executives and board members from being sued personally for any errors or omissions related to their work for the company or as part of their responsibility on the company's board.

generally accepted accounting principles (GAAP)   Actually thousands of very detailed opinions developed over the years to establish how various transactions should be reported in the financial statements. The Federal Accounting Standards Advisory Board produces and manages GAAP rulings.

gross domestic product (GDP)   Represents the monetary value of goods produced during a specific period of time, such as a quarter or a year, and shows how fast the economy is growing. The U.S. government releases its GDP numbers quarterly.

growth stocks   Stocks in companies that focus primarily on growing the company. They rarely pay dividends and instead reinvest all profits in future growth. Companies start paying out dividends to their investors only when they no longer have good ideas for investing all the money they make into plans for future growth.

initial public offering (IPO)   The first time a stock is sold on the public markets. Companies sell stock to raise cash for the company operations and growth.

intrinsic value   Based on the internally generated cash returns of a company. When analyzing numbers for a stock, the common way to find intrinsic value is to calculate a discounted stream of net cash flows to find out what those cash flows are worth in today's dollars.

monopoly   Occurs when only one company serves a particular market segment. For example, Microsoft has been charged with using its computer operating system monopoly unfairly to crush competitors.

over-the-counter market   Made up of hundreds of securities firms and banks that trade bonds by phone or electronically.

preacquisition costs   For a builder, these involve the options for the purchase of land and the surveys and other work done before the purchase of that land. If a builder decides not to buy the land, those costs are lost.

secondary public offering (SPO)   When the company sells shares of stock directly to the public sometime after the IPO.

secured debtors   Debtors who have loaned money based on specific assets, such as a mortgage on a building. The asset has been promised as a guarantee against the debt. If the company doesn't pay a secured debt, the debtor could foreclose on the asset and take the property, much like banks are doing to homeowners who can't pay their mortgage.

speculative homes   Homes built before the builder has a signed contract from a buyer who wants to buy the home.

stock market index   A basket of stocks whose price is closely watched for upswings and downswings in the market.

subsidiary   Any company for which a majority of the voting stock is owned by another company, known as the holding company.

unconsolidated subsidiaries or affiliates   Involve the ownership of less than a controlling share in another company. To list an unconsolidated subsidiary or affiliate, the company must own less than 50 percent but more than 20 percent. If the company owns less than 20 percent of another company's stock, its ownership is tracked as a marketable security.

volume discounts   Offered to retailers by a manufacturer to encourage the retailers to buy a large number of the manufacturer's product, to save a certain percentage of money off the price.

yield to call   The total return you will receive until the bond is called. Some bonds are issued with the right to call the bond, which means the issuer can buy back the bond before it matures.

yield to maturity   The total return you will receive until the bond matures.

Resources

Business Magazines

Business Week (www.businessweek.com)

Forbes (www.forbes.com)

Fortune (money.cnn.com/magazines/fortune)

Daily News Sources

Bloomberg's (www.bloomberg.com)

Investor's Business Daily (www.investors.com)

The London Financial Times (www.ft.com)

Marketwatch (www.marketwatch.com)

The Wall Street Journal (www.wsj.com)

Economic Data

Consumer Confidence Index (CCI)—This index is released monthly by the Conference Board, a nonprofit business group. The CCI surveys the results of the spending of more than 5,000 households and gauges the financial health, spending power, and confidence of the average consumer. You can read the monthly press announcement from the Conference Board at www.conference-board.org/economics/consumerConfidence.cfm.

Durable Goods Report—This report by the Census Bureau provides data on new orders received from more than 4,000 manufacturers of durable goods. Durable goods are higher-priced capital goods orders with a useful life of three years or more, such as cars, semiconductor equipment, and turbines. You'll find more than 85 industries represented in the sample, which covers the entire United States. This report gives you an indication of business demand. You can view this report monthly at www.census.gov/indicator/www/m3/adv.

National Bureau of Economic Research—You can see a chart of the peaks and troughs for business cycles throughout history at the National Bureau of Economic Research's website, www.nber.org/cycles/cyclesmain.html.

Stock, Bond, and Mutual Fund Research

Analysts' Call—Listen in on analysts' calls and find out about upcoming calls. Two websites make it easy for you to find out what is available: Vcall (www.vcall.com) and BestCalls (www.bestcalls.com).

Bankruptcy—You can find out a lot about the inner workings of a company during bankruptcy: the bankruptcy court requires regular filings about a company's financial position, and you can access that information on the Internet. For more about bankruptcies, go to the website of the U.S. Bankruptcy Courts (www.uscourts.gov/bankruptcycourts.html).

Fitch Ratings—The youngest of the three major bond-rating services is Fitch Ratings (www.fitchratings.com). John Knowles Fitch founded Fitch Publishing Company in 1913. The company started as a publisher of financial statistics. In 1924, Fitch introduced the credit ratings scales that are very familiar today—AAA to D.

Moody's Investor Service—Moody's specializes in credit ratings, research, and risk analysis. Its analysts track more than $30 trillion of debt issued in the U.S. domestic market, as well as debt issued in the international markets. In addition to its credit rating services, Moody's publishes investor-oriented credit research, which you can access at www.moodys.com.

Morningstar—One good source for independent analysts is Morningstar (www.morningstar.com), which is one of the leading groups that rates mutual funds for individual investors. Morningstar also assigns analysts to rate stocks. In addition to individual stock ratings, you can find stories on Morningstar's website about which stocks mutual fund managers are buying and why they're buying them. Don't buy stock based on these stories; read the financial reports yourself and do your own analysis of these reports.

Securities and Exchange Commission—If you can't find company reports at the company's website, you can always find them at the Securities and Exchange Commission's website (www.sec.gov).

Standard & Poor's—You've probably heard the name Standard and Poor's mentioned before. It's well known because of the S&P 500, which is a collection of 500 stocks that form the basis of this stock market index. Each year, Standard and Poor's reviews the list and tweaks it by adding some stocks and taking off others. Many mutual funds base their portfolios on this index, which is seen as one of the best indicators of stock market performance. When a stock is added to the list, its stock price usually goes up; when it's taken off the list, its stock price usually drops. You can find the list on the company's website at www.standardandpoors.com. You do have to pay fees to use Standard & Poor's if you want to access their confidential services, but they're much more reasonable than those of an independent analyst that you might hire as an individual—depending on the information you need, these fees can be as low as $100 per year.

SmartMoney University—Dow Jones' SmartMoney University (www.smartmoney.com/university) offers excellent self-directed courses that help you learn more about investing using stocks, bonds, and mutual funds.

Yahoo! Finance—Yahoo! Finance (http://finance.yahoo.com) is a great place to research stocks. You can get historical pricing, statistics, links to the companies' websites, insider trading information, and many other features that make this a one-stop shop for basic stock research.

Stock and Bond Purchase Tips

Broker survey—Each year SmartMoney does a survey of online brokers to find the most up-to-date information about how well online brokers serve their customers. Go to http://www.smartmoney.com/brokers to find the results of the latest survey.

Direct stock purchase—You can find stocks that are sold directly to investors, by-passing brokers, on many different websites. Two good ones to check out include Drip Central (www.dripcentral.com) and ING Direct's Sharebuilder (www.sharebuilder.com).

Mortgage bonds—These bonds are based on mortgages. They used to be among the safest bonds, but the subprime mortgage mess tainted some of these options. For safety, when picking a mortgage bond or mortgage bond fund, be sure you are buying bonds or a portfolio of bonds backed by one of the two key government enterprises—Fannie Mae (www.fanniemae.com) or Freddie Mac (www.freddiemac.com).

Treasury bonds—You can buy U.S. Treasury securities directly from the government at www.treasurydirect.gov/tdhome.htm. If you don't want to buy individual securities, you can also choose to buy mutual funds that specialize in Treasury securities. Be sure to look at the details of the portfolio, though, to be sure the fund is investing only in government-backed securities.

Value Investors and Strategies

Warren Buffett—You can read the full owner's manual and Buffett's annual reports at www.berkshirehathaway.com. You'll learn a lot about how Buffett invests by reading his annual reports.

Dogs of the Dow—When you consider a Dogs of the Dow strategy, it's a safety strategy, not one that will get you the highest return in a bull market. You can find out more about the Dogs of the Dow online at www.dogsofthedow.com.

Mario Gabelli—You can find out more about Mario Gabelli and his style of investing by reading the prospectus for his mutual funds. If you don't think you're ready to handle this on your own, you can buy shares in one of Gabelli's mutual funds and let him do it for you. The big disadvantage of Gabelli's mutual funds is that their management fees are high—but you might find that premium worth it, given the success he has had with Private Market Value. To look at his mutual fund options, go to www.gabelli.com/indiv.

Appendix C

Financial Statements

In this appendix, you will find two sets of financial statements for builders: Company A and Company B. The information in this appendix is used to analyze the companies in Chapter 11.

For each company, you will find the following:

- Balance sheet

- Statement of operations (income statement)

- Statement of cash flows

Company A Balance Sheet (in Thousands)		
	December 31, 2007	December 31, 2006
Assets		
Home Building:		
Cash and Cash Equivalents	$900,337	$632,524
Inventory	$5,572,655	$6,095,702
Equipment	$84,265	$99,089
Accounts Receivable	$135,910	$160,446
Contract Receivable	$46,525	$170,111
Mortgage Loans Receivable	$93,189	$130,326
Customer Deposits Held in Escrow	$34,367	$49,676
Investments in and Advances to Unconsolidated Entities	$183,171	$245,667
Deferred Tax Assets	$169,897	
Total Assets	$7,220,316	$7,583,541
Liabilities and Stockholders' Equity		
Loans Payable	$696,814	$736,934
Senior Notes	$1,492,306	$1,491,167
Mortgage Company Warehouse Loan	$76,730	$119,705
Customers' Deposits	$260,155	$360,147
Accounts Payable	$236,877	$292,171
Accrued Expenses	$724,229	$825,288
Income Taxes Payable	$197,960	$334,500
Total Liabilities	$3,685,071	$4,159,912
Minority Interests	$8,011	$7,703

Stockholders' Equity		
Preferred Stock (None Issued)		
Common Stock	$1,570	$1,563
Paid in Capital—Common Stock	$227,561	$220,783
Retained Earnings	$3,298,103	$3,193,580
Total Stockholders' Equity	$3,527,234	$3,415,926
Total Liabilities and Stockholders' Equity	$7,220,316	$7,583,541

Company A Statement of Operations (in Thousands Except Per Share Data)			
	Year Ended		
	12/31/2007	12/31/2006	12/31/2005
Revenues			
Completed Contract	$4,495,600	$5,945,169	$5,759,301
Percentage of Completion	$139,493	$170,111	
Land Sales	$11,886	$8,173	$34,124
Total Revenues	$4,646,979	$6,123,453	$5,793,425
Cost of Revenues			
Completed Contract	$3,905,907	$4,263,200	$3,902,697
Percentage of Completion	$108,954	$132,268	
Land Sales	$8,069	$6,997	$24,416
Interest	$102,447	$121,993	$125,283
Total Cost of Goods Sold	$4,125,377	$4,524,458	$4,052,396
Selling, General and Administrative	$516,729	$573,404	$482,786
Goodwill Impairment	$8,973		
(Loss) Income from Operations	$(4,100)	$1,025,591	$1,258,243
(Loss) Earnings from Unconsolidated Entities	$(40,353)	$48,361	$27,744
Interest Income	$115,133	$52,664	$37,141
Income Before Taxes	$70,680	$1,126,616	$1,323,128
Income Taxes	$35,029	$439,403	$517,018
Net Income	$35,651	$687,213	$806,110

Earnings Per Share			
Basic	$0.23	$4.45	$5.23
Diluted	$0.22	$4.17	$4.78
Weighted Average Number of Shares			
Basic	155,318	154,300	154,272
Diluted	164,166	164,852	168,552

Company A Statement of Cash Flows (in Thousands)			
	Year Ended		
	12/31/2007	12/31/2006	12/31/2005
Cash Flows from Operating Activity			
Net (Loss) Income	$35,651	$687,213	$806,110
Adjustments to Reconcile Net (Loss) Income to Net Cash Provided by (Used in) Operating Activities			
Depreciation	$29,949	$30,357	$20,345
Amortization of Initial Benefit Obligation	$1,291	$1,957	$3,802
Stock-Based Compensation	$27,463	$27,082	
Excess Tax Benefits from Stock Compensation	$(15,915)	$(16,110)	
Loss (Earnings) from Uncon-solidated Entities	$40,353	$(48,361)	$(27,744)
Distribution of Earnings from Unconsolidated Entities	$23,545	$10,534	$13,401
Amortization of Unearned Compensation			$200
Deferred Tax Provision	$(289,203)	$8,773	$26,763
Inventory Impairments	$603,845	$152,045	$5,495
Decrease (Increase) in Assets and Liabilities			
Increase in Inventory	$(18,273)	$(877,746)	$(1,025,421)
Origination of Mortgage Loans	$(1,412,629)	$(1,022,663)	$(873,404)
Sale of Mortgage Loans	$1,449,766	$992,196	$873,459
Receivables, Prepaids, and Other Assets	$133,515	$(147,766)	$(39,169)
Customer Deposits	$(84,683)	$(36,530)	$109,506
Accounts Payable	$(195,594)	$51,885	$314,949
Current Income Taxes Payable	$1,388	$63,045	$126,404

Net Cash Provided by (Used in) Operating Activities	$330,469	$(124,089)	$334,696
Cash Flows from Investing Activities			
Purchase of Property	$(14,975)	$(41,740)	$(43,029)
Purchase of Marketable Securities	$32,299	$—	$115,029
Investment in Consolidated Entities	$8,260	$(113,134)	$(40,428)
Net Cash Used in Investing Activities	$25,584	$(154,874)	$31,572
Cash Flows from Financing Activities			
Proceeds from Mortgages and Notes	$1,507,865	$1,614,087	$1,125,951
Principal Payments of Loan Payable	$(1,632,785)	$(1,316,950)	$(1,198,736)
Proceeds from Stock-Based Benefit Plans	$20,475	$15,103	$44,729
Excess Tax Benefits	$17,715	$16,110	
Purchase of Treasury Stock	$(1,818)	$(109,845)	$(118,767)
Change in Minority Interest	$308	$3,763	$3,940
Net Cash (Used in) Provided by Financing Activities	$(88,240)	$222,268	$(142,883)
Net (Decrease) Increase in Cash	$267,813	$(56,695)	$223,385

Company B Balance Sheet (in Thousands)		
	December 31, 2007	December 31, 2006
Assets		
Home Building:		
Cash and Cash Equivalents	$12,275	$43,635
Restricted Cash	$6,594	$9,479
Inventories	$3,518,334	$4,070,841
Accounts Receivables	$286,221	$307,331
Property Plant & Equipment	$106,792	$110,704
Prepaid Expenses	$174,032	$175,603
Goodwill	$32,658	$32,658
Definite Life Intangibles	$4,224	$165,053
Total Home Building	$4,141,130	$4,915,304
Financial Services:		
Cash and Cash Equivalents	$3,958	$10,688
Restricted Cash	$11,572	$1,585
Mortgage Loans Held for Sale	$182,627	$281,958
Other Assets	$6,851	$10,686
Total Financial Services	$205,008	$304,917
Income Taxes Receivable	$194,410	$259,814
Total Assets	$4,540,548	$5,480,035

Liabilities and Stockholders' Equity		
Home Building:		
Land Mortgages	$32,415	$49,772
Accounts Payable	$515,422	$582,393
Customers' Deposits	$65,221	$184,943
Liabilities from Inventory Not Owned	$189,935	$205,067
Total Home Building	$802,993	$1,022,175
Financial Services:		
Accounts Payable	$19,597	$12,158
Line of Credit	$171,333	$270,171
Total Financial Services	$190,730	$282,329
Notes Payable	$2,161,294	$2,100,883
Total Liabilities	$3,155,017	$3,405,387
Minority Interests	$63,728	$132,485
Stockholders' Equity:		
Preferred Stock	$135,299	$135,299
Common Stock	$746	$740
Paid in Capital—Common Stock	$276,998	$253,262
Retained Earnings	$908,760	$1,552,862
Total Stockholders' Equity	$1,321,803	$1,942,163
Total Liabilities and Stockholders' Equity	$4,540,548	$5,480,035

Company B Statement of Operations (in Thousands Except Per Share Data)			
	Year Ended		
	12/31/2007	12/31/2006	12/31/2005
Revenues			
Home Building:			
Sale of Homes	$4,581,375	$5,903,387	$5,177,655
Land Sales	$141,355	$155,250	$98,391
Total Home Building	$4,722,730	$6,058,637	$5,276,046
Financial Services	$76,191	$89,598	$72,371
Total Revenues	$4,798,921	$6,148,235	$5,348,417
Expenses			
Home Building:			
Cost of Sales	$4,109,610	$4,741,410	$3,951,944
Inventory Impairment	$457,773	$336,204	$5,360
Total Cost of Sales	$4,567,383	$5,077,614	$3,957,304
Selling, General and Administrative Expenses	$539,362	$593,860	$441,943
Total Home Building Expenses	$5,106,745	$5,671,474	$4,399,247
Financial Services	$48,321	$58,586	$48,347
Corporate General	$85,878	$96,781	$90,628
Other Expenses	$14,596	$48,852	$18,565
Intangible Amortization	$162,124	$54,821	$46,084

Total Expenses	$5,417,664	$5,930,514	$4,602,871
(Loss)/Income Joint Ventures	$(28,223)	$15,385	$35,039
Loss Before Taxes	$(646,966)	$233,106	$780,585
State Taxes	$7,088	$1,366	$44,806
Federal Taxes	$(26,935)	$82,207	$263,932
Total Taxes	$(19,847)	$83,573	$308,738
Net (Loss) Income	$(627,119)	$149,533	$471,847
Less: Preferred Stock Dividends	$10,674	$10,675	$2,758
Net (Loss) Income Available to Common Shareholders	$(673,793)	$138,858	$469,089
Per Share Data	$(10.11)	$2.21	$7.51
Shares Outstanding	63,079	62,822	62,490

Company B Statement of Cash Flows (in Thousands)			
	Year Ended		
	12/31/2007	12/31/2006	12/31/2005
Cash Flows from Operating Activity			
Net (Loss) Income	$(627,119)	$149,533	$471,847
Adjustments to Reconcile Net (Loss) Income to Net Cash Provided by (Used in) Operating Activities			
Depreciation	$18,283	$14,884	$9,075
Intangible Amortization	$162,124	$54,821	$46,084
Compensation from Stock Options	$24,434	$23,428	$12,690
Amortization of Bond Discounts	$1,072	$1,039	$715
Excess Tax Benefits	$(2,341)	$(7,951)	
Gain (Loss) on Sale of Assets	$1,849	$428	$(3,681)
Loss (Income) from Joint Ventures	$28,223	$(15,385)	$(35,039)
Distributions from Joint Ventures	$3,998	$15,038	$28,868
Deferred Income Taxes	$85,612	$(151,072)	$(20,823)
Inventory Impairment Write-Offs	$457,773	$336,204	$5,360
Decrease (Increase) in Assets:			
Mortgage Notes Receivable	$99,354	$(70,638)	$(1,790)
Restricted Cash, Receivables, Prepaids	$6,400	$58,527	$(102,005)
Inventories	$33,625	$(920,346)	$(645,280)
Increase (Decrease) in Liabilities			
State and Federal Income Taxes	$(43,308)	$(90,888)	$(22,556)
Customers' Deposits	$(110,446)	$(73,503)	$168,682
Accrued Liabilities	$(45,900)	$20,724	$13,949

Accounts Payable	$(31,667)	$4,447	$50,065
Net Cash Provided by (Used in) Operating Activities	$61,966	$(650,710)	$(23,839)
Cash Flows from Investing Activities			
Net Proceeds from Sale of Assets	$1,539	$384	$8,495
Purchase of Assets	$(37,777)	$(51,506)	$(317,777)
Investment in Joint Ventures	$(30,088)	$(29,113)	$(141,448)
Distributions from Joint Ventures	$33,932	$5,691	$1,320
Net Cash Used in Investing Activities	$(32,394)	$(74,544)	$(449,410)
Cash Flows from Financing Activities			
Proceeds from Mortgages and Notes	$8,590	$69,386	$128,291
Net Proceeds (Payments)— Credit Agreement	$206,750		$(115,000)
Net Proceeds (Payments)—Line of Credit	$(99,038)	$71,315	$10,440
Proceeds from Senior Debt		$549,910	$595,287
Proceeds from Preferred Stock			$135,389
Principal Payments on Debt	$(178,593)	$(120,930)	$(128,380)
Excess Tax Benefits	$2,341	$7,951	
Preferred Dividends Paid	$(10,674)	$(10,675)	$(2,758)
Proceeds from Sale of Stock	$2,962	$1,347	$294
Net Cash (Used in) Provided by Financing Activities	$(67,662)	$568,304	$623,563
Net (Decrease) Increase in Cash	$(38,090)	$(156,950)	$150,314

Index

financial reports, 37
  analyzing, 43-45, 131-132
    current ratio, 138-139
    discounted cash flow,
      135-136
    earnings per share, 136
    intrinsic value, 132-134
    operating ratio, 139-144
    P/E (price to earnings),
      136
    price-to-book ratio,
      136-138
  annual reports, 38-39
    auditor's letter or report,
      38-40
    introductory paragraph,
      40
    opinion paragraph,
      41-43
    parts, 38
    red-flag words, 39-40
    scope paragraph, 41
  big-bath charges, 43
  cookie-jar reserves, 44
  creative acquisitions, 44
  expenses, 44
  materiality, 44
  MD&A (management's
    discussion and analysis),
    109
    allowance for doubtful
      accounts, 119
    capital resources,
      115-116
    company operations,
      110-115
    environmental and
      product liabilities, 118
    impairments to assets,
      117-118
    pension plans, 118
    restructuring charges,
      117
    revenue recognition, 117

    SEC expectations, 110
    stock-based
      compensation, 119
  oversize assets, 44
  revenue recognition, 44
  undervalued assets, 44
financial statements, 91
  accounting policy changes,
    92-96
  analyzing, 8
  annual reports, 38
  business make-up, 102-103
  mergers and acquisitions,
    99-100
  new borrowing, 96-98
  pension benefits, 100-102
  reading, 8
  red flags, 105-107
  retirement benefits,
    100-102
  significant events, 104-105
  small print, 92
  standing commitments,
    96-98
Financial Times, 177
financing activities,
  statements of cash flows, 78,
  85-89
    buying back stocks, 86-87
    discontinued operations,
      88-89
    foreign currency
      exchanges, 89
    incurring new debt, 88
    issuing stocks, 86
    paying dividends, 87
    paying off debt, 88
Fitch, John Knowles, 154
Fitch Ratings, 154
fixed-income funds, 189-190
fixtures, current assets, 55
float (cash), 225
Forbes, 178
foreign currency exchanges,
  89

formats
  balance sheets, 50
    account format, 50-51
    financial position
      format, 51-52
    report format, 51
  income statements, 63
    multistep format, 64-65
    single-step format, 63
  statements of cash flows,
    79-81
formulas, balance sheets, 48
Fortune, 178
Freddie Mac, 166
full-service brokers, 180-181
funds, bond mutual, 169-170
furniture, current assets, 55

G

GAAP (generally accepted
  accounting principles), 41,
  260
Gabelli, Mario, 9-10, 257-261
GDP (gross domestic
  product), 26-27
General Portfolio Operations,
  234
*Global Convertible Investing:
  The Gabelli Way*, 202
Graham, Benjamin, 4, 9, 202,
  237-238, 250-255
  Intelligent Investor, The, 14
Greenberg, Glenn, 10,
  264-271
gross profits, income
  statements, 69-70
growth and income funds,
  188-189
growth funds, 188
growth stocks, 249-250
GTC (good till canceled)
  orders, 183

H

History of Railroads and Canals of the United States, 155
hockey sticks, analyst calls, 157
hybrid funds, 191
hybrid trade zone (convertible bonds), 201

I

impairments to assets, MD&A (management's discussion and analysis), 117-118
income, nonreporting, 73-74
income statements, 61-62
  cost of goods sold section, 62, 68
  costs, 68-69
  earnings per share, 74-75
  expenses, 70-71
  expenses section, 62
  formats, 63
    multistep format, 64-65
    single-step format, 63
  gross profits, 69-70
  net income or loss section, 62
  profits, 72-74
  revenues, 65-68
  sales or revenues section, 62
income taxes, financial statement notes, 93
independent analysts, 151-152
indexes
  CCI (Consumer Confidence Index), 30
  Standard & Poor's Industrial Index, 11
  VIX index, 232-233
indirect method, statements of cash flows, 79

individual bonds, 166-169
industries, choosing, 7, 14
inflation risks, 206
ING Directs Sharebuilder, 250
initial public offerings (IPOs). *See* IPOs (initial public offerings)
insurance
  errors and omissions insurance, 71
  expenses, 71
intangible assets, balance sheets, 55-56
Intelligent Investor, The, 14, 238, 250-255
interest expenses, 71
interest rate risks, 208
interest rates, bonds, 172
international funds, 191
intrinsic value, 226
  capital expenditure requirements, determining, 134
  companies, 3-4
  market prices of assets, determining, 134
  profit margins, determining, 133-134
  sales growth rates, determining, 132-133
  stock, finding, 132-134
introductory paragraph (financial reports), 40
inventories
  accounts payable turnover, determining, 143-144
  accounts receivable turnover, determining, 141-142
  current assets, 53
  inventory turnover, determining, 139-141
  statements of cash flows, 82
inventory turnover, determining, 139-141

investing
  activities, statements of cash flow, 78, 84-85
  defensive investing, 237-246
    bonds, 242-243
    cash, 243-245
    portfolio asset allocation, 241-242
    risk tolerance, 238-241
    stocks, 243
    time constraints, 238-241
investment analysts, 147-148
  bond analysts, 152-153
  buy-side analysts, 148-149
  independent analysts, 151-152
  sell-side analysts, 149-151
investments
  bonds, 165
    bond mutual funds, 169-170, 243
    bond unit investment trusts, 170
    convertible bonds, 195-202, 245
    corporate bonds, 166
    individual bonds, 166-169
    investment bonds, 166
    investment strategies, 171-172
    issuance, 166
    long-term bonds, 243
    mortgage bonds, 166
    price, 172-173
    redeeming, 196
    short-term bonds, 243
    tax-free bonds, 243
    taxable bonds, 243
    U.S. government securities, 166
    yield, 173-174

S